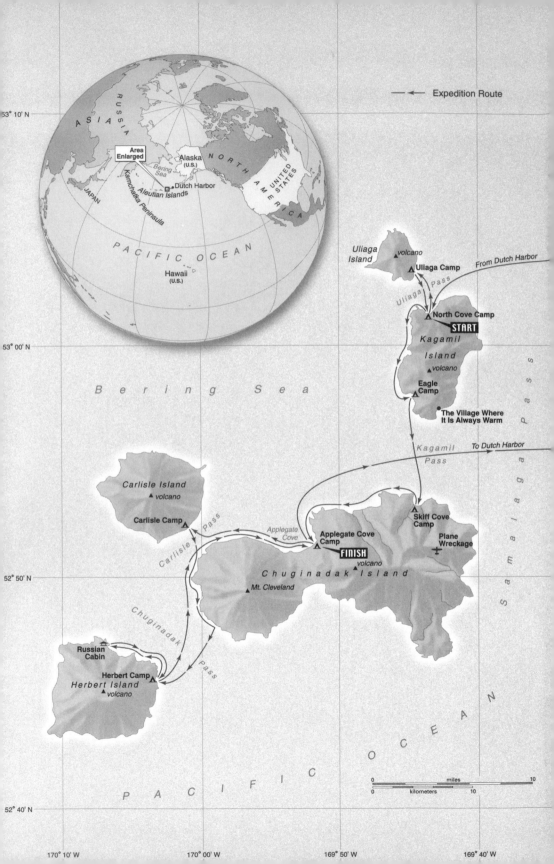

53° 10' N

Area
Enlarged

A S I A

RUSSIA

ASIA

JAPAN

Kamchatka Peninsula

Bering
Sea

Aleutian Islands

Alaska
(U.S.)

Dutch Harbor

NORTH AMERICA

UNITED STATES

P A C I F I C   O C E A N

Hawaii
(U.S.)

Expedition Route

Uliaga
Island

▲ volcano

Uliaga Camp

From Dutch Harbor

Uliaga
Pass

△ North Cove Camp

START

Kagamil
Island

▲ volcano

Eagle
Camp △

● The Village Where
It Is Always Warm

53° 00' N

B e r i n g   S e a

Kagamil
Pass

To Dutch Harbor

S
a
m
a
l
a
g
a

P
a
s
s

Carlisle Island

▲ volcano

Carlisle Camp △

Carlisle
Pass

Applegate
Cove

Applegate Cove
Camp △

FINISH

△ Skiff Cove
Camp

Plane
Wreckage

volcano

C h u g i n a d a k   I s l a n d

52° 50' N

▲ Mt. Cleveland

Chuginadak

Pass

Russian
Cabin

Herbert Camp △

Herbert Island

▲ volcano

miles   10

kilometers   10

P A C I F I C   O C E A N

52° 40' N

170° 10' W   170° 00' W   169° 50' W   169° 40' W

BIRTHPLACE OF THE WINDS

Adventuring in Alaska's Islands of Fire and Ice

BIRTHPLACE OF THE WINDS

Adventuring In Alaska's Islands of Fire and Ice

Jon Bowermaster

ADVENTURE PRESS

NATIONAL GEOGRAPHIC
WASHINGTON, D. C.

Also by Jon Bowermaster

*The Adventures and Misadventures
of Peter Beard in Africa*

Governor

with Will Steger

Crossing Antarctica
Saving the Earth
Over the Top of the World

Library of Congress Cataloging-in-Publication Data

Bowermaster, Jon, 1954-
    Birthplace of the winds : adventuring in Alaska's islands of fire and ice / Jon Bower-
master.
        p. cm.
    ISBN 0-7922-7506-3
    1. Sea kayaking--Alaska--Aleutian Islands. 2. Bowermaster, Jon,
1954---Journeys--Alaska--Aleutian Islands. I. Title.

GV776.A42 B69 2001
917.98'4--dc21   00-053416

Printed and bound by R. R. Donnelley & Sons

Interior design by Melissa Farris and Suez Kehl Corrado

For Brigitte

ONE

A long spit of rock and sand juts out into the Bering Sea from the rustic Alaskan fishing town of Homer. We've arrived at its point after a drive of 3,180 miles, from the Sierras of California. Stepping out into the cruel, cold wind whipping off the ocean, we wonder if we haven't made a wrong turn somewhere.

Instead, as we lean into the wind and shiver, we—my friends and expedition teammates Sean Farrell and Barry Tessman—are staring into our own immediate future. Later this day we are headed another 1,000 miles west, deep into the heart of the Bering Sea. From there we will proceed even farther in the pair of 22-foot-long kayaks currently strapped atop Barry's pickup truck.

"Geez," is the only sentiment I can muster as a mini-tornado of seaborne dust nearly knocks us to our knees, "maybe we should have stayed home. Whose brilliant idea was this, anyway?"

Barry and Sean had picked me up at the small airport in Prince Rupert, British Columbia, five days before. They'd left from California and I'd flown in from France. Having been on the road more than a week, we are all a little tired and grumpy. On the one hand, it feels good to arrive at this juncture. Finally, after months of brain-numbing exchanges of e-mails and various pleadings, budget crunching, schedule juggling, etc., the real adventure is about to begin. On the other, when that cold wind blowing off the ocean smacks us, it is a literal wake-up call. If it feels this cold here, how is it going to feel when we are on the water in our kayaks in the middle of a long crossing between islands, wet, exhausted, and lost in a fog?

An 18-hour ferry ride out of Prince Rupert delivered us at midnight on a Saturday in Haines, where an old Alaskan buddy met us at the dock with a cooler stuffed with dried salmon. We would be cramming the plastic-wrapped fish into every spare nook and cranny of our kayaks, for both its protein and salty taste. After a wet sleep on his forested front yard we began the 1,000-mile drive from Haines to Homer. It was absolutely essential we arrive in Homer on time, two-and-a-half days later, in order to board the four-day-long ferry that would carry us out into the Aleutian Islands and drop us in the remote fishing town of Dutch Harbor. That ferry runs just once a month. If we missed it, the trip was over before it began. During the ensuing drive we stopped just once to sleep, pulling off the road onto a dirt track leading to snow-covered mountains. Despite the urgency it was a beautiful drive, though classic Alaskan territory—sharp-peaked mountain ranges, crystal-blue rivers, deep fields of snow—before dropping down through the stunning Kenai Peninsula.

The plan was to spend four to five weeks kayaking among and climbing the volcanic peaks of a little known group of islands called the Islands of Four Mountains. Though the logistical trail was nearing an end, we were still several thousand dollars short of the money we needed, which wasn't overly bothersome. When was the last time you heard of any expedition leaving home with a positive cash balance? Christopher Columbus was on his knees before his queen until minutes before sailing away; polar explorer Ernest Shackleton and his *Endurance* left harbor to much hoopla as he set off for the South Pole, yet he snuck back into London under the cover of night to arrange his last minute financing— by selling serialization of his adventure to a newspaper.

The bottom line—and the allure, to be honest—is that no one in the world knows much of anything about where we are headed. Few travel past, and even fewer stop at those remote islands. Most people I'd asked during the previous year, even Alaskan residents, had never heard of the Islands of Four Mountains. Admittedly, they are a blip on the map in the middle of a big, cold ocean. Those that had heard of them threw up their hands when asked how to get there. We'd managed to get this far.

Now we are faced with a new, potentially disastrous situation. We are to meet our fourth, Scott McGuire. He was to have flown into Anchorage earlier this morning and caught a commuter plane down to Homer, where we plan to pick him up. He is a sales rep with Teva, which means driving his decal-covered mobile home up and down the California coastline selling shoes, and this was high season for him. He had to stay on the job until the last possible minute. Now, only a few hours before the once-a-month ferry to Dutch Harbor is to depart, there is no sign of Scott.

Of all of the unknowns we face, Scott is actually one of the biggest. He is the youngest of our foursome at 27 years old, and none of us has traveled with him before. He used to be a kayak guide in the Channel Islands off California's coastline, and Barry and I had made an early morning, fog-heavy crossing with him from Ventura to the island of Anacapa a couple years before. He didn't stick around for the rest of that trip, but caught a ferry back to the mainland soon after we arrived. Since then I'd seen him twice, just briefly.

Son of a California banker, Scott had done a short stint with the Marines. Since then he'd worked as a commercial fisherman and diver off the coast of California as a kayak guide and Necky Kayak sales representative. His biggest adventure to-date was paddling the length of Baja California with an ex-Marine buddy. Tall, smart, a strong paddler on the ocean or white-water rivers, with good outdoor skills, we had invited him to come with us for two reasons: his hours spent in a sea kayak and his idea of going to the Islands of Four Mountains in the first place.

But on an adventure like this one—alone, dependent on each other, where every time we paddled we'd be putting our lives at serious risk—it was reasonable to ask, How does this person react in serious situations? With Scott, we had no idea. That we can't find him now is hardly encouraging.

Sean went to the small airport in Homer early this morning as planned. Not seeing him, he asked the plane's attendants if they'd seen a tall, dark-haired stranger on the flight, but they had not.

Now, standing on the wind-blown spit, we debate our options. What if he doesn't show? Maybe he changed his mind at the last minute. We wonder out loud about who we might replace him with. We have two, two-man boats; three of us is definitely an unworkable number.

"What about Jeff Hancock," Barry throws out. He is an outfitter based in Dutch Harbor who had been very helpful during the past months as we had queried him about everything from ferry schedules to the kind of bait we might have luck with.

"Or those other guys we talked with in Dutch, the high school teacher or the museum curator?" suggests Sean. When word got out that we were going to try to kayak in a place where few had journeyed in the past couple centuries, we had some compelling inquiries from men who would have been happy to join us.

"The only problem with any of those guys is that we have no idea what kind of kayakers they are, or what kind of travelers they might be," I say. "What if we invite them, then get out there to discover they are intolerable for one reason or another. It's not the kind of place you want to end up tenting with, or kayaking with, some kind of schizophrenic, or paranoid, or hypochondriac...you get my drift."

We still hope that Scott is just late and can catch the once-a-day plane from Anchorage to Dutch Harbor. (We, unfortunately, can't take that plane—our kayaks are far too long to squeeze into even the largest baggage compartment.) But none of us know him well enough to know if this disappearing act is par for the course.

Two months before, in April 1999, we all met to spend a weekend on a warm lake in the Sierra of California, mostly to practice our at-sea rescues. Overdressed for the California climate in shiny new drysuits, we overturned the big, empty kayaks just offshore of Lake Isabella, near Barry's home in Kernville. We tried to roll them back up, which should work in theory but in practice was extremely difficult. We practiced ejecting ourselves from the boats, then working together as two-man teams to roll them over, crawl back in, pump them out and start paddling again.

After our days of practicing it became apparent just how difficult righting these same boats in the middle of the Bering Sea would be. There, they would be much heavier, loaded with 400 to 500 pounds of shifting equipment and food. Water temperatures would be about 40° colder. If we went over in the Bering Sea, we would most likely be capsized due to fierce winds and waves. In theory, we should be strong enough, experienced enough to compensate, to rescue ourselves. We are all strong paddlers and out on the calm lake flipping the boat back right side up, then swinging ourselves up and into the boat had been relatively easy. But even as we practiced on Lake Isabella, I was filled with foreboding. A knot that would last for several months began to grow in my stomach that weekend. It whispered to me that *out there*, in the middle of the icy ocean, with the winds and sea whipping, the cold sapping our strength, all the practicing in the world wouldn't count for a thing. The bottom line is, if one of our two boats overturns—a strong likelihood where we were going, a place known as the Birthplace of the Winds—we will die. I am sure of it. We will never be able to right our boats and climb safely back inside.

My worries were further fueled by the variety of horror stories we heard daily as we prepared for the expedition. Numerous recountings of Alaskan fishermen swept off their boats into the Bering Sea and never seen again. Internet checks to a NOAA (National Oceanographic and Atmospheric Administration) weather buoy anchored off the coast of Alaska that reported five-to-six-foot swells, 38° air temperatures, 35° water temperatures, 16 mile an hour winds, resulting in a wind chill of 25°. Talks with experts on hypothermia. If any of us end up in that water during our five-week journey by sea kayak to the heart of the Aleutian Islands, we guess at the outside we'd have 20 minutes to live.

Our concerns about Scott's willingness to be a good team player first surfaced during that weekend. An admitted loner, late on a Friday night he threw a small fit when Barry, backed by me, explained that we didn't want him bringing a camera on the trip. In the back of his mind Scott saw this adventure as a launching point for a career as a photographer. What we didn't need was him focusing on making photographs when we needed him to concentrate on other responsibilities. My account of the expedition, with Barry's pictures, would be published by the National Geographic Society; the Society's Expeditions Council was our primary source of funds. Making pictures is Barry's job, and the magazine is expecting him to come back with the best work he's ever done. We needed Scott to focus on the kayaks, the paddling and our camps. To us it seemed a clear definition of responsibilities. To him it was as if we were denying him a golden opportunity. Though he finally accepted the decision, it was not without a certain amount of pawing of the dirt and harrumphing. His attitude that weekend worried us; in the middle of the Bering Sea, surrounded by vicious winds and 35° waters, is not the place to throw a fit. We are hoping we won't experience a repeat of his Kernville scene.

Finally we spot him. A scant three hours before we have to transfer our pair of kayaks and 1,000 pounds of gear and food onto the ferry, we drive past a shuttered restaurant on the spit and spot Scott sitting on the stoop. Bundled in Gore-Tex® and fleece to keep out the raw, windy day, he is carrying just a small backpack. It turns out he's been in town since early morning, having caught an earlier flight and then hitchhiking into town rather than waiting at the airport. He trusted that at some point he'd spot our very obvious rig—the only one with two kayaks strapped to its camper—or simply meet us at the ferry.

"I was worried maybe you guys hadn't made it," he says as he climbs into the truck.

As we drive toward the ferry, I breathe a sigh of relief. One less thing to worry about. Then I catch myself looking out the window at the seething, wind-lashed bay beyond. Great, I say to myself, now all we have to deal with is the Bering Sea.

TWO

A light rain has fallen all day, and as the 150-passenger ferry pulls away from our first stop, Kodiak's small harbor, the rain picks up. As we steam into night, the four of us standing at the rail watching Kodiak disappear, the fog thickens, swallowing the fishing boats and the processing plants. The ship's purser announces over the p.a. that if anyone has a tendency for seasickness, now would be a good time to visit her office and borrow the appropriate pills.

The ride from Homer to Dutch Harbor takes more than four days, and it passes through some of Alaska's most wild, most wind-and rain-swept scenery and seas. We have staked out a section of plastic seats on the upper deck, outside beneath a small roof. Cabins are small and expensive, so we've opted to sleep on the metal floor. Sleeping bags and pads are spread between the rows of chairs, bags of oatmeal and bread and peanut butter scattered about. We take hot showers for the first time in a week and spend the first day reading books, writing, napping. It promises to be a long four days, especially if this cold drizzle keeps up. The boat makes stops in Chignik, Sand Point, and False Pass. Only a small contingent of characters, including a solo kayaker from Japan humping a folding boat in his backpack, will ride out the entirety of the trip. A few seniors are actually doing the round trip for the scenery.

We left Barry's pickup behind in Homer. As we loaded our monstrous pile of gear by hand into the car-level deck of the ferry, a slightly disgruntled boathand had asked as our gear filled up two car spaces, "How long you boys going to be gone? The rest of the year?"

I pick a seat overlooking the bow of the big boat and watch the silver-gray fog lower until it matches perfectly the color of the sea. Enwrapped in the ashen night, a silent wind picks up and a strong rain begins to fall. Soon it is blowing horizontally in between the decks, threatening to soak our sleeping bags, books, etc. I move to another chair fully behind a plastic windshield, where the four-foot-tall picture window offers a protected view of the roiling seas. Every time someone around me gets up, I change seats, edging closer each time to the overhead heater, glowing red in the misty night. The heavy boat bucks as we head into the wind, whitecaps and swirl whipping across the top of the sea.

"It's windy out there," reports Barry, pulling his head out of the weather after a quick surveillance, his head and jacket fully drenched. "And I'm afraid it's all downhill from here." We agree to adopt this as the first motto of our expedition: "It's all downhill from here." As we head into the west, every hour until we crawl into our sleeping bags on the floor, the conditions grow wetter, windier, colder.

Despite this introduction to Alaska's foulest weather we are in good shape. We made every deadline to date. Our biggest question mark now is Scott Kerr, the hunting guide in Nikolski who had promised to carry us out the final leg to the Islands of Four Mountains. We'd finally gotten him on the phone from Kodiak. He'd just returned from a six-week camping trip and acted surprised to hear we were on our way. He was even more surprised to hear we hoped to meet up with him in just a few days. He explained his boat was "not there," but offered no more detail or excuse. His answer did not fill us with optimism, but until we got to Dutch Harbor there was nothing we could do.

We need Kerr both for his knowledge of the Islands of Four Mountains and for his service. Nikolski is 40 miles from our final destination. He wants $800 to carry us out there and pick us up. Don Graves, the commercial fisherman who's agreed to take us the 125 miles from Dutch Harbor down to Nikolski, wants $2800 each way. I'm carrying just enough money to cover both those costs. Now we're beginning to worry that Kerr's low price may reflect his business attitude.

"Maybe he's lived in that Indian village a little too long," poses Sean, who did most of the long-distance negotiating with Kerr. "I'd hate to think that his attitude is that if we show up, he'll help us whenever he gets around to it."

"To me it sounds like he and 'schedule' don't have a very close relationship," I reply. Wouldn't it be ironic if it was our very last link—and most irreplaceable link—that failed?

As I write in my journal, the boat's lights come up and the captain announces a rough night ahead. "Small craft warning,

ten-foot rolling seas…hold onto your bunks. Tomorrow's forecast? Gale force winds. Have a good night!"

We were headed out into the middle of nowhere thanks to the
offhand inspiration of one of the grandfathers of sea kayaking,
an adventuresome Scot named Derek Hutchinson. A progenitor
of the sport and prolific author about its how-tos, Hutchinson
traveled to Dutch Harbor in the early 1970s with four others
intent on paddling along the seacoast south out of Dutch Harbor.
His goal was to paddle from Dutch to Nikolski, including a 10-
mile crossing between Unalaska and Umnak islands.

In what now are extremely rudimentary boats, using paddles
that look like they were carved on the spot from lodgepole pine,
the team forged its way to Nikolski. For three weeks they camped
along the rocky coast staying within easy reach of shore. When
I met Hutchinson later, on a sandy beach in Port Townsend,
Washington, his memories of his Aleutian trip were not particularly inspiring.

"There were really only two things wrong with that trip," he
explained as he took apart his four-piece, self-designed paddle.
"The fact that for many days the wind blew so hard it rained horizontally. And that I traveled with the biggest bunch of assholes
I've ever paddled with. Otherwise it was great."

Our inspiration for venturing out to the Islands of Four Mountains was based on a throwaway remark Hutchinson had made
earlier at a lecture. In 1998 Scott McGuire went to see the
curmudgeonly icon talk in Santa Barbara. During his Aleutian
paddle, on a rare clear day, Hutchinson had glimpsed the volcanic peaks of Chuginadak and Carlisle through his binoculars,

some 40 miles across Samalga Pass. Afterward Scott introduced himself and asked him if there was somewhere in the world he wished he had kayaked. "The Islands of Four Mountains," was his immediate answer. His comment sent Scott to his atlas to find out exactly where these dream islands were.

Once found, he came to Barry and me. Scott knew we were looking for an extreme kayak expedition—something to test our paddling skills and ourselves. He also knew that I had strong connections with National Geographic, which might be convinced to finance such a relatively expensive (for sea kayaking) trip.

I did get financing from National Geographic's Expeditions Council, plus a grant from Mountain Hardwear and many favors called in from a wide and varied bunch of friends in the outdoor industry, who helped out with everything from the kayaks to a 50-meter rope. We raised nearly $20,000 in cash and another $25,000 worth of equipment. The former was needed to pay for ferry rides, to charter Scott Kerr's fishing boat, to pay for airplane rides in and out of Dutch Harbor after the trip, for food, gasoline and miscellaneous unsponsored necessities such as VHF radios and drysuits. The latter included myriad pieces of equipment from Skanoraks to stoves, compasses and dry bags.

Harder than raising the money was simply the getting out there. The big Necky kayaks were way too cumbersome to squeeze into any kind of airplane, which meant they had to be driven from Kernville, California, where we'd tested them. Barry's house on the Kern River was turned into our base of operations, and during the spring of 1999 everything from PFDs and throw-bags to freeze-dried food (enough for 35 days) and wetsuit booties arrived at his gate thanks to a legion of overnight shippers. Everything had to be packed into his pickup truck and driven, and ferried, nearly 4,000 miles to Dutch Harbor.

Using his home as our base camp was natural. My friendship with Barry goes back a decade. We'd met in the southernmost airport in the world, in Punta Arenas, Chile. He'd just come off a grueling trek around the peaks of Torres del Paine, the mountainous park in Chile's south. I had been rafting and horsebacking with friends through the same park. I was headed north, to the infamous Rio Bi´o-Bi´o to join the biggest raft trip ever to run the river. Fifty people had been invited, many of them environmentalists and politicians from both the U.S. and Chile. The idea was to run the threatened, Class V river as a protest against the government's plan to block it with a series of five dams, an effort that ultimately proved far too late.

We had everything we needed for that week-long trip except for enough experienced river guides. When I spotted Barry across the airport everything about him said "river guide." California-blond, biceps like oaks, sunglasses hanging on Chums around his neck, T-shirt, Patagonia shorts, Tevas. I approached him, introduced myself and asked him if he'd ever guided. It turned out he'd just come off leading environmental and cultural rafting trips in Russia and Costa Rica. At the time he was just beginning the transition from guide to photographer, but he readily signed on and traveled with us down the Bi´o-Bi´o. Since then we have traveled together literally around the world on expeditions and magazine assignments, from Nicaragua to Tibet.

He is strong but gentle, and an incredible athlete. I've long joked that I like traveling with Barry because I know he'd always be able to get me out of trouble, if necessary. His response to that line is always the same: "I take great comfort in knowing that I can outrun you. I'll get away, you'll be left behind and they'll quit the chase." The irony is that to date the only serious injury we've suffered in each other's company happened in Guatemala. Barry got up early to photograph the sun rising over Lake Atitlan and in the morning darkness fell into a cement drainage ditch, fracturing his pelvis in three places. I half-dragged him to the closest hospital, in the nearby hills, where they charged us $12 for the exam and X-rays and another $25 to build crutches big enough for the oversized gringo.

On his own he once spent several months in Siberia photographing aboriginal tribes only to have all his film seized by the KGB just before his train crossed into Finland. They claimed he'd been photographing "sensitive" defense sites, a nonsensical charge that nonetheless meant he had to spend two months in Moscow lobbying to have his film returned.

The best word to describe Barry is solid. That's a key ingredient when you're about to put your life in each other's hands in the middle of the Bering Sea.

As for Sean, he and Barry are old friends. They went to different schools in Santa Barbara and met on the job at the local Patagonia store. They couldn't be more different physically. Barry is big and blond. Sean is compact and Irish-red. Yet they've been friends and adventuring partners since their early twenties. For them, this trip included the opportunity to spend time together, somewhat like a pair of reuniting frat brothers.

A vastly experienced ocean sailor and pit-bull tough lawyer in Orange County, Sean was a welcome addition for two good reasons: I knew he would never complain, and we needed his expert navigational skills. Having sailed across the Atlantic Ocean several times using just the stars and a compass, he'd be able to steer us through the thick fogs that would be inevitable in the Aleutians. (We were actually looking forward to kayaking in the fog, since heavy fog meant less wind, thus calmer seas.) On the logistics side of this trip, Sean had taken prime responsibility for figuring out the calendar that would deliver us from road to ferry, ferry to road, all the way to Dutch Harbor, no easy assignment.

How did he get six weeks away from his law firm job to join us? He simply walked into one of the partners' offices and explained he was going on an adventure and he'd be back. "Some of my colleagues were mystified that they let me go," he explained, "but I find the direct route usually the best. If you want something, don't ask, just tell them." Unconcerned with such Orange County status symbols as fancy cars (he drives a Isuzu Trooper with a bashed-in front end) and expensive homes (he lives in a smallish two-bedroom apartment hard by Interstate 405) he could literally afford to walk away from his job if the bosses questioned his "commitment to law."

And what did I bring to this party? Mostly organizational skills, the connection with the National Geographic Society and the good humor and patience necessary to hold an expedition together from wistful idea to safe arrival back home. A writer-cum-adventurer, I'd learned about expeditioning at the feet of some masters. In the mid-1980s I'd hooked up with polar explorer Will Steger just after he'd successfully led a dog team to the North Pole without resupply. In the years that followed we wrote several books and traveled around the world together, from posh hotels in Tokyo and Chicago to icy glaciers in Greenland and Antarctica. I'd watched up close as he and his partner Jean-Louis Etienne raised—and spent—$12 million to cross Antarctica by dogsled (3,741 miles in 221 days). Four million dollars went for building a super-structured sailing boat shaped like a walnut so that it would pop out of the frozen sea rather than be crushed by it. When not traveling with Steger I had also made first descents of rivers in Chile and China and worked and traveled on six continents.

Reputations are funny things. Among my hardest-core adventuring pals, I'm viewed more as a "writer" than an "adventurer." Of this foursome headed into the Aleutians, I was the leader, but more for simply pulling off the organizational task of getting us here. On my past travels I'd often been the outsider, writing about something somebody else had dreamed up and organized. Here, the ultimate responsibility for pulling this off was on my shoulders.

The sea raged throughout the night, and the early morning hours delivered a torrential rain. Sean made the mistake of sleeping too close to the opening of our little three-sided solarium and woke in a rain-soaked sleeping bag. By mid-morning it is still gray and cold, but the sea has calmed.

Spread out in the aisle next to us is a 40-year-old Japanese engineer named Hdeki. We'd watched him board in Homer, lugging only two backpacks. One carried paddling gear and clothes, the other a folding kayak, a Canadian-made Feathercraft. From Tokyo, he was headed for Dutch Harbor as well, where he hoped to spend two months paddling solo around the shoreline of Unalaska. He proudly showed us his inspiration, a dog-eared copy of a paperback book, in English, *Mother Earth Father Sky*, by Sue Harrison. Translated into

Japanese, this romance novel, set in a much earlier century, replete with healthy-looking Aleut men and maidens on the cover, was apparently hugely popular in Japan. He'd come to see for himself the region where the book was set, in the heart of the Islands of Four Mountains, to soak up some of the romantic ambiance on its pages. We were a little skeptical. While we admired his alpine, minimalist approach to kayaking, we wondered if he realized just how cold and lousy and formidable this place could be? He was an experienced sea kayaker, so we trusted his kayaking skills. We weren't so sure about his survival skills.

"Some people think sea kayaking is like paddling floating lawn chairs," said Barry, after we'd spent an hour talking with the Japanese paddler. "Not that guy, he gets it. But where we're headed is sea kayaking at its most remote, most challenging. One slip, and that's it."

The ferry boat is pushing 25 miles an hour through the black Bering Sea. The farther west we get, as impossible as it seems, it grows more foggy, more wet. We joke darkly that this may be as good as it gets.

"What if we are out there and we are pinned in our tents for a month or more by rain and wind," I pose to Barry and Sean as we clamber down the metal stairs to the ship's small bar.

"We better hope there's a good bookstore in Dutch Harbor so we can bulk up our library," is Sean's reply.

We stop for an hour in Chignik, and tramping around in the village doesn't brighten our mood. Translated as "Big Winds," the tiny fishing port is situated on an exposed tip of land jutting into the ocean. The town has the reputation of having the worst weather in the United States.

We trudge along its single, narrow, muddy road, desperate to stretch our sea legs despite a cold, blowing rain that turns to sleet as we walk. "Perfect spot for a summer vacation house, don't you think, Jonny B?" Sean jokes. A boathand directs us to the town's bakery, where some savvy local caters to the once-a-month ferry with fresh cream cheese Danishes and cinnamon rolls. The only other store in town is an all-in-one stop, stocked with everything from groceries and foul weather gear to, incongruously, rubber flip-flops. Sean buys a pair.

"A great show of optimism," I offer as he plunks down his two bucks for the black thongs. Since pulling out of Homer, our feet have been encased in heavy Extra Tuff rubber boots and liners. It's hard to imagine a day in the near future where we'll be wanting to expose our toes to the elements.

"C'mon, it's almost summer," Sean says, defending his purchase. We walk back to the dock carrying brown paper bags full of sticky rolls. Our pants below our rain jackets are soaked from the blowing rain. "Can you imagine what it's like out here in the middle of winter?"

"Unforgiving? Untenable? Unrelenting? Take your choice."

Pulling away from Chignik, we stand on deck with one of the boatmen. He's telling us that usually when they arrive here, the ferry has to attempt several landings before successfully docking, thanks to the heavy seas and gale-force winds.

As we travel west, the big ship angles a route taking us farther south. With slightly warmer temperatures it grows only wetter, foggier.

By mid-morning the fog finally began to lift, and for the first time we can see the tops of the islands we have been passing since leaving Homer. Gulls fly overhead, and an occasional playful sea otter pokes its head above the waves as we pass. Dolphins jump and swim alongside the bow, and a cry of "Bear!" comes from the other side of the ferry, signaling either crew or passenger has spotted one of the big brown guys ambling on land. Most of the 100 or so passengers are along just for the ride, destination-less. They will either fly back from Dutch Harbor or return by the next ferry, lured simply to see for themselves this remote part of the country.

We are playing the trip like recovering alcoholics: one day at a time. No need to get too worked up about what may or may not transpire in the next days or weeks, since there's nothing we can do from here. It is hard to stay "fresh," mentally or physically, during such a period, and we hold mini-triathlons on-board of push-ups, pull-ups, and beer drinking.

For me, the closer we get to Dutch Harbor, the less intimidated I am by the conditions, the remoteness, the place. Taking the slow route out here has been a good way to adjust to this unforgiving environment.

Just off the port side, as we motor through the tides that race across False Pass, a trio of beluga whales break the surface. The Aleut name for False Pass—*isanax*—means simply "the pass." Its English name was earned because early mariners thought the channel impassable. Today it is a well-traveled part of the marine highway. Its population of 90, mostly Aleuts, work as salmon fishermen. A cannery, once the town's biggest employer, burned down in 1981, taking 130 jobs with it.

False Pass is an important spot on the map for us because the Aleutian Island chain officially begins there. We witness the transition from southeast Alaska to the Aleutians outside on the deck. The air temperature has grown balmy, into the 50s, and the wind has virtually stopped. I use the word "virtually" with purpose since it never truly stops blowing out here.

Late in the afternoon we climb to the bridge to talk with Captain Rob Crowley, a 20-year-veteran of the Alaskan Marine Highway. I want his perspective on just how fast the weather can change out here, and he offers good advice, mostly about simply being patient. "The people who get in trouble out here are the ones who hurry. It is not a place where you want to make snap judgments. My best advice is that you rely mostly on your gut. If it doesn't feel right, if something's telling you not to travel that day…don't. Instinct has saved lots of folks out here."

Stroking his salt-and-pepper beard, he peers over the bow of his big boat. Back home in Kodiak, he explains, he's just bought a couple kayaks for himself and his wife. It turns out he has as many questions about how to handle them as we do about how he runs his big ship.

Suddenly he points his finger at a place back off the stern. "Look behind us," he says, "and you can see just a sliver of robin's egg blue. That's something you won't see often in these parts. It's known as 'the sky.' "

THREE

"To live on a treeless island in the Bering Sea is to live between broad sheets of water and sky, to become accustomed to open space and to forces—wind, ice, tides—wiping out what is peripheral, rootless, impossible."—Sumner MacLeish

The Aleutian chain remains one of the loneliest and least-known spots on earth. Caught in a cross fire between cold and warm air circulating above the Bering Sea and the north Pacific Ocean, the islands are continually sculpted by winds of exceptional velocity and persistence. As the international navigational guide, *The Coast Pilot*, has noted, "No other area in the world is recognized as having worse weather in general than that which the Aleutian Islands experience."

The war between water and land is never ending. Waves fracture themselves on the rocky coast and sizable tides devour the sand beaches, daily changing the shape of an island. Fierce winds accelerate down the side of a volcano, gaining 100-mile speeds in a matter of minutes and turning the sea into a fury sinking the strongest boats and most experienced sailors. There are four seasons: a long autumn, or berry time; an endless season of snow and rain storms; a short moment of white flowers; and a few short weeks when the world is both green and hidden in fog.

The Aleut called the Alaskan subcontinent Alaxsxag, which literally means "the object toward which the action of the sea is directed." Alaska is an abbreviation of Unalaska, derived from the original Aleut word *agunalaksh*, which means "the shores where the sea breaks its back." When it was theirs, the Russians called their American possession *Bolshaya Zemlya*, "the Great Land."

There are increasingly fewer corners of the world, edges of civilization, white spots on the map, where 20th-century man hasn't made his particularly heavy presence known. It is a rarity in this modern day to still find the kind of remoteness we were headed into, especially one with an U.S. address. The heart of the Aleutians is 850 miles southwest of Anchorage, smack in the middle of the 885,000 square miles of the Bering Sea, the nutrient-rich waters that divide Alaska and the Russian Far East.

Half basin, half range, the Bering Sea is bordered east and west by Siberia and Alaska. To the north, through the narrow Bering Strait, lies the shallow Arctic Ocean; to the south, through the many passes of the Aleutian Islands, is the great Pacific Ocean, deepest in the world. At its eastern edge is Unimak Island, 500 miles farther west than Hawaii; the Andreanofs are due north of New Zealand; and Attu, westernmost point of the American continent, is only two hundred miles from Russian Kamchatka. The entire sea is home to 20-foot waves and, in the north, big ice.

During the ice ages, when massive continental glaciers absorbed so much of the Earth's water, this area was left high and dry by a receding sea, allowing the migration of animals and people from the Asian continent. At one time, many millions of years ago, the Aleutian Islands were the peaks of a range of tall mountains. Glaciers, snow, and ice then surrounded the mountains. Over many thousands of years as the temperatures of the earth warmed up, much of that ice and snow melted. As it fled it created giant lakes—what we now call our oceans—that rose up and up, toward the tops of the mountains. Finally, when the water stopped rising, all that was left showing of the mountains were the very tops, the Aleutians, a chain of 120 volcanic peaks strung like a diamond necklace between Kamchatka and Alaska.

These islands are formed at the juncture of two massive continental plates—the Aleutian and the Pacific—that are slowly moving toward each other. Where these plates meet and the earth buckles, the land is pushed upward, forming islands where it breaks the ocean's surface. Beneath the sea, the land falls away sharply, forming the Aleutian Trench, where the Aleutian plate moves under the Pacific plate. Sixty miles south of Unalaska Island, near where we will be kayaking, the Aleutian Trench plummets to a depth between 14,000 and 24,000 feet.

The Aleutian chain is divided into six groups of islands, each group separated by a gap of open ocean ranging from 20 to 50 miles. The Fox Islands have the largest landmass and are closest to the Alaska Peninsula. They include the island of Unalaska and the biggest town in the chain, Unalaska/Dutch Harbor. Just southwest are the Islands of Four Mountains.

The Andreanof Islands, which include Amlia, Great Sitkin, Adak, Kanaga, and Tanaga islands, are home to the small Aleut village of Atka, on Atka Island. Atka, resettled after it was nearly destroyed by starvation during the Russian occupation, suffered another trauma during World War II, when the village was evacuated and then burned to the ground by the U.S. military. Islanders returning from internment camps after the war rebuilt the town on its ancient village site. Adak, on Adak Island, is an abandoned Navy base that once held 100,000 men. Recently decommissioned, Adak has been returned to the Aleut through the Aleut Corporation, which dreams of developing its huge airport and deepwater port into a major way station between Asia and the North American continent.

The Delarof Islands are a smattering of tiny islands, more mountaintops in the submerged mountain range that makes up the chain. From there it's a leap to the Rat Islands and a very broad jump to the Near Islands, which include Attu, just 200 miles off the coast of Kamchatka.

I spent the better part of a year learning about the Aleutian region, through libraries and conversations. I came away convinced this is still the least-known part of our planet. Though geologists have worked in Alaska since late 1800s, the huge landmass of Alaska is not very well mapped. Complete geographical mapping on a scale of one mile to the inch, comparable to that done in much of the lower 48 would take more than 100 years and large sums of money. Present geological mapping has been done only at a reconnaissance level. Entire mountain ranges go unnamed and unexplored. On maps the region is still marked UNKNOWN. Few records exist documenting the Aleutians, the longest network of active volcanoes in North America. Sizable earthquakes are frequent along the chain, but most of the violent eruptions and earthquakes that have shaped it are unrecorded.

(This one in Kodiak, however, was described by an early Russian explorer: "During this period the volcano formed a new crater in its side which is still smoking....After the first tremors the sea receded suddenly from the shore and Koniagas and Russians ran to the mountains. A few minutes later a mountain of water poured over the land. This tidal wave tore one vessel from its mooring and set it on the roof of a hut, some huts were washed away entirely. There were two more tidal waves the same day. Strong quakes occurred from time to time over a period of 17 days causing mountains and shores to crumble and cliffs to fall, forming many separate crags.")

Where the two oceans meet, the Pacific and Bering Sea, is an extraordinarily rich waterscape. Record numbers of plankton, more than a million metric tons of pollack, sole, cod, halibut, and salmon are caught each year in the Bering Sea. Seabirds mass by the hundreds of millions—puffins, murres, fulmars, kittiwakes, cormorants. Bald eagles are more common than ravens. It was once home to the world's largest concentration of marine mammals, vast colonies of sea lions, seals and sea otters. Although the islands are treeless, they are carpeted with wildflowers (buttercups, chocolate lilies, lupine, wild iris, and orchids), lush grasses and mosses.

The islands have always been a link between two worlds. Over this ancient land bridge it is believed nomadic tribes from Asia and even Africa migrated to the American mainland. According to historian Corey Ford, the native Aleut are supposed to be descendants of the original inhabitants of the island of Nippon, who were driven from their homeland by swart barbarians from the south called Japanese. They settled in the Aleutians, living in sod-covered *barbaras* with giant whale ribs for rafters, hunting seals and sea lions and using sea otter fur for their clothing.

Aleuts once lived throughout the archipelago, but now they inhabit just five of the 120 islands. The entire chain is an International Biosphere Reserve, and all but 16 of the named islands are included in the Alaska Maritime National Wildlife Refuge, created in 1980. Attu, the westernmost island, one of the bleaker ends of the earth, is home to merely 22 coast guardsmen whose lonely task is to maintain a loran station to broadcast navigational signals for ships and aircraft.

It seems strange, but the more developed Alaska and the rest of the United States have become, the more the Aleutians have been forgotten. Many times as I prepared this expedition I explained to people that we were headed out to the Aleutians. They would listen, nod their heads, then inevitably ask, "Where are the Aleutians exactly?"

Besides the Poles, this part of the globe was the last section explored by outsiders. Russians—followed by the English, Spanish, and Dutch—arrived for the first time in 1741. Two hundred and sixty years later there are still wide gaps of missing information. The best map of the Aleutian Islands I could find, copyrighted in 1995 by the Alaska Geographic Society, acknowledges that: "To date, the Aleutian Islands have not been completely and accurately charted."

In part this lack of "knowns" is what lures me to this place, far "out there" into a land of volcanoes and earthquakes, hurricane winds and cold water. From a distance, it doesn't seem all bad, especially if you like extremes including lousy weather, tidal waves, earthquakes, and volcanoes. It rains most days, and the tops of the volcanoes are covered with snow almost year-round. But that's not why I have come. I have come because I sense that on those rare days when the skies are blue and the seas calm, it must be one of the most beautiful, maybe even magical places on Earth.

"To me, the Islands of Four Mountains are the most impressive and most beautiful of all the Aleutian Islands. Their volcanoes are all symmetrical, most of them are snow-clad and they appear to rise directly from the sea," wrote Harold McCracken in 1930 in *God's Frozen Children.* The lyrical name—the Islands of Four Mountains—is given to a small group of volcanic islands smack in the heart of the Aleutians. Few pictures, virtually no writings, exist to describe the five islands. Three retain the names given them by the Russians, shaped from their original names—Chuginadak, Kagamil, Uliaga. The other two were named more recently, in 1894, by the U.S. Navy—Carlisle (after John G. Carlisle, Secretary of the Treasury) and Herbert (after Hilary Abner Herbert, Secretary of the Navy).

The first people to live here, going back more than 5,000 years, were the Unagan—which translates literally as "the first" people. They were renamed by the Russians, who called them Aleuts. They had their own names for this small group of volcanic islands. The chain was known as Unigun, the islands as Kigalga, Kagamiliyax, Tanax angunax, Ulyaganx, Chagulyax.

Treeless, animal-less, rugged promontories and hidden reefs, kelp-strewn beaches, interminable rain and fog and mystery mark the islands. The last permanent population left several hundred years ago. During the past two centuries, since marauding

Russian fur hunters chased out the Aleuts, fewer people have visited them. They've been itinerant home to a small handful of Russian and American fox trappers—who introduced the animals to the islands, then hunted them almost to extinction—and even a U.S. Army team of meteorologists and a radio team during World War II. The tallest volcano is Mount Cleveland, on Chuginadak Island, rising 6,000 feet straight out of the sea and still smoking.

Throughout the first half of the 18th century the Russian Navy searched for eastern routes to China and India. Explorers, led by Vitus Bering, who became the first to fully trace the southern route of the island chain, followed those boats. Pushing east, looking for trade routes and trade partnerships, Bering named the chain the Catherine Islands, for Catherine the Great. By the mid-1700s entrepreneurs, traders, and fur hunters followed the sailing route along the southern side of the small chain.

As the Russians sailed past these volcanic peaks they would have seen four big mountains: Herbert, Carlisle, then the two volcanoes on Chuginadak. That is, the Islands of *Four* Mountains. Only when they had sailed past Chuginadak, looking back off the port side of their wooden ships, would they have spotted the smaller volcanoes on Kagamil and Uliaga. At the time each—from the tiny Uliaga to the big, twin peaked Chuginadak—boasted a community of about 100 Aleuts, seafaring people whose lives depended on the nutrient-rich, sea mammal-wealthy region.

The islands sit on the dividing line between the Bering Sea and the Pacific Ocean, one of the wildest, windiest, stormiest spots on the planet, an inhospitable place for man. Especially for man in extra-light, thin-skinned kayaks. One veteran Russian navigator, who'd sailed for 50 years, described a storm he sat out off the Islands of Four Mountains in the late 18th century: "The storm lasted continually for 17 days—I had never seen an example of the same, long, incessantly violent storm."

This dividing line is known as the "Birthplace of the Winds," a breeding ground for storms. Cold air blowing off the Siberian landmass meets the moisture-laden air of the warm Japanese current. It creates a succession of lows, like jets of steam from a teakettle, which shoot eastward along the Aleutian chain. The channels that separate the islands—the heavy waters we will have to kayak across—are renowned for unpredictability. Fast, marked by big currents, strong tides, ten-foot standing tide rips and constant winds, they were our major concern. Hundred-mile plus winds are common; on Attu Island they once lifted a B-52 off the runway and dumped it over like a Tinker toy. Winds of 170 miles an hour were recorded in nearby Unalaska in 1989.

We were going to explore the islands in a way much like those early Aleut people had, by kayak and foot. Our primary goal was to travel to all of the islands. We went knowing that the strong winds, powerful currents, and fast-moving tides could be so opposing we might never move from the first island. That was a strong possibility—being pinned down in our tents for a month, unable to push our kayaks into the water even once. We had a host of unknowns. We didn't know how cold it would be, how stormy, if we'd find places among the steep cliffs to pull our boats ashore, if the currents might not be too strong to paddle across, if the winds and rain would relent long enough to allow us to climb the volcanoes. My dream was to stand atop Mount

Cleveland and look out over all the islands, gazing as far as 100 miles out to sea on a blue-sky day.

Over the course of the 12 months prior to our June 1999 arrival on Kagamil, I had sought information from the experts I thought would be most helpful, Alaskans mostly. What I had learned was exactly how little is known about this small group of islands—for one simple reason. They are hard to reach, and once there, they are difficult to explore. Everyone told me essentially the same thing: we were in for the trip of our lifetime. Even the resident expert on the Aleutians at the Alaskan Volcano Observatory said when I called him in Anchorage, "When you get back, you'll know more about the place than we do."

One small comfort was that we knew people had kayaked out there before. The Aleut had depended on the seas for their lives, and their sophisticated *baidarkas* were the forerunners of our fiberglass kayaks. No one had made these crossings since because…well, because you just can't get any place more remote, more difficult to reach, more difficult to survive.

FOUR

T he ferry pulls into Dutch Harbor at 6:30 on a dark Saturday morning. Jeff Hancock, Tennessean by birth, Alaskan by residence for the past decade, meets us at the dock to help us lug our boats and gear to his warehouse on the town's main drag. We figure we have about 24 hours to unpack and repack everything for our ride to the islands.

Dutch Harbor is the colloquial name for the town of Unalaska, population 4,000. Its Dutch Harbor is a tiny islet reached by a 500-foot-bridge, known as "The Bridge to the Other Side." It is the last outpost; the next town of any size is in Siberia.

No one ends up in Dutch Harbor by accident. It is definitely the end of the road, a last outpost, the "playground of earth's last great hunter-gatherers," a last refuge for human wildlife drifting westward. It is still a place where men go to prove themselves or lose themselves. The town is home to the Bering Sea fishing fleet and a kind of last vestige of the Old West. My friend Jeff Dickrell, who teaches history at Unalaska High School, says it is the only place he knows where the place to buy the cheapest beers is on the once-a-day plane out of town.

During the mostly dark and rainswept days of summer we were in town I got a pretty good feel for the place. I was quickly educated that the filthy-looking birds scavenging the parking lot outside the hardware store were young male bald eagles. I came away sure there are a good many reasons to love and hate Dutch Harbor.

We spend our Saturday, after a fueling of Alaskan-strength coffee, running around town in Captain Don Graves' falling-apart pickup truck. We buy plastic buckets to hold a potential food cache, a couple of windproof lighters, some last-minute food, and a list of groceries for Scott Kerr. A bottle of cooking oil had opened onto several of our sleeping bags, so Sean mounted a cleansing operation. Our gear is spread all over Hancock's dusty warehouse space, for which we are thankful. Without his offer we'd be sorting and repacking in the rain on the dock.

As we drive back and forth on Dutch Harbor's main road, it is easy to see this is a world dedicated to seafood. Dirt roads are lined with crab pots—500-pound steel-and-wire cages used to capture 300 million pounds of snow crabs each year. Dozens of boats ranging from 90 to 200 feet are tied up side by side with small trawlers. Sleek factory trawlers come to offload frozen product and get back out to sea. A half-dozen rusty Japanese refrigerator ships await their cargo. It is essentially an industrial town set in the middle of some of the most savagely beautiful wilderness on the planet. Its raison d'être today is fish processing, turning halibut and salmon into chunks, slices, and steaks for a hungry, mostly East Asian clientele.

Fishing has always dominated Dutch's economy. Situated 850 miles southwest of Anchorage, the harbor is cut into the north side of the mountainous Unalaska Island, creating the finest, most ice-free harbor in the Aleutians. Captain James Cook named the harbor when he spotted a Dutch ship anchored there in the 1700s. Known as "the rock" or "the end of the world," Unalaska is where our journey begins.

The Aleut first settled here for the natural deepwater harbor, the abundance of marine life and birds and lush tundra, with its abundant harvests of berries, greens, and medicinal plants. The Bering Sea owes its bounty to its continental shelf, one of the world's largest. The submerged shelf of land extends from the shore to the start of deep water and supports a rich ecosystem. Its relatively shallow waters and mostly smooth floor make good conditions for all kinds of fishing.

The scenery then, even more than today, must have been spectacular. In the near distance, Makushin Volcano steams, and the emerald green tundra blankets the angular volcanic escarpments rising abruptly from the sea. The Unagan called their most populated harbor located at the mouth of a river teeming with salmon—Iliuliuk, translated as "to live in harmony" or "curved bay." By 1775 they'd set up a trading settlement. Journals of those early visitors recount the ease of fishing. In three or four hours the men could "fill their boats with *holybut* of an enormous size." Archaeological excavations of Aleut sod houses on the hills above town have unearthed artifacts from Iliuliuk going back 6,000 to 8,000 years.

The Russian explorers first arrived here in 1759; and fur trappers followed, brutally enslaving the local hunters to harvest fur

seals and sea otters and making Iliuliuk the first permanent settlement in Russian America. Soon after, the arrival of Russian
Orthodox Church missionaries helped ease relationships
between Aleuts and Russians. Father Ivan Veniaminov, later can-
onized as Saint Innocent, settled on Unalaska in 1824. With Aleut
Ivan Pan'kov, a fluent Russian speaker, he wrote a Russian-Aleut
grammar. Veniaminov may be the best historian of Aleut life and
culture for very few histories of the Aleuts exist. His book, *Notes
on the Islands of the Unalashka District*, is the seminal history of
the region, and I had read it, underlined, photocopied and passed
it around to my teammates. Very few histories of the Aleuts exist;
Veniaminov observed them up close for 20 years, and he wrote
about everything from their religious ceremonies to clothing
and what they ate.

When the Americans purchased Alaska from the Russians in
1867, many Aleuts living still in Unalaska were moved permanently north to the desolate Pribilof Islands, commanded to
harvest fur seals for the Americans. During the Gold Rush in
the late 1800s the island became a way station for ships. They
reloaded with water and coal stored on Unalaska on their way
north to Nome.

Mount Ballyhoo, named by Jack London, overlooks town. I wonder where the desire to live in this hard, beautiful place comes
from and guess that it is slightly different for every one that
arrives. Some are lured by fishing. Others because it is the ultimate end of the road. A hardy few stay for the rare beauty. Going
back centuries, it has lured a tough crowd. One old Aleut told a
historian that if the Russians had not arrived in the late 1770s,
introducing disease, murder, and enslavement, the natives would

have most likely killed themselves off with their interminable fighting. During World War II the town was a home base for U.S. soldiers sent to fight the Japanese who had taken over some of the western Aleutian Islands. Thousands on both sides died from frostbite and hypothermia.

It can be an extremely beautiful place, surrounded as it is by the deep blue Bering Sea and a long line of snow-capped volcanoes. But more often it is a dismal, cold, miserable place…and that's on a day locals consider nice.

The Russian fur traders may have been the first to cash in on the Bering's ecosystem in the mid 18th century, hunting sea otter and seal skins. Within a hundred years those stocks were depleted. Today, a more modern, allegedly smarter man threatens to similarly destroy the region's economic base.

In the not-so-distant past Dutch Harbor was the place to come if you wanted to cash in on the biggest boom of commercial fishing in the U.S. For a few years at the end of the 1970s and beginning of the 1980s, Dutch Harbor was the busiest fishing port in the country. In 1975 the Aleutians were not even mentioned on the National Marine Fisheries Services list of top ports. But 1,000 miles to the east, crab stocks were being depleted around Kodiak's rich processing center. As a result, fishermen began looking for other resources along the Aleutian chain. A year later Dutch Harbor replaced Kodiak as the number two port of the nation in the dollar value of seafood landed, $48 million in crabs alone. By 1978 it had become the top-money-making fishing port in North America. Crab fishing proved so lucrative that captains of crab boats were making $10,000 before lunch.

The immediate result was that local crab fleet increased from 130 vessels in 1978 to 236 in 1981. Unalaska grew from 500 residents to 1,000, then 4,000. Competition grew so fierce that the Bering fleet fished in the worst weather. By then the industry was grossing more than $100 million. Unalaska's city budget grew from $350,000 to $11 million.

Crab season sent the boomtown into overdrive. Airports, hotels, restaurants and bars filled with fishing crews and processing workers. A small police force worked overtime on cocaine-and-alcohol-related trouble. High season overlapped with the region's worst winter weather, which resulted in weeks-long airplane delays, stores emptying their shelves, banks running out of cash.

Books have been filled with anecdotes about fishermen who earned $30,000 in a month on a crab boat, or the boat owners that retired to Seattle or the Caribbean, after several long, hard seasons of highly profitable Bering Sea fishing. Yet other wannabes died trying to make a million, vanishing forever in the cold Bering Sea, accidentally getting trapped inside one of the 700-pound crab pots as it whistled toward the bottom, or by spending all that fast-earned money on drugs, booze, and tattoos. Then, in 1982, the crab boom was over. That year the catch was less than one-fortieth of 1980, and the season was closed by emergency. Some blamed the drop on rising sea temperatures hampering breeding; others pointed to flagrant overfishing.

Today, with crab populations down, fishermen still make a living, but hardly the riches of recent history. More than a dozen ships still sit in harbor waiting to be filled with *sirimi*, or "crab," almost all destined for Japan. Seven different seafood processing plants are still scattered around the perimeter of the harbor, processing pollock, king crab, opilio crab, salmon, halibut, cod, herring roe. That adds up to more than 600 million pounds of seafood a year, valued at more than $135 million.

The smoky, always dark Elbow Room, Dutch's best-known landmark, is still open. It is a giant human crab pot packed with unsavory-looking creatures in woolly beards and baseball caps, moving back and forth through the smoke and the din. The bar has Plexiglas windows to discourage them from being used as an exit during fights. According to author/fisherman Spike Walker, during the boom days of the early 1980s a "tidal wave" of narcotics rolled over Dutch Harbor. Thousand-dollar nights on the one-bar town were not uncommon, with $175 rounds for the house common, chased by $150 grams of cocaine. Legend has it that Jimmy Buffett once played the tiny room, and was taught to fly by local pilot legend Tommy Reeve.

We spend an hour in the Elbow, washing down our last supper before heading out the next day, swapping tales with Hancock and a few of his friends. One thing jumps out at you in Dutch: This is definitely not a place to come if you're searching the opposite sex, at least not if you're looking for a woman. In the good old days $200 hookers used to be flown in from Anchorage or Seattle during peak season. Now the prettiest girl in town is most often in the band at the Elbow Room, most often from Anchorage or Seattle. Dutch Harbor's number one pick-up line, I'm told, is: "Even if I was in Seattle, I'd still be attracted to you."

Midnight finds us drinking homemade beer in cans the size of small kegs in the Hancock's upstairs apartment. I am about to fall inelegantly onto my Therm-A-Rest pad spread on the floor. Then all of our so far perfectly timed logistics fell apart with a single phone call.

It did not come as a complete surprise. We'd had suspicions for several days that our last travel link—Kerr, the hunting and fishing guide who was to escort us the final 45 miles out to the Islands of Four Mountains—had a loose wire or two. We'd all been silently crossing our fingers he'd get them reconnected before we arrived.

We had assumed, based on several long-distance phone calls during the past few months, that he was waiting for us to arrive in the tiny, 4,000-year-old Aleut village of Nikolski, where he lived with his Aleut wife, Agrafina. For months we'd been negotiating with him, and now we were counting on him to motor us out and drop us off on one of the islands. We hoped we might even talk him into planting a food cache on another of the islands before heading back to Nikolski. We also hoped he'd come back out and pick us up a month or so later.

Kerr had lived in the area for the past decade. A native of New York's Mohawk Valley, he was the only white man, and the youngest of any race, living in the hard-drinking-cum-strictly-religious town of 26. His reputation in Dutch Harbor was as a boatman extraordinaire, if not always reliable. All we wanted was for him to show us a good first beach somewhere in the islands and drop us off. The map we had for the chain was extremely limited, so any insider knowledge about this little-known place was worth whatever price he was going to demand.

We were curious about Kerr, as we were about Nikolski. We were fascinated to learn that the oldest known settlement of the Aleut world, dating back 8,750 years, had been excavated at Anangula Island, four miles offshore from Nikolski. For Kerr the village offered cheap living; he could fish and hunt ducks, geese, and the occasional reindeer, which had been put on the other end of the island in the early 1900s. There was a single store in town, and a Russian Orthodox priest visited once a year. On the rare clear days a flight arrived from Dutch Harbor.

"This country, you just can't get it out of your blood once you get it in. There may not be many beautiful days, but the ones you get make up for the rest," Kerr had said to a reporter a few years before, which made him sound like the kind of man we would like. "I'd heard from a friend there was absolutely nothing here. I moved here just because that was where the boat was going. Built a cabin at Anderson Bay. No roads, no signs, no intense social structure. If I could do anything in the world, it's what I'm doing now. Trapping in the winter, guiding in the summer."

Agrafina grew up in Nikolski and returned after high school in Kodiak. Her mother works as a janitor at the village clinic; her dad is a mechanic at the power plant. They live in a comfortable three-bedroom house with two dogs and a rack outside for drying fish, since they put up most of their own food. Working for money generally means leaving the village, sometimes for several months at a stretch. Scott takes jobs longshoring and crewing on commercial fishing boats. Agrafina works for Aleutians West Coastal Resources Area, counting sea lions at nearby rookeries and conducting water-quality interviews with Dutch

Harbor seafood processors. Together they'd formed a tour company, Aleutian Island Adventure, hoping to cater to people interested in the area's history, scenery, and wildlife. That business, I hear, is very slow.

Our plan had been to hitch a ride with a commercial fishing boat captain out of Dutch Harbor—Don Graves, aboard his *Miss Pepper*—down to Nikolski. The route hugged the shore, and Graves felt comfortable making the delivery as long as the weather wasn't too bad. Our hope was to spend a couple days in Nikolski, packing out our boats and doing a little paddling. In other words, we wanted to acclimatize ourselves to the near-freezing ocean, powerful winds and constantly changing weather before heading out into the middle of nowhere.

After a few of those mini-keg-sized beers Sean managed to get Kerr on the phone, just a dozen hours before we were to load onto Graves' boat. Sean hung up the phone in Hancock's darkened upstairs shop and reported the bad news to me.

"He says he doesn't have a boat," he said in a stunned voice. Sean had been our main link with Kerr, and I could tell he felt responsible, guilty.

I too was stunned and couldn't respond immediately. Could it be that our last link—our only ride out to the IFM—would be the end of the trip? "Where the fuck is his boat?" I asked quietly.

"He says he never really had a boat," said Sean. "He was hoping to be able to borrow the tribe's 24-footer, but apparently he never formally asked them. Now it's up in dry dock. Can't be put in the water for days, maybe weeks. He did ask if we got that far if we could drop him off some groceries, dog food, chewing tobacco."

"That's ballsy," was all I could answer.

Sean and I chose the only rational option given the dire news. We popped another of those keg-sized home-brews. After traveling 4,000 miles to get here, it looked like our last, most tenuous, most important link had collapsed. Not only might we not get off the beach at Kagamil, we might never get out at all. If we failed to get out to the Islands of Four Mountains, we'd be stuck here for another month, or until the ferry returned.

In shock, we don't pause more than five minutes before getting Don Graves on the phone and beginning a not-so-subtle, 13th-hour negotiation for him to carry us all the way to the Islands of Four Mountains.

More than a month before he had agreed to carry us to Nikolski. We were due to leave with him aboard his *Miss Pepper* in less than 12 hours. He had long ago explained he had no interest in crossing Samalga Pass to the Islands of the Four Mountains. His reasoning was straightforward. He had a new, untested boat he'd bought to run fishing charters. It had fewer than 100 hours on its single diesel engines. He didn't want to take it into treacherous waters he'd never crossed before, most likely at night. He had boated out of Dutch Harbor for the past 20 years. He had a good job at one of the processing plants, a wife and two kids at home. Risking his boat, and his life, he said softly over the phone, was not something he wanted to consider.

Along with our realization that Kerr would not help us, it dawned on us that now our permits to visit the Islands of Four Mountains, arranged by him, were to have been issued by Dara Johnson in Nikolski. If Kerr doesn't have a boat, there is no reason for us to make a stop in Nikolski. At midnight we realize not only do we not have a ride, we also don't have permission. Nor do we have a clue, especially at this late hour, with Sunday dawning, whom to ask.

Listening to our negotiations from the kitchen, our new friends—Hancock, high school history teacher Jeff Dickrell, pilot Burke Mees, photographer Dan Parrett—are sympathetic. My guess is, they are a little skeptical about our plans anyway. They are tough, experienced guys who know this region well. They bid us good night and good luck, agreeing on one sentiment: "You're going to have your hands full." Our second motto of the expedition is born.

As they drive off, the exhaust of their pickup trucks hanging in the cold night air, I walk into the damp warehouse and crawl into my sleeping bag, exhausted. As I try to fall asleep, I'm not certain how we'll continue. I'd used my last card with Don Graves—money—and we agreed to talk first thing in the morning. The more than $8,000 I'd agreed to pay him for taking us out, and picking us up a month later, was more than I'd carried with me. He wasn't gouging us; the price was based on his standard boat rate, $165 per hour. We figured with good luck the run out would take 12 hours each way, or 24 hours boat time. He'd have to do that twice in order to pick us up. It was expensive, but we'd asked around—there were no other options. If Graves would take us, tomorrow, on our schedule, it would be worth the money.

I haven't slept well for a month now, since leaving Paris on May 31. There's been that knot in my stomach since Barry's house in Kernville, and that goes back to mid-April. Being less than a day away from departure has only made the knot thicker.

We may be getting ourselves in over our heads, in an exceedingly remote place. A certain amount of fear is good, makes you cautious. But how much is too much, before it becomes crippling?

FIVE

"**T**here came to us from the island a Chukchi in a leather boat, which had room, but for one man. He was dressed in a shirt of whale intestines which was fastened about the opening of the boat in such a manner that no water could enter even if a big wave should strike it."—first written account of natives in kayaks, by Russian sailor Michael Spiridovinich Gvozdev, in 1732, near King Island

Migration through the Aleutian Islands occurred as far back as 15,000 to 50,000 years ago, when the sea level was as much as 350 feet lower, linking Siberia and Alaska into a huge Arctic grassland called Beringia. Asiatics drifted across the Bering Sea land bridge in pursuit of mammoths, mastodons, and other large herbivores. Others arrived via the chain of volcanic mountains in big skin boats. Emigrating in small bands, over generations they continued as far south as the southern tip of South America. The ancestors of today's Indians came first, followed by the progenitors of the Aleut and Eskimo.

From 15,000 to 25,000 years ago, the Unagan people inhabited all of the Aleutian Islands. They lived in villages built in protected coves along the seacoasts. No one is 100 percent sure where the people we now know as the Aleut came from. Most scholars believe they came from Siberia and Mongolia. Others are convinced they came from Japan; still others, from Canada and Alaska.

Aleut legend holds that their roots are in a place called "Ta-nam Annuna," somewhere on Asia. The island of Chuginadak, one we'll visit, was originally named for that place, thus its centuries-old moniker as "the birthplace of the Aleuts." Another folk tradition claims the Aleut "descended from a dog that fell from the sky on the Island of Umnak," which adjoins the Islands of Four Mountains. Wherever they came from, they would have arrived in boats carrying 20 to 30 people, made from wood and the skins of seals. They came as all explorers do, looking for new land, a new place to raise their families. Tracing the exact history and culture of the Aleut is difficult because they had no written language—and because the Russians did such a pervasive job of eliminating them.

When the white man arrived, the Aleutian chain was one of the most densely populated parts of Alaska. The Aleut inhabited all of the major islands, the Alaska Peninsula as far east as Port Moller and the Shumagin Islands south of the peninsula. The name Aleut stems originally from the Koryak or Chukchi languages of Siberia, and it appears to have been quickly adopted by Aleut people themselves. About 400 abandoned Aleut villages are listed in state records, and certainly more exist. Only a fraction have been studied, due to the expense of working and researching out in that cold, uninhabited, faraway place.

Before the outsiders came, the Aleutian Islands were home to at least eight distinct social tribes from the different island groups who were among the most advanced aboriginal settlers. They spoke different dialects and exploited the vast richness of the sea around them, enjoying a high standard of living, developing art, music, and natural medicine including mummification.

Their lives were dictated by the sea, it provided them with food as well as materials for clothing and tools. They built their drift-wood and tundra homes near the best beaches, choosing sites where they could most easily pull their kayaks ashore. If possi-ble, they built on an isthmus with beach on either side, better for observing the seas, keeping a contant eye out for invaders and quick escapes

The Danish navigator Vitus Bering, serving Russia on his historic voyage of 1741, made Alaska known to the world. Spon-sored by Peter the Great, Bering came upon the islands during an exploration of the Pacific coastline.

Bering's pair of sailing ships first encountered Aleut war-riors in their baidarkas in the Shumagins, near Adak Island. Disdaining trinkets and cloth, the Aleuts wanted the sailors' metal knives. They were already familiar with iron, having obtained pieces washed ashore from shipwrecks or through aboriginal trade channels. Ironically, Aleut shamans had pre-dicted that white men would arrive from beyond the sea and that the Aleut would become like them, adapting their customs and manners.

Bering's voyage marked the culmination of a great Russian eastward expansion. With little government assistance Russian fur hunters—the so-called *Promyshlenniki*—had gradually penetrated Siberia and brought the great territory under control. Those who continued on were mainly private individuals interested in more fur. Few settled permanently in Alaska. They were the ones who gave "Russian America" its unique character. Though they greatly influenced the lives of the people living here, at no time was more than a fraction of the native population or land under Russian control. Yet today there are reminders of the Russians all over the map of the Aleutian Islands: Baranof Island, Constantine Harbor, Davidof Island, Vsevidof Island, Seredka Bay, Pogrommi Volcano.

The wooden sailing ships carrying Russian explorers—outlaws, mercenaries, entrepreneurs, however you view them—sailed along the southern side of the Aleutians, headed for America. When they stopped on the islands, the Aleut were not sure what to make of these new people. On some islands the Russians were welcomed like friends. On others the natives were angry and scared. They had a right to be. The Russians brought the Unagan people epidemics, violence, starvation, and slavery.

In his thorough account of the Aleuts, *Baidarka,* author and kayak builder George Dyson succinctly sums up the period of colonialism: "The Russians were outlaws. They had been thrown out in the different revolutions, and they moved east across Siberia. You had to be tough to cross Siberia on foot. You couldn't be just an ordinary man. Most of those who reached the Pacific died on the coast. Only a few made it across the ocean, the toughest of the toughest. A lot of them had been rich people before they were thrown out. They were into the money thing. The trip was to go and find a tribe of Aleuts to enslave. Then you went off with them to kill fur seals."

The most compelling discovery made by Bering and the Russians was the plethora of fur-bearing animals they passed along their route. Their richest find was the fur of the then-abundant sea otter. When word spread back to Siberia about the abundance of seal life in the islands, Russian fur traders started flocking to the Aleutians. They had wiped out their own fur bearing mammals in Siberia and on the Pacific coast.

Driving the quest for sea otter pelts and other furs, for which the Chinese paid top prices, was the Russian desire to acquire exotic goods from Chinese merchants. Russians came to the Alaska coastline because mammals here were plentiful. Some got along with the Aleut, trading fairly for sea otter pelts and other valuables such as walrus tusks. Others forced native hunters to hunt for them by taking their wives and children hostage. Hunted first was the sea otter, then when they were depleted, the fur seals, which migrated through the Aleutian chain each spring and fall. Hundreds of thousands of fur seals were killed because their dense fur—300,000 hairs per square inch—provided warmth for the wealthy. Demand for the skins spread through Europe and eventually across the Atlantic.

The Aleut had a very different culture. They could not have been more different from their invaders. Their clothing was made from fish skin and bird feathers. They wore bones and plugs in their nose and sometimes even dangled whole birds from an earlobe. They lived underground in smoky communal long houses, surviving on a diet of mostly raw fish and sea mammals, berries, eggs, and birds.

The Aleut were not peace-pipe smoking, nature-admiring, spiritual tribal folks content to be left alone out in the middle of nowhere. As Dyson points out, one reason the Aleuts shared little boat-building knowledge from island to island was because they were usually at war, "effectively preventing the free exchange of nautical ideas and making speed, rather than armament or carrying capacity, the measure of a boat." Veniaminov claimed, "The Aleuts had battles at sea…only when they came unexpectedly upon an enemy. However, having a superiority over the Kad'iak people in the speed of their baidarkas, the Aleuts sought out the latter…they moved in ferociously to drown him without mercy until the vanquished begged for peace." The men usually had several wives, and wars between groups often started over claims to women. Vengeance and feuds were common excuses for fights, and they often took prisoners in raids on their neighbors to use as slaves. Slaves and criminals were treated brutally, sometimes tortured to death.

Among the early accounts written by the first Russians was that of navigator Andrean Tolstyk, who visited the islands in 1760 and wrote about the locals, "They live in holes dug in the earth, in which they make no fires, even in winter. Their clothes are made like shirts, of the skins of guillomots and puffins…. They catch cod and turbot with bone hooks and eat them raw…. In the severest weather they make no addition to their usual clothing. In order to warm themselves in the winter, when it is very cold, they burn a heap of dry grass over which they stand to catch the heat under their clothing. And whenever they pass the night at a distance from home, they dig a hole in the earth and lay themselves down in it, covered only with their clothes or mats of platted grass. They are without the least appearance of decency, and seem but few degrees removed from brutes."

Another Russian wrote: "These savages…dwell in large caves from forty to eighty yards long, from six to eight broad and four to five feet high.…Although no fires are ever made in these caves…both sexes sit naked. They feed upon the flesh of all sorts of sea animals, and generally eat it raw.…Marriage ceremonies are unknown and each man takes as many wives as he can maintain. These women and their children are not infrequently bartered in exchange for commodities—often a bladder of fat is the price.…When they want to glue their stone arrows to the shaft, they strike their nose until it bleeds and use the blood as glue."

This condescension led, typical of the era, to the slaughter of the natives. The first Aleuts were murdered in 1747, when 15 warriors refused to surrender some metal to Russians for inspection. As the fur trade peaked between 1760 and 1780, so did the violence, particularly in the larger islands. During the Promyshlennikis the Russians "took" village after village, forcing Aleuts into slavery or killing them outright.

The natives were not passive victims. Repeatedly, they banded together to kill shiploads of their unwanted visitors. Some of the Aleut put on wooden armor and tried to fight off the newcomers with bows and lances. Observed Ken Brower in *The Starship and The Canoe*, "Putting aside old feuds, they united against the fur hunters and succeeded in killing a few, but the reprisals were always more terrible." The Russians retaliated by killing hundreds of warriors, attacking villages and destroying baidaraks, spears, and other tools vital to survival. In a particularly savage incident, a Russian sailor lined up a dozen Aleuts and shot a bullet through the first. The bullet stopped in the ninth, giving the Russian empirical evidence of his gun's strength. The Russian government disciplined some traders for mistreating the Aleut, but complaints took a long time to reach St. Petersburg. "God is high above, and the Czar is far away," was an unofficial motto of the campaign.

Ultimately defeated, the Aleuts became partner-slaves, joining massive Russian fur hunts that scoured the coast of Alaska and ranged as far south as Baja California. Escorted by support vessels rarely larger than 80 feet long, sea otter hunting fleets ranged as far afield as northern Japan, with permanent detachments stationed in southeast Alaska, northern California, the Pribilof Islands, and Commander Islands and the Kurils. "Nothing was left them but that bleak adventure. Aleut men between the ages of 18 and 50 were subject to the draft," continues Brower. "The lucky ones were allowed to work on shares, keeping half their catch. They hunted sea otter on Kodiak Island and were attacked by the Eskimos there. They hunted Prince William Sound and were attacked by those Eskimos too."

The initial two decades of hostilities between Aleuts and Russians gave way to another two decades of coexistence. In 1799 the Russian American Company was granted a monopoly over all Alaskan commerce, and Aleuts discovered themselves dominated by a ruthless bureaucracy.

Before the Russians arrived in the Aleutians the islands had been one of the most densely populated regions of aboriginal America. The sea around was wild but rich, and the Aleut survived well off it, supporting a population as large as 25,000. Within 40 years after the Russians arrival at least 80 percent of the Aleut population was lost. Smallpox, measles, tuberculosis, venereal diseases, and pneumonia—as well as Russian guns—drastically reduced the Aleut population to 2,247 in 1834 and to 1,400 in 1848. That year a smallpox epidemic struck, further reducing the number of Aleuts to approximately 900.

The Russians were no more kind to the animal life. Stellar sea cows, discovered by Russians in 1741, were eradicated 27 years later.

The decades that follow resulted in a literal blitzkrieg against the sea otter. Amassing up to 800 baidarkas at a time, the Aleut hunters—who outnumbered the Russians by 100 to 1—swept through the seas. Organized under the banner of the Russian American Company, the entire battallion was controlled by a single Russian *peredovshchik,* who collected the pelts from the hunters and kept a record of their catch. The peredovshchik was also in charge of trade with the inhabitants of the regions through which they passed, "bartering furs from those people from whom the company does not dare take them." It was war, against the animals, but also anyone whose path they crossed. "The Aleuts and their Russian masters were attacked at every opportunity by the Tlingits, the warlike people who guarded the top of the Inside Passage. Hundreds of Aleuts were killed when the Tlingits sacked Old Sitka in 1802," reports George Dyson. These annual voyages encompassed over 2,000 miles and only the toughest were able to survive the trip. "Many such paddlers, once they have made two such journeys, fall into a fever and are completely without strength." In a season, 200 men would drown en route to Kodiak from Sitka.

These hunting journeys were hard on the boats as well. After a storm or enemy attack, crippled baidarkas were cannibalized to repair the less injured craft. Aleuts spent the winter building new boats in preparation for next year's hunt. Baidarkas were built by the thousands, requiring a massive number of seal skins.

Numbers taken from the traders' journals tell the harrowing tale of the hunts. During the reign of the Russian merchant/hunters Shelikhov and Golikov, for example, between 1743 and 1780, 35 Russian companies hunted furs in the region. The accumulated take was valued at 4,522,844 rubles. Between 1781 and 1797, 11 companies took another 2,799,669 rubles' worth.

During the powerful reign of the Russian entrepreneur Baranov, between 1797 and 1820, hunted and exported from Russian America were: 72,894 sea otters, 34,546 river beavers, 59,530 sea otter tails, 1,232,374 fur seals, 36,362 blue fox and large quantities of walrus tusk, varieties of fox, and other furs to the value of more than 16 million rubles. Frigates built in Chugach Bay ran constant shuttles between Kodiak and Okhotsk, each carrying accounts like this: 3,467 sea otters, 3,350 beaver tails, 1,115 river otters, 1,515 black foxes, 1,615 silver foxes, 1,659 red foxes, 290 river beavers, and 200 sables.

As the Russians continued to explore farther into the continent, news of their discoveries spread around the world. In the late 1700s more explorers came from as far away as Sweden to claim lands in the North Pacific. The Spanish sent five expeditions at once, two overland and three by sea, in order to prevent Russian penetration into California. Perhaps the best known sailor to arrive in the Aleutians was Captain James Cook, desperately searching for a route from the Pacific to the Atlantic. He landed at Unalaska in 1778 and his reports of abundant otters and fur seals brought more British and Americans. The English government offered a 20,000 pound reward for the discovery of the Northwest Passage. For this reason Russians purposely made bad maps—they didn't want anyone else following in their fur-rich footsteps.

Yet, by the 1860s, with the Crimean War depleting government coffers back home, the Russian Empire lost whatever small interest it had in the Aleutian Islands. In 1867 the tsarist government of Russia signed a treaty with the United States, selling the right to govern Alaska and its people for $7.2 million. Ratification of the treaty was barely approved by a U.S. Congress, which was struggling with issues closer to home than acquiring such faraway territory.

At the time, that's all Alaska seemed to be—a cold, faraway place. Who could have imagined the vast stores of minerals lying just below the surface? The treaty increased America's landmass by fully 50 percent and checked a westward-expanding Canada.

By the time the U.S. purchased Alaska in 1867 the Aleut were, as documents of the day worded it, a "civilized tribe." Their lives didn't improve much under the Americans, who put them to work hunting seals in the still animal-rich Pribilof Islands to the north. The new Alaska Commercial Company, which acquired the assets of the Russian American Company, similarly "drafted" Aleuts to hunt sea otters and fur seals. Another 100 years of captive Aleut labor and seal killing followed, now under the jurisdiction of the U.S. Department of Treasury and the U.S. Department of Commerce. Revenue from this commercial seal harvest quickly paid for the original cost of Alaska and generated many millions more. No long-term plans were made for conserving the remaining seal herds, though the ultimate goal of the Americans proved to be the same as the Russians: Profit.

Helping the native people was far down the ladder of responsibilities. Skins became so scarce the Aleuts had trouble finding enough to build and repair their *baidarkas.*

During World War II, the last remaining Aleuts were evacuated from the chain after the Japanese bombed Unalaska/Dutch Harbor and occupied Attu and Kiska islands. Given just hours to pack a suitcase before they were shipped off to southeast Alaska, they were interned there in concentration camps for the duration of the war.

Only a very few descendants of those last islanders ever returned. Today only five of the 120 islands in the chain are inhabited, home primarily to migratory birds and a small number of marine mammals. Virtually all of the mammal life has been hunted out.

In December 1971, President Richard Nixon signed the Alaska Native Claims Settlement Act, and a vast restructuring of power began in the state. One of the most pronounced impacts of the act on a local level was the transfer of land that had been for sale on Amaknak and Unalaska to Aleut people. In 1971 they were given 1.3 million acres and $38.2 million.

Under the act, regional and local native corporations were formed. In Unalaska/Dutch Harbor the Aleut Corporation and the Ounalashka Corporation began to enroll members, to organize themselves, to formulate goals, to define the relationships with commercial, municipal, and state institutions.

Today, all of the Aleutian Islands are part of the Aleutian Wildlife Refuge, loosely administered by Aleut people. There is steady talk, but to-date little action, on accessing the remote islands for new economic resources. There are some who would push the Aleut Corporation to protect their Bering Sea resources and others who would like to utilize them by selling long-term leases to oil companies. Another option is bottom fishing around the islands' perimeters, which some think could create between 8,000 to 20,000 new jobs. Another possibility being explored is the potential on the volcanic islands for geothermal energy. Already $5 million has been invested in exploratory drilling on Makushin volcano and other promising sites are on Akutan, Atka, and Umnak. Despite any economic potential, the Aleutians remain as they have been for centuries: isolated, quiet, and virtually untouched.

SIX

One of two things happened during the night. Either sleep gave Don Graves a boost in confidence, or he'd spent the night spending the money we'd offered him. Just before eight o'clock the phone rang in Jeff Hancock's shop, upstairs from where we slept. Graves was calling to say we would leave as soon as the conditions were right—which meant a prediction without high winds and rain in the forecast. That could be the next day, or in a few hours. We agreed to load our gear and tie down our kayaks atop his shiny new boat—the 38-foot *Miss Pepper*—right away, so we'd be ready to leave on short notice. Graves figured the 300-mile round-trip would take between 24 and 30 hours, stopping only to offload us, and he recruited a trio of friends for the ride. Two were master electricians. The boat was relatively new, with just one long test run under its belt, and Graves' biggest worry was suffering an electrical problem in the middle of Samalga Pass. If the boat were to die out there, it would float a long, long way before seeing land. We helped him tie a rubber Zodiac atop the cabin just in case.

During the week Graves is a research and development manager with UniSea, one of the giant fish processors based in Dutch Harbor. The *Miss Pepper* is his weekend and vacation job. The boat's name comes from a nickname for his daughter, Sirahna. Mostly he, or a hired captain, takes clients from the lower 48 sportfishing, a great day trip for willing clients. As a bonus to the nearly guaranteed great fishing, during the run in and out of the harbor you are likely to see pods of whales—killers, orcas, minkes, California grays, and humpbacks. On a good day the skies are heavy with birdlife—black-footed and short-tailed albatross, whiskered auklets, eagles, puffins, and laysan.

The *Miss Pepper* currently holds three world records for halibut: a 395-pounder caught on 80-pound line; a 459-pounder on 130-pound line and, in 1998, a 222-pounder caught on 16-pound line, landed by a 100-pound lawyer from San Diego. She had returned earlier this summer with her fiancé, who proceeded to land a 228-pounder on 16-pound line. A few days later Graves' wife, Chris, landed a 247-pound halibut on 13-pound line.

We knew all about these big fish. Sean and I had gone into a bait store the day before and asked about what kind of fishing we might expect where we were headed. While not relying on catching fresh fish, we weren't against it. We had a few collapsible rods and were curious what kind of bait we should consider.

The craggy-faced guy behind the counter listened to our story about traveling by kayak. He eyed us as if we were out of our minds. "If I were you, I'd bring along a really big gun." He had a point. Even if we were to land one of those giant halibuts—they average over 150 pounds—we'd never be able to land them, certainly not from our kayaks. Shooting them would be the only way.

We met Graves and his wife at noon for a midday breakfast. He'd been monitoring the forecast and announced over sausage, eggs, and pancakes that we should leave in a matter of hours. Though it was Sunday, we had managed to find the name of a federal ranger in Kodiak we could fax a request for "permission" to visit the Islands of the Four Mountains. There was no way we would receive an answer, or formal permit, but this way if anyone asked—and we doubt they would, since we didn't anticipate seeing anyone these next four or five weeks—at least we could honestly say the paperwork had been filed.

The boat loading was done calmly, under a gray sky, with the help of Jeff Hancock and friends. We were about to cast off the lines when a bearded man came running down the dock. It was Bob Adams, a sailor who I knew had visited the Four Mountains nearly a decade before. He'd picked up archaeologist Lucy Johnson off Carlisle back in 1990. I'd been trying to reach him for several months, but we hadn't connected. Graves quieted the engines while we stopped long enough to look at our maps with him, testing his memory of possible harbors and camps. This was as close as we'd come to talking with anyone who'd actually been out to the Islands of Four Mountains. It was unfortunate that the meeting had to be so rushed.

"You'll see, it's a very mysterious, magical place," Adams said as I rolled up our maps. "I think because of all the Aleutian history out there. At one time there were lots and lots of Aleuts living there. What happened to them? Where did they go? Even the Aleuts don't have any clear idea. But when you're out there, it feels very different, more spiritual, than any other place in the Aleutian chain.

"You're going to one of the most special places in the world," were his last words as we pulled away. "Just be careful."

As we pulled out of the slip, the sky was dark and gray. The day had grown cold. We made one last stop at the town's main fuel dock to load extra barrels of diesel fuel. Graves' two electricians boarded there, carrying small gym bags with extra clothes. We felt overdressed in our Windstopper and Gore-Tex®. Graves and his assistant captain, Tony, were wearing blue jeans and T-shirts. The difference was that we'd be wearing these same clothes every day for the foreseeable future. If fortune was in our favor, they'd be back home for dinner Monday night.

An hour out, just around the ironically named Cape Cheerful, the sun comes out. It's the first time in five days, since leaving Homer, we have seen the sun. It's also the first time we can see the snow-capped volcanoes that line Unalaska Island, the greening tundra on the hillsides, as well as the waterfalls spouting from the cliff walls. With the sunlight the knot in my stomach loosens slightly. I am encouraged even more when Graves picks his sunglasses off the dashboard and snugs them squarely onto his nose. It's amazing how empowering a good dose of sunlight can be.

As we rock in 12-foot swells, under bright skies, a trio of dolphins jumps alongside the boat. When an albatross crosses our starboard, Graves gives me a big thumbs-up. "It's always a good sign to start your trip with the blessing of a white albatross," he says. Just as the words are out of his mouth, a splash of cold sea water blows in his cracked-opened side window, soaking his gray sweatshirt.

We pass Cape Wilson, Bishop Point, and Cape Kovrizhka. The sea calms down a bit as night sets in. I feel as if the adventure has truly begun, and I study the faces of my three teammates under the cabin's interior lights. Sean, most comfortable of any of us on a big seagoing vessel, makes coffee, sponges up the countertop, hangs up fallen rain slickers, stays busy. Barry, not benefiting from the advantage of Dramamine, sits at one of the two cabin tables looking slightly green thanks to the pounding of the seas.

Scott stares out the front window. I think back to a conversation he and I had on the ferry out from Homer. We were talking about what we each expected from the trip. For me, as well as hoping to support my lifestyle by selling a story or two about the trip to one magazine or more, I saw the trip as an incredible confidence booster. If I could pull this off—if we could pull this off—it would allow me, I envisioned, to undertake a variety of future expeditions, whether more physically challenging, logistically difficult, or simply more expensive.

"I'm bothered by this feeling that what I really want out of this trip is something to brag about when I get home," he said to me on the ferry. "That's the wrong motivation," he admitted. "But what else is there? I mean we're not going out here to add to any scientific body of work. We're putting ourselves into a very dangerous situation, and for what? That's got me thinking." He conceded that probably the biggest challenge for him was simply to work together with three others. Most of his previous traveling had been done solo, or with one other. He was used to making all the decisions, and it was becoming clear that he balked at a more democratic dispersion of responsibilities.

As *Miss Pepper* slammed into a growing sea, I am also concerned about Scott's willingness to be a good member of a team. He is certainly prepared on the physical side, with more kayaking experience than Sean or I. Tall, strong, and physically tough, I wasn't worried about him on that front. But in terms of simple life and travel experience, especially working with a team, he was far behind the rest of us. Alone, on a bench seat next to Graves, Scott peers out the window over the bow. We are headed to a place where your life is truly in your own hands, a place where we had no one to rely on but ourselves. I wonder how we would fare as a team, if we would return from this experience as friends. One thing I know for sure is that this is not the place to prove who is the biggest, strongest, smartest man.

After a couple hours of bumping through the seas, the *Miss Pepper* pushed by big side winds, the ride smooths out and we head straight south, paralleling the coastline of Unalaska Island. I crawl into the forward bunk below, pin myself against the bow and try to get some sleep.

That is nearly impossible. *Miss Pepper* rocks hard in high seas. Crawling up into the cabin, I peer out the darkened windows. All I can see are black waves, matched by an ominous sky. I can hear our fiberglass kayaks banging against the boat's wheelhouse. Though they are tightly secured by cam straps and rope, 12 hours of the heavy rock-and-roll of the Bering Sea threatens to unleash them. It is midnight, and we are making our way at full throttle down the coastline. Soon we will turn hard to the west, heading across the 25-mile wide Samalga Pass, which separates Umnak from the Islands of Four Mountains. This extremely deep pass, which is rich with nutrients and thus a prime fishing area for the early Aleuts as well as those who followed, has a reputation for being extremely rough. It is one of the primary passes where the Pacific Ocean and Bering Sea meet, blending into a rich and risky melange of food growth and turbulence.

In a hasty, last-minute call from Dutch Harbor earlier this morning we had convinced Scott Kerr to meet us off Nikolski and accompany us aboard the *Miss Pepper* out to Kagamil, where we would be dropped off. Graves has no idea where he could safely drop anchor and unload us. We had leaned on Kerr to make the crossing, point us to the best drop-off point, then return to Nikolski with Graves.

He'd agreed, in return for us bringing him $88 worth of groceries, Purina dog food, and Red Man chewing tobacco. Just after midnight Graves calls out to me, saying we were nearing Nikolski. Though he brought along a co-captain, Tony, he quickly found out that the latter didn't have the quite the right touch necessary to handle the boat in these heavy seas. The few times Graves tried to hand off to him the boat veered violently right or left, pushed by the seas, causing everyone—especially the boat's owner, Graves—to look at one another with panic. Now, after nearly eight continuous hours at the helm, Graves' eyes were red, his hair was standing up straight, and his gray sweatshirt was stained with coffee spilled from his Styrofoam cup each time the boat bucked after slamming into yet another giant wave.

I grab the VHF radio and try to raise Kerr. No response. I try again. "*Miss Pepper* to Scott Kerr. Come in, Scott Kerr, come in." After several tries he finally picks up. Groggily he asks, "What's your intention?" as if we hadn't explained it to him a dozen times.

I shout over the roar of the boat and the sea that we are near Nikolski and that we'll be off shore within a half hour. Then we lose communication. I can only assume he is on his way. (He later admits that when he heard the radio, he was very tempted to ignore it, roll over, pull Agrafina closer to him, and go back to sleep.)

At 1:00 a.m. we pull into a wave-socked bay; a half-dozen lights a mile toward shore indicated Nikolski. Because Graves does not know the entry through the rocky bay, it is too dangerous at night to get any closer. Soon we spot a giant, single headlight coming at us through the sea—Kerr in an 18-foot metal skiff. He pulls alongside, trying desperately not to bang into the *Miss Pepper* in the heavy seas. He is not alone. As he had headed down to his boat, he'd knocked on the door of a sleeping neighbor—introduced as Rex—saying he needed help. Rex was barely awake; he thought he was coming out on a grocery run.

Once they are aboard, it takes several passes to safely tie the skiff off the back of the boat. Empty .410 shells rattle around on its floor, making me wonder, What had these boys been hunting? We would be pulling the skiff behind, through the heavy seas, and Kerr is concerned that it not end up upside down, being dragged. Though he made the rendezvous, he doesn't appear happy to be here. When he pulls back the hood of his forest green sweatshirt, wild, long, unkempt hair billows from beneath his ball cap. Around his waist he wears a rope belt loaded with knives and a heavy flashlight. He smells of woodsmoke and tobacco.

After brief introductions he returns to his earlier question: "What are your intentions?" Apparently Kerr still has not gotten the message. He thought we were bringing him his groceries and then crashing on his floor. Unrolling our maps, I focus on getting as much information out of him as possible in the limited hours we have together. First we tackle the question of the initial landing. Graves' navigational system says we were 43 miles away from a sand beach on the north end of Kagamil, where Kerr says we'll have no problem going ashore. It will take us another 3 to 4 hours. In the dim light of the boat's interior we study the maps together, us asking questions, him giving back little more than grunts.

The final few hours of the 15-hour, 150-mile trip are spent trying to stay seated and picking up maps, coffee makers, donuts, and rain gear as they fly around the cabin. The metal skiff tied off the back of the boat kept banging dangerously in the rough seas.

I try to sleep sitting up. Scott Kerr admits to feeling slightly seasick and lies down on a bench. So much for our expert guide.

Rex, lightly dressed considering the conditions, in blue jeans, hooded cotton sweatshirt and a Carhart vest, complains it is too hot in the cabin. For the bulk of the ride he stands on the back deck. I stand with him for a while and ask what it is that motivates him to live way out here. "Oooh, I been in some sit-eee-ations, that's for sure, some real sit-eee-ations," was all he would say. Turning away he mutters, "It's hot out here, ain't it? Just like Florida."

Just after six in the morning Don Graves studies his depth gauge and throttles back. We know we are near land, but the fog is so thick we cannot see the shoreline. I look over his shoulder at the screen. "North Cove is a half mile inland," he says, referring to the mile-long beach on the top of Kagamil. "I can't risk getting any closer. I'm dropping anchor."

Only in the past two hours have the four of us finally fallen into varying forms of sleep—fitful, deep, wave-rocked—and we are now barely awake. I stumble to the back of the boat for my first glimpse of the Islands of Four Mountains, only to find that I can barely see my hand in front of my face. No time for a cup of coffee either, though the seas have calmed. We must download the boat as quickly as possible so that Graves can turn around and head back. He's anxious to get going due to the fog. As we would soon experience firsthand, fog is good for boating, accompanied as it generally is by calm seas.

Sensing Graves' hurry, Barry and I hustle to pull our heavy bags of food and gear out of the below-deck storage compartments and toss them into Kerr's metal skiff. Scott and Sean climb atop the wheelhouse and begin unleashing our kayaks. Kerr and Rex will run the first load into the beach, offload, and return for a second. "Not too much weight," Kerr yells as we hurriedly throw big blue and orange bags into the little boat. Then he reverses gears, "C'mon, let's get as much of that stuff in here as we can."

He still seems a little put out to be out here at all. He asks why we don't unstrap the rubber Zodiac from the roof and use it as our shuttle craft. We argue that taking his skiff makes more sense since all we have to do is pull in its leash, load it, and take off.

Within short minutes after *Miss Pepper's* anchor settled into the rocks below, things fall apart. Badly.

Barry and I, in rain gear and rubber boots, jump atop the dry bags filling the skiff. Rex mounts the front end, riding the boat like a broncobuster, lit Marlboro dangling from his lips. Kerr jerks the small outboard to life and we are off. This doesn't look so bad, I think. Calm seas in a heavy fog, a wide black sand beach in front of us. As we near land, though, the waves grow big and it is quickly apparent we are too heavy. The skiff is riding low and waves crash over the bow, soaking Rex.

Surfing onto the sandy beach, the metal boat buries its nose in the sand. Even as Kerr yells from the back of the boat—"Get everything out of the boat, now!"—surf continues to crash over its stern, threatening to sink it. Barry, Rex and I struggle with the heavy bags. Before we can get everything out of the boat, allowing Kerr to reverse back through the surf, the boat is half filled with seawater and being pushed sideways, perpendicular to the breaking waves, which means it fills even faster.

Kerr, who'd put on a red survival suit before we left the boat, jumps out of the skiff into waist-deep water, desperately trying to drag his metal boat around so that it faces into the waves. We join him in his fruitless effort, even as the boat continues to be pushed farther onto shore and take on more water. Within minutes it is too heavy to budge, burrowed deep into the sand, filled to the top with ocean. Refusing to accept that he's just swamped his boat, Kerr begins bailing between waves. It is a losing battle. Great, I say to myself. Here less than 30 minutes and we've already sunk a boat. Kerr can't be pleased either. He certainly didn't plan on spending the day, or possibly longer, out here with us.

Watching us through binoculars, Sean and Scott were not impressed by our landing. We could see that Graves had come back up top to watch the debacle taking place onshore. He'd crawled into a bunk as soon as we set anchor, hoping to catch a couple hours' sleep before beginning the drive back. Now he'll never get any sleep.

Meanwhile, as Sean and Scott unload the kayaks, another minor disaster brews up, which we cannot see from shore. As they untie the boats the big blue hatch cover in the center of the red kayak—a nearly invaluable piece of equipment, for which we carry no spare—blows off into the sea. Apparently during the night the leash that kept it tied to the boat came loose. As soon as the boat is unstrapped, the wind catches the hatch cover and it takes off like a fiberglass Frisbee.

Sean watches it flutter to the surface and begin to sink, just four feet from the boat. Without hesitation he strips out of his fleece jacket, shoes, and pants. Quickly down to his underwear, he dives into the 36° Bering Sea. He has only one shot to catch it as it falls. Diving into the deep waters again is not an option. Kicking hard, he comes within a finger length of the square cover…but cannot grab it. Ten feet below the surface he turns and shoots back up to fresh air. Catching Scott's eye, who has watched the scene unfold in disbelief, he shrugs with disappointment.

Barry and I pace the shore, unable to discern without the help of binoculars what's going on out on the boat. We can see four men outside, waving their hands, but have no idea what has transpired. We are also searching the beach for the best spot to land the kayaks, since they'll have to be paddled in rather than pulled by Kerr's skiff, which now is completely filled with sand and water. I've already run through some options with Kerr. Leave the skiff here, buried in the sand, until he can return another day and dig it out. Camp out with us while *Miss Pepper* makes its return, unbury the skiff, then motor it back to Nikolski—requiring incredibly calm seas and no wind. "I know guys who could do it," says Kerr, almost as if he is looking forward to the challenge. For now we continue to bail, hoping that when the tide begins to recede, we will be able to empty it, turn it back toward the sea and get it back to the *Miss Pepper*.

Meanwhile, Rex is nearly hypothermic. Shivering in his soaked jeans and cotton sweatshirt, he hides behind a big rock onshore, trying to stay out of the slight breeze that threatens to turn him into a Marlboro-sucking popsicle. He's shivering noticeably, his lips already turning blue, when I hand him a Gore-Tex® jacket to help cut down on the wind burn. I begin to gather driftwood for a fire, knowing that the only way to dry him completely is to get him out of his soaked clothes. Knowing that he has a dry change of clothes on the *Miss Pepper* gives him some comfort, as does the knowledge that a case of beer and a couple small bottles of Southern Comfort are on board. "That's all I need, something to warm up the old heater," he says. While Barry and I pace, trying to figure out what is taking those guys so long to get in the kayaks and paddle in, Rex and Kerr talk about the big fire they'll build once they get back to Nikolski, and how many six-packs they'll drink in front of its roasting embers. Just like Florida, I think, just another sit-eee-ation.

One more ominous sign soon follows. Barry digs one of our two VHF radios out of the dry bags, hoping to raise the *Miss Pepper* and find out what the delay is. Though sheathed in a protective plastic case and loaded with what we assume are new batteries, it barely has enough strength to reach the boat just a half mile offshore. We are prepared for the cold and wet to suck up batteries. We also know that the radio will be of extremely limited help to us, given that we don't expect to see any passing boat or airplane traffic and that the nearest responder is more than 40 miles away, at Scott Kerr's house in Nikolski. Actually, we are in one of the few marine spots on the planet where the VHF is of almost no good.

The radio signals used by VHF marine radios are similar to those of commercial FM radio stations. Their relatively short range of communication is limited to not much farther than a direct line of sight between transmitting and receiving antennas. Reception range in miles is also geographically limited, by the earth's curvature, to approximately 1.2 times the square root of the antenna height in feet. The bigger the antenna, the better. The hand-held units we carry have a low output to begin with, and the fact that we are calling from essentially sea level is another limit. Hand-held models work far less efficiently from the seat of a kayak than they do from the deck of bigger boats.

We should be able to communicate with large ships or sailboats (as long as they have an antenna on the mast) within 10 miles, or when in sight on a clear day. Chances are, we won't be able to reach a power boat just five miles offshore. Reaching the Coast Guard, which is what most small boaters use as a last-case backup, is out of the question. We are in one of those radio "blind spots," beyond reach. Even if we climb the big hill behind us, it is unlikely we'll be able to be heard in Nikolski. We brought the radios along on the slim chance we saw, and needed to contact, a passing boat. The ominous part is that they apparently don't work very well even for that.

Two hours after we left the mother ship, we see Scott and Sean finally crawling into the big, tandem kayaks and heading toward shore. Using hand signals, we guide them to a smooth landing and share travails. Sean is not in as bad shape as Rex, who is now lying on the beach hugging himself. But his plunge was a wake-up call. "The only good thing is that it wasn't as cold as I'd expected," he says as we drag the kayaks high onto the beach. "I really thought I'd hit the water and immediately turn into an ice cube. That's the silver lining, I guess." They managed to fashion a replacement hatch cover out of the pair of plastic buckets we brought along when we thought we might be leaving a food cache on one of the islands. The luckiest thing is that it was the hatch cover that was lost. If it was the neoprene cover that stretches tightly over the big hatch in the middle of the boat, we'd be in big trouble. We are carrying no spare neoprene covers and no piece of clothing we have in our bags can be cut for the same purpose. Without the fiberglass cover, we can make do. Without the neoprene cover, every time the boat is on the water it will be at risk of sinking.

The tide starts to withdraw, and the five of us—Rex taking a deserved pass from standing in the cold water—are able to bail out the skiff and turn it around. Though it filtered water and sand, the engine springs to life after a couple pulls. With a gruff wave and no spoken goodbye, Scott Kerr and Rex are history. We watch them putt out to the *Miss Pepper*, glad they will not be joining us here for an undetermined number of days. Despite the solitude of the place, or maybe because of it, we are anxious to finally be alone here on the Islands of Four Mountains.

We spill a half bottle of white gas onto the damp driftwood, and a warming fire comes to life. Two and a half hours after we've arrived, we watch the *Miss Pepper* motor away into a thickening fog.

SEVEN

"**N**ature failed to provide (the Aleuts) with the material necessary for boats, that is, wood. But on the other hand, as if in compensation, she gave them greater ingenuity for the perfection of a special new kind of fleet: the baidarka."—Ivan Veniaminov, 1840

Why had we come to this remote place? One big lure is that we are kayakers, and the Aleut invented the kayak. They called the boats *ikyaks*, and when the Russians arrived they dubbed the strange boats baidarkas (from the *baidara*, which plied the rivers of the Ukraine). As we ventured onto the Bering Sea for the first time, I thought often about what it must have been like for the Aleut who depended on kayaks for their livelihood.

The boats we will paddle—though built of carbon fiber and Kevlar rather than driftwood and seal skin—are designed from the model refined by the Aleut thousands of years before. While we will be the most recent to kayak among these islands, certainly the first in 150 years to kayak the dangerous passes that separate Kagamil and Chuginadak, Carlisle and Herbert, we will hardly be the first. Imagining what it must have been like to be out on these same seas in a tiny seal-skin-covered boat occupied me for many hours during the days we made our way toward the Islands of Four Mountains. During the few hours we'd stopped in Anchorage on our way here, I had slipped away from my teammates and spent a couple hours in the cool halls of the Anchorage Museum of History and Art. A grand, silent room was filled with full-size dioramas of Aleut life. In one hung a 15-foot-long baidarka, surrounded by the tools of the day: arrows, bow, spear, spear launcher, lance, dart. They also had a stove lamp, which they fired with whale blubber, a ballast stone, a bailing tube (shaped like a bowling pin), a double-bladed paddle, and a gut parka laced together with sinew and grass (the grass would swell when wet and seal the needle holes). Despite the rudimentary materials, none of the pieces would look terribly out of place on a modern-day sea kayak rigged for an expedition.

Another diorama showed the interior of one of the homes—*barbaras*—in which 30 to 40 family members lived together, protected from the fierce winds by the structure's being mostly underground. Before leaving the house in the morning, by climbing up a ladder and out a manhole, each hunter customarily paid deference to a figurine suspended from the ceiling. Called the "image of the deity," it is a crudely carved wooden doll, which they obligingly asked for protection, especially if they were going to spend the day, or coming days, on the sea.

The kayak was the most important possession the Aleut had. Perhaps historian and kayak builder George Dyson wrote the best account of the relationship between man and his boat. His *Baidarka* is not only a story about that relationship, but a guide to how he built his own boat based on their model. His inspiring effort, and research, is required reading for anyone who wants to understand just how important the kayak was to these people.

Every able-bodied adult man had at least one kayak. Each village's strength was expressed in the number of kayaks available. Their relationship with the sea pervaded their manners, quickened their minds, and exterminated incompetents. Their relationship with their boats was so intense that over generations they became shaped to the demand of kayaking vast distances, developing huge upper bodies from relentless paddling and bowed legs that allowed them to sit confined for hours. To endure the long hours of concentration and stillness necessary if the arduous and time-consuming pursuit of seals and sea otter was to be successful, young boys started training early. Righting the boat was an important skill, and boys' shoulders also had to be strengthened to achieve maximum velocity and accuracy with the throwing board or atlatl, which was used to cast darts and harpoons at birds and marine mammals. Kayak hunting on the open sea—the Aleuts' primary form of subsistence—has to be the most skilled and demanding form of hunting practiced by man. Training was so complete that Smithsonian archaeologist William Laughlin once suggested, "It was not possible to tell whether the kayak was made for the Aleut or the Aleut for the kayak." Ironically, most Aleuts—even the very best kayakers—could not swim.

For more than 5,000 years, Aleut Indians plied the islands in these craft made of animal skins and bones. The ancestry of the kayak is not clear. Dyson suggests they may go back as far as stuffing an animal skin with willow branches, a practice in Asian and American hunting cultures. The Aleut perfected the craft, building the frames out of driftwood and covering them with seal skins. Of the three primitive boats of North America—the dugout, the bark canoe, and the Arctic skin boat—the last are the most remarkable for effective design and construction under conditions in which building materials were both scarce and limited in selection. They evolved curiously split bows, sterns that were wide at the top but V-shaped at the bottom, and bone joints that made the vessels 100 times as flexible as a boats. The soft, elastic skin made the Aleut boats flexible, bending over the waves rather than plowing through them. With their keen knowledge of winds, waves, and tides, they propelled the boats as if they were born to them instinctually. "When such a *baidarka* was in motion, almost every part was in movement…. The keel is always in three pieces in order that the *baidarka* may have movement when on the run or, as they say, that it may 'bend' over the wave," writes Dyson.

Superior celestial navigation skills allowed the Aleut to travel hundreds, even thousands of miles across open water to destinations now named Barrow and Hawaii. The best of them could sustain 10 miles an hour on the open ocean, in boats ranging from 15 to 30 feet long. Many were lost at sea, and even the best hunter kayakers were sometimes overturned. Most often they went out with a partner, so if one boat flipped he could be pulled to shore by his friend. If caught in open sea by a williwaw, or long storm, several hunters would lash their boats together to ride out the storm.

"The Aleuts were a rude people, compared to their cousins the Eskimos, but better seaman," Ken Brower wrote. "No inter-connected system of inland fjords, no bulwark of seaward archipelagos, to protect them. They ventured into storm-breeding seas in canoes so light they could be carried under one arm. Made of animal skin stretched over wood frames, they were the finest hunting canoes in history.

"While the Eskimos liked to stay within sight of land, Aleuts kayaked over the horizon regularly, and on purpose. They went as far as the Kamchatka Peninsula, Japan, San Francisco and Baja California."

The Aleuts' relationship with their boats was not without some oddity. "They have no particular word for curses," Hieromonk Father Gideon of Kodiak observed. "When he is most passionately enraged a Kodiak man will say, with an air of great importance: 'Your father did not own a baidarka and was not a hunter, and I did not wear a hair sealskin parka!'" If a man in the polygamous society slept with a woman, he was obliged to share his affections with the kayak the next morning. If he did not, it was believed, the boat would become jealous, break, and not return the hunter to his village. The result was an elaborate session of rubbing the kayak in the morning before going out to sea. They believed that whales and sea otters could immediately detect any hunter who had "dallied" with women and promptly avoided such an imprudent person. Sea lions, oddly, were apparently less discriminating. A one-month avoidance of women was neces-sary before sea otter hunting but none for the sea lions.

Those early boats were extremely sophisticated. The cover most often was made from sea lion skins, pulled over a frame of whale bones or driftwood tied together with baleen and hinges carved from polished ivory or bone. As many as 60 small animal bones were strategically inserted into the framework as joints so that every part of the ikyak was in motion as it forged through the sea. As opposed to bark canoes, Aleuts built the frame first, then sewed skin around it. A birch bark canoe was built by forcing a framing system into an assembled cover.

To serve as covers, the bearded seal skin and skin of sea lions were first piled and "sweated" until the hair became loose. Then the skins were scraped until they were clean. They were thin and light, and could be air dried and stored until ready for use. The skins had to be well soaked in blubber before being stretched over the frame of a kayak, or umiak. The holes in the hide were punched with bone awls. The sewing needles were made from small bones in the wings of gulls. The thread was sinew. The boat had to be reoiled after a week in the water, and after several years of use the skin had to be replaced entirely. The Eskimos claimed that walrus skin, though strong, was not as good as the bearded seal or the sea-lion skin for boat covers, as the latter two held the oil longer and did not become water-soaked as quickly as the walrus hide. The paddler's seat in most kayaks consisted of a portion of heavy skin with fur attached. The fur seat was sometimes as long as the paddler's legs. Great care was exercised to avoid getting dirt into a kayak, as it might chafe the hide cover.

"They lashed their frames together with sinew or twisted gut," writes Brower. "The skirts of intestine were laced at the bottom to the manhole rim and fitted at the top with drawstrings. They went to sea with repair kits of animal fat, which they smeared over leaky seams. Carried hollow bones for sucking water from their bilges. Lashed harpoons, lances and fishing gear to their decks. In heavy seas they were known to join two baidarkas together to make a catamaran, then raise sail."

The Russians influenced baidarka construction by providing the Aleut with steel tools. According to Dyson, the Russians also homogenized the baidarkas design by forcing large hunting parties to undertake extended voyages in search of sea otter pelts, thus bringing together builders from previously isolated islands.

The Aleut also had larger canoes—called umiaks or baidaras—walrus-skinned vessels that carried as many as 40 persons, used for ferrying passengers or freight or carrying war parties. The Russians soon outlawed them because they were big enough to carry war parties and created in its place the three-holed kayak, all the better for the Aleut paddlers to transport a Russian trapper or priest. Years later the Russians tried to take baidarkas to warm weather locales, like Mexico, Hawaii, and Micronesia, only to have the hot sun melt the whale-fat that waterproofed their seams.

That won't be a problem for us. Our boats were modeled after those early ikyaks. Their boats were about 13 feet long, weighed 30 pounds when empty, and were made for one person. Our boats are 22 feet long, weigh 100 pounds when empty, and are made for two persons. They used primarily seal skins, ours are fiberglass sheathed by Kevlar. The clothes and tools they used for paddling were very similar to ours. The Aleut carved double-bladed paddles, similar in shape to the ones we are using. The wooden pipes they used for emptying water from inside the kayaks, the waterproof shoes they wore—many of the things they created are still used today, using slightly different materials.

As for our dress, despite the obvious differences—Gore-Tex®
versus seal intestines, as a starter—their desire was the same as
ours, to keep the cold water and wind away. Aleut hunters wore
waterproof shirts—*kamleikas*—made by stitching together strips
of sea-lion intestine and stomach linings. The shirt was long and
pulled tightly and tied over the cockpit of the kayak to keep the
water out (much like the neoprene spray skirts we wear). Under
the hunter's intestine rain parka was a second parka of sea-lion
hide, with drawstrings at the neck and sleeves. The soles of his
waterproof boots were made from sea-lion flipper and uppers
of sea-lion esophagus. Like us, man and kayak became a water-
tight unit, with as little skin as possible exposed to the elements.

One major difference is our hats. Ours are flimsy cloth ball
caps, with the trade names "Necky," "Oobe," "Teva," and "Aleutian Adventure Sports" stitched onto them. The Aleuts' headgear,
by comparison, were pieces of art, carved from wood and decorated with bird's feathers, sea-lion whiskers, and beads. The beautiful visors and elongated hats worn by men were painted in
striped, curving designs of different colors and decorated with
painstaking artistry. "One of these hats might be worth more than
the hunter's other pieces of equipment, including his boat, combined," Dyson noted. "Highly prized in this regard were bristles
from the beard of the sea lion, considered as trophies of the hunt
giving an indication of their bearer's rank."

The ornamentation of the hats was not designed solely to
impress other Aleuts. They had sea otters in mind. "Since the
Aleuts believed the sea otters to be transformed human beings,"
wrote Veniaminov, "they made every effort to decorate their
baidarkas, their *kamleikas*, and their spears as finely as possible,

supposing that the sea otter, loving women's handiwork, would come of his own accord."

But the primary reason for wearing hats has always been the same—to keep the sun, wind, spray, and rain out of your eyes.

EIGHT

"**K**agamilyax is an elongated island, made up of rather low mountains and hills, with a small sandy cove on its north side. This island in the past flamed and smoked, but nowadays the subterranean fire works within in secret. Midway up the mountain on the south side, sulphur, always in a hot state, is found, and at the place where it is collected underground noise is heard, and steam rises from the ground while hot springs flow from the foot of the mountain."—Ivan Veniaminov

Our first real glimpse of the Islands of Four Mountains provides little sense of the place, since all of this first day we are bathed in fog. We comb the wide black sand beach for driftwood, build a blazing fire, and construct a log barrier that we can sit behind to escape the wind, then scout for tent sites. We anticipate this will be one of the few beaches we will find drift—there are no trees on any of the islands—so we plan to take advantage of it. Sean finds a rusted oil barrel half-buried in the sand that we dig out and turn into a cooking table. It is cool—40°F—with an on-again, off-again rain and a constant wind of ten miles an hour, making the wind chill factor below freezing.

We spend the rest of the day making camp and talking about what should be our next steps. Sean and Barry put up their tent in the black sand. Scott and I hike our orange-and-gray tent to the top of the bluff and bury it in the protection of the sea grass. We've teamed up in twos, to share both kayaks and tents. That arrangement makes it easier to pack up if we stick together, even though my preference would be to switch off tent partners. Too much proximity breeds either mini-cliques or out-and-out hostility. But once a paddling and camping rhythm has been established, we decided we'd stick with these pairings. I'm fortunate to be teamed with Scott, in that his devotion to order— everything has a place, the same place every day—assures that we'll spend little time searching for missing tent stakes or packages of pasta. The downside is that if everything doesn't end up back in its correct place he tends to become irritated.

Because of the unpredictable weather and the uncertainty of when, where, and how we would land, we arrived with no firm logistical plan. Now that we are here, we would like to chart some kind of logical route that will take us from island to island. But it will take a little while to get a good feel for the islands and the weather, to discover just what they will allow us to do. Our itinerary is free-form, our plan to proceed one day at a time. The only limit we have is that the last word we'd shared with Don Graves was that he should return sometime the week of July 7. He will meet us at Applegate Cove, the only other long, sandy beach in these islands, on Chuginadak. I paid him for the ride out and I hoped he was needy enough, and conscientious enough, to come back for us.

Though the Aleut left behind little written history, folkloric evidence remains of their special attraction to the Islands of Four Mountains, particularly their habit of mummifying their dead and burying them, along with their kayaks, in the warm thermal caves that line the coasts of Kagamil and Chuginadak.

Kagamil is remarkable in that, on its western side, are the caves that contain mummies. Wrapped in sea-grass blankets and suspended in cradles, next to the mummies lay their entire possessions: mats, parkas, sea-otter remains, spears, various bundles. It is reported that when the mummies were found many of their belongings appeared quite whole. The Aleut believed it was bad luck to touch them and that those who had, even with just the tips of their spears, were stricken with open wounds all over all their bodies and died after long agony. Scott Kerr had told us he knew where some of the caves were, but that they were long ago buried by rock slides and overgrowth.

What a strange, hard life it must have been for those early Aleuts, surrounded by a ruthless sea, a bitterly inclement climate, a barren land, all combining cruelly in an attempt to drive the little group of humanity from its unfriendly adopted homeland.

It seemed clear why the tribe would want to preserve the earthly remains of the one who had been leader and godfather to his people. Particularly clear because the chieftain's spirit was to them an entity as real as the wind, which was quite invisible. According to Veniaminov, the Aleut believed that the souls of the dead, or shadows as they called them, remained invisibly among their relatives and loved ones, accompanying them on both land and sea, and that they were able to cause various good as well as evil. For this reason the living asked their help in danger and especially in wars undertaken for the revenge of some dishonor to their family.

No one is sure exactly how this science arrived in the Aleutians. Mostly the early tribes buried their warrior dead in the labyrinth caves around the bases of volcanoes. The bodies were carefully eviscerated, stuffed with wild rye (elymus), and placed in a sitting position, the knees drawn up under the chin, the arms folded, the head bent forward in an attitude of brooding contemplation. The natural heat of the volcano dried and preserved the mummies. Landslides and geologic disturbances sealed the entrances to the caves and locked away their secrets forever. Where this process of mummification originated is not known. The late Dr. Alex Hrdlicka, curator of anthropology in the Smithsonian Institution, estimated their age to be more than 3,500 years. The art, he believes, was practiced in only two, widely separated places in the Americas: the Aleutians and Peru. Perhaps wanderers bringing the original secret from Egypt crossed the land bridge and migrated down the west coast of the continent to South America.

Waldemar Jochelson, who'd explored Kagamil in the 1910s, related how the Aleut viewed the mummies and their spirits: "The Aleut regarded the mummies as bewitched after death and called them asxi'Nan, which properly means 'the departed ones.' The asxi'Nan were hung up in caves in troughs resembling large cradles which were attached to crossbeams resting on two posts. Colored posts were placed in front of the entrance, which was also painted in different colors. The asxi'Nan were busy throughout the night;

they rose, hunted, prepared food for themselves, had feasts and festivals, and in the morning resumed their squatting position."

The asxi'Nan was supposed to serve as a house for the dead man's spirit. The Aleuts believed that nearly ever night, when darkness came, he and other chieftains, all immortal, would leave their "houses" to go forth once again on hunting expeditions, using the weapons and other things which their tribesmen had thoughtfully left with them. If the hunt was successful, a feast was held, with festivals and dances, around the entrance to their cave. These lasted until dawn, when the spirits returned to their resting places. When storm or darkness overtook native hunters, they often reported catching glimpses of these weird performances by the dead.

Nor were the Aleut the only ones who believed in the mummies' spirits. I read an account by an early 20th-century sailor who passed by the islands where we were headed one foggy night: "The Islands of Four Mountains is the only place they put them [mummies]. That's why their ain't a livin' soul that'll stay on them islands even today. It's a mighty dangerous thing for anyone to go lookin' for them mummies, though. They're sorta like gods to the natives—got some sorta supernat'ral power about 'em. The old Aleut medicine men say that anybody that goes into the caves will have the worst kind of bad luck the rest of their days; and anybody that molests 'em or takes 'em away is sure to die in a very short time. It may just be one of them native yarns.... There's just one white man that I know of who ever took any of the Aleut mummies out of the caves. He was a Swede trader out on the islands that found a couple of them and started in his little schooner with a lot of other Alaskan stuff to sell at the Frisco

Fair. He never got there with the mummies or his boat, and never was heard of afterward. Anybody out that way will tell you about it. Some funny things happen, you know. I'd be kinda careful, if I were you, if you figure on monkeyin' around to try and find any of them Aleut mummies."

SHIIIT!! I am out of my kayak and I can't breathe, something's choking me from behind, can't catch my breath, can't squeeze out a sound though I'm trying to shout at the top of my lungs over the surge of cold wind and whitecaps swirling around my head.

I'm not sure if it's the cold of the 35° water cutting off my air supply, or the fact that my yellow life jacket has been pushed up around my neck during the struggle to free myself from the cockpit of my upside-down kayak. Bare hands, squeezed tight at the wrist by the neoprene sleeves of my drysuit, are numb, though I've been in the water only a minute. How did this, my worst nightmare, happen on what began as a relatively calm day here in the Aleutians: Aswim in the middle of the Bering Sea, my kayak floating overturned two waves away! Why a nightmare? Any kind of help is literally days away; certain death by hypothermia will arrive within minutes.

As I struggle I flash back to what *should* be happening rather than this nightmare scenario, running through the litany of stay-calm-and-save-yourself rescue patter I've heard, read, and pronounced myself many times during years of kayaking and whitewater rafting. "Never let go of the boat." Too late for that. "Hang onto your paddle." Let that go when I realized it would take both hands to try and pull off my spray skirt. "Don't panic."

Nice try! I can already feel my feet going numb in those lousy zippered booties and they can barely kick, which means—with failing arm strength and feet too weak to kick—that adrenaline-fueled panic is the only chance I've got. "Stay still—flailing, even trying to swim after your boat, saps your energy in this cold." Given that I probably have less than another few minutes to live, now is not the time to ball into a turtle float and relax. No one is going to save me. Me saving me is the only way out of this mess.

We'd been paddling for two hours, hard into the wind-whipped waves blowing from the south, off the Pacific Ocean. The waves had grown as we paddled, breaking repeatedly over the bow of our superlight carbon fiber and Kevlar boats. We plowed into each wave, literally burying the bow as we made progress, moving forward strong stroke by strong stroke. Land—the tiny, treeless island with an Indian name—was two miles off. Each stroke meant dipping hands into the nearly frozen Bering Sea, so that after just minutes on the sea they were already cold, like blocks of wood.

Even if I could reach our overturned boat—it's cream-colored underside just strokes beyond my reach — I'm not sure I could unlock my fingers to grab onto it.

I'm not alone out here. Somewhere nearby Scott must be in the same predicament. Grabbing for the plastic whistle which should be fixed on a lanyard to my life jacket's neoprene shoulder strap…I can't reach it. During the struggle to free myself it's apparently been pushed over my shoulder. Reaching back awkwardly a dozen times my hand can't quite grab it. I want to blow the whistle since my voice isn't cooperating. I try again to scream over the roar of the wind and waves…but nothing comes out. I'm already in shock

Carlisle Island—one of the five Islands of Four Mountains—rises to nearly 6,000 feet, straight out of the Bering Sea.

Along the road in British Columbia, Sean Farrell stretches his arms during a break on our 3,200-mile drive from California's Sierra Mountains to Homer, Alaska. We have to drive—our 22-foot-long kayaks are too big to put on an airplane.

Captain Don Graves and his *Miss Peppers* carry us from Dutch Harbor out to the Islands of Four Mountains. It is a trip across dangerous Samalga Pass that Graves has never made before, one he says "scared him to death."

We spend our first four nights camped at the black volcanic sand beach known as North Cove on Kagamil, mostly waiting for the wind and seas to calm.

Sean Farrell prepares to unpack a just-packed kayak after a fierce storm blows in, just as we are ready to push off North Cove. This storm is a reminder that patience is the most important piece of equipment we carry with us.

Scott McGuire and I paddle away from Uliaga, dressed for the conditions in two layers of Gore-Tex®, neoprene-and-fleece hats, and rubber gloves. Temperature this day, with windchill, is 25°F.

We spend most of our time, on land or sea, with our hoods cinched up tight to ward off the near-constant rains and winds. Here, we paddle toward Carlisle Island.

Sean prepares dinner outdoors—a rarity, thanks to the wind and rain—at Eagle Camp on the southern end of Kagamil.

During our attempt to climb to the top of Kagamil's volcano, we were turned back from the peak by falling rock and sliding scree. This is not a place to fall and break a leg, or cut yourself on the sharp volcanic rock all around.

Sean uses a GPS, compass, maps, and his watch to chart several possible routes each time we attempt one of our seven crossings.

Given the cold water and dangerous conditions, every time we paddle it is with the same motto in mind: "Paddle for your life."

from the cold and panic, but because of the shock and panic I do not comprehend why my voice box isn't working.

I'm desperate to see one of my three teammates bob up on a parallel wave. One of them, Scott, is for sure in the same predicament as me, since we were paddling the same boat. Sean and Barry, in the second boat? Who knows if they're upright or not. Stroking hard, riding the waves, I reach out with a frozen hand, am within a stroke of the overturned boat, trying to keep my saltwater-swollen eyes out of the water, trying to catch a glimpse of Scott's yellow PFD. There's no sign of him hanging on to our boat, he's not there trying to right it and climb back in, as we'd practiced over and over. And where the fuck is that other kayak?

Scott's last shoutings—Brace, Jon, brace! Right! Hard! Now! Now!—ring in my ears as I swim atop the rough sea. Just before we went over our 22-foot-long kayak had been smacked hard from the right by a rogue wave, one we didn't see and couldn't have anticipated and, despite both of our efforts, leaning far into the giant wave and slamming our paddles into the churning sea, we were unable to keep the heavily loaded boat upright. The actual turning over happened in slow motion, as it always does. I swallowed a mouthful of saltwater just as the boat went over, slammed by yet another broadside wave. The next minute was spent in an upside-down mildly controlled panic. For about 30 seconds I waited, upside down, for a signal from the back of the boat—a knock on the hard shell indicating it was time to attempt a coordinated Eskimo roll. The best case was to roll the boat back upright without coming out of it. That knock never came. As my lungs neared explosion-level from holding my breath, I reached for the tab to release my spray skirt.

Nothing cooperated. The neoprene-and-Kevlar spray skirt, so efficient at keeping out the cold water, was snugged so tightly around the coaming that it now threatened to trap me inside. I tugged again and again at the loop that should have released it but nothing budged. It was as if an unseen vacuum was sucking back in the skirt. When I finally stripped the front of the skirt away using a combination of pulling and kicking with my knees, I pushed myself out of the overturned kayak and surfaced, spluttering for air, choking, only to swallow a mouthful of salt water.

A long five minutes after we capsized I kicked my feet and pushed my head up above the waves, looking for our yellow-and-cream kayak, which had now disappeared from sight. At one point it had been just an arms-length away, just beyond reach. As I reached for it the six-foot seas and 30-mph wind pushed it just as fast, countering my every effort. Scott! I yelled, weakly. I could barely hear my own voice. Not ready to give up I kept stroking to where the boat had been, swallowing seawater with every stroke. My arms were finished, could barely lift them out of the water. Physically I could feel myself giving up, the shock of the cold making me dizzy, weak. I knew I should try and preserve my strength in this cold water, but it ran against human nature to just float and wait in such a foreboding situation.

Where is that other kayak? When we planned this expedition into the middle of the Aleutian Islands, 150 miles from the nearest town, we purposely opted for two, tandem kayaks so that we'd be able to look out for one another in just such an occurrence. That I can't see the second boat says to me it must have been dumped as well. All four of us must now be in the same shit, swimming for our lives on the crests and troughs of nearby waves. And where is Scott? At my right ankle I can feel water seeping under the twisted rubber gasket and into my Gore-Tex® dry suit.

Treading water I kick myself up again, scanning the tops of the growing waves for boat or man. I can see the yellow kayak, now several waves away, far beyond my reach. Gone. I am so frightened by what I now regard as the inevitable—drowning, within another couple minutes—I can't even get a squeak out of my saltwater-ravaged throat. The winds whip a cold spray all around me. Despite the massive ocean that surrounds me I am as parched as if I were crawling across the Sahara. I try to scream as loud as I can, again and again and again, but nothing comes out.

I wake up.

Thanks to this nightmare, a version of which has haunted me since April, the knot in my stomach is definitely back this morning when we wake in our tents, which are sagged, heavy with dew. Out of the tent shortly after seven, I walk in a big circle through the tall grass atop the cliff. I would like to say I gazed out over the ocean, to take stock of the day, but the fog is so thick by the time I get 20 steps from my tent, even it is lost in the fog.

There's no sense waiting, though. We've agreed to attempt our first two crossings today. As we cook a big pot of oatmeal in a gray drizzle, hoods pulled up masking our faces, gone is the lighthearted patter of yesterday. Then, we were happy to finally be here. Now, the reality dawns that we have to get out onto the sea and see what's like.

Putting compass and ruler to map, we estimate the meat of the pass separating Uliaga from our camp on Kagamil is just 2.5

miles across, as the crow flies. Given the push and pull of current and winds, we'll probably end up paddling between four to five miles, beach to beach. Yet the distance is not what gives us pause. The risk we run is that if we are blown off course or unable to reach Uliaga thanks to unexpectedly strong currents or a sudden storm, we'll easily be pushed far from land. From the beach we try to judge just how fast the current is moving. We can see it running from west to east and guess it's traveling at seven miles an hour…or so. We'd been warned by boat captains who'd sailed through these Aleutian passes that the rip tides and currents are unpredictable, dangerous.

"His doom is sealed."

Why has this phrase of the old Russian priest Veniaminov—spoken about an Aleut kayaker who found himself tossed from his kayak—lodged itself in my head on this particular morning? And why is it repeating itself over and over as we break down camp and ready for our first crossing? Everyone's mood is made even more tense by the fact that we cannot see Uliaga through the fog. Except for a couple moments yesterday when a small parcel of the island made itself visible through the clouds, we have yet to see the island. Truth is, we haven't really seen much of Kagamil either. Steep walls rise behind our tents, higher than a thousand feet. Along the shore to the west we can see several offshore rock spires jutting straight out of the sea, and guess they are what the maps indicate as Candlestick Point. As the morning lengthens, the fog lifts for a few minutes more and with binoculars we can make out a beach of smooth rocks on the eastern edge of Uliaga where we hope to be able to pull our boats up for an exploration of its 2,500-foot volcano.

What we are undertaking is expeditionary kayaking at its most risky. Simply making the crossings in our heavily loaded boats is our first and major concern. Unlike a big mountaineering trip—with accompanying sherpas and literally tons of gear—we will have no base camp, no assistants. The four of us will be carrying everything we need for five weeks—food, paddling and climbing gear, emergency and first aid equipment, tons of camera gear. Every time we paddle we will pack the boats with everything we've brought. We cannot risk leaving food and gear behind in case one of the big Aleutian storms we anticipate arrives out of nowhere. Imagine if we are not able to get back to our "base" for a week or more, pinned down by 70 mile an hour winds and rain. What if we left behind food, sleeping bags, or tents? We didn't want to be separated from what we considered to be a very thin lifeline. As a result, each time we paddle it means packing everything into the two boats. Since we skipped our couple days of boat-loading practice in Nikolski, today will be a test to see if everything we've brought actually fits.

My mood ranges from confidence to slight panic as we tear down camp and begin to load the boats. I am hesitant in part because it has been more than three weeks since I've been in a kayak. That was in the calm, protected seas off Brittany. We'd relied on that stop in Nikolski to give us a chance to try out our paddling systems. We'd only been together in these big boats a few times. Scott and I had spent a day paddling around the oil-rigs off Santa Barbara, our one shot at practicing together. Now, here we are, in the middle of the Bering Sea. I took the water temperature this morning, and it was a frosty 38°.

Any confidence I have is because I know we are a strong team. Scott and Barry are like human motors in the back of a kayak, the former tall and rangy, with extra-long reach, the latter built like a real-life gladiator. We'd opted for two tandem boats rather than four singles for two reasons. If the weather turned bad midway across a pass or someone tipped over, we would only have to worry about keeping track of or rescuing one other boat rather than three. Second, we hoped that if conditions got bad fast, we could hustle these superlight boats—even when heavily loaded— out of the way of whatever was coming.

We aren't lacking in safety or protective gear. It is funny to watch us dress this first morning, struggling into our multiple layers. First comes a 200-weight Polartec fleece bunny suit. Over it goes a full-length Gore-Tex® drysuit, snugged at wrists, ankles and neck by super-tight rubber cuffs. If it is a cold day—today we consider warm, the temperatures in the low-40s, with a slight breeze— we will add another Gore-Tex® Skanorak, neoprene-and-fleece skullcap, neoprene gloves. On our feet we wear three layers of neoprene and rubber. We have brought along Buck Rogers-like helmets, which we'll wear this first day out, just in case the landing on the other side involves rough surf and big rocks.

Despite all that, I can't stop thinking about what it is like to fall out of a boat *in* the Bering Sea. It is not a place I want to spend any time at all. We should be able to roll these big boats, weighing between 700 and 800 pounds when fully loaded, back up if we go over. But that's more theory than reality. If the boats are dumped and we end up swimming, it will be absolutely essential to get back in the boats in less than ten minutes before hypothermia begins to slow our hearts and every other organ.

For safety, our paddles are leashed to our boats, and so are we. If the kayaks turn upside down, we don't want to be separated from either. On our Personal Flotation Devices—PFDs, or life jackets—we each wear a strobe light to signal potential rescuers and carry flares, whistles, and a signal mirror in a velcroed pocket, as well as a waterproof box of matches and a few energy bars. One person in each boat also carries an EPIRB (Emergency Position Remote Beacon), an electronic global emergency beacon that if triggered will send a distress signal to the nearest ship or plane. We've jokingly dubbed the EPIRBs "body finders," since the closest rescue would come out of Dutch Harbor, 150 miles away. By the time they'd picked up our distress signal, we would most likely already be dead, afloat in the cold ocean. Not a pretty picture, but this is the reality of the conditions and a reminder of just how far we are from help.

On the positive side, as I watch Sean with his compass and GPS survey the maps he holds on his knees, I am again made confident. Religious in his preparation, yesterday afternoon and again this morning he sat down on a piece of driftwood, binoculars in hand, and worked out a series of three optional targets for us, waypoints. Our plan is to set out following what he estimates to be the most direct route. But because we cannot easily read the speeds of the currents and tides from the beach, he has mapped at least two more optional routes dependent on how we are pushed by the sea and winds. The winds are easier to judge than the currents. If looking through the binoculars we see whitecaps in the pass, it probably means far too much wind for us to paddle through. If it is foggy, like this morning, it means less wind and fewer whitecaps.

The bottom line, if such a thing exists out here, is we have come to a place where there are no rules. Tide tables are handy to have, and so are the various wind and weather measuring gauges. We feel like we have plenty of experience. But a lot of our success or lack of it out here will depend on good luck. I am also convinced the most important thing we have is something each boat captain we'd met on our way traveling out here had recommended: Patience.

It takes a couple hours to find a place in the boats for all our various dry bags. The longer we're out here, the easier this packing-up will get, as we learn what fits where, and as we eat some of the food. Thanks to his giant bag of camera gear, Barry's red-topped kayak resembles something the Beverly Hillbillies might have constructed, with dry bags, an ice ax, rubber boots, and a bag of paperback books bungied—dangerously—to the deck. Dangerous because if the boat goes over, they'll never be able to roll it back up with all this extra paraphernalia hanging off it.

As we push off the beach for our initial foray, we paddle into thick fog. I feel vastly overdressed, in three layers, and the silver-and-black helmet on my head seems more intimidating than necessary. It is the first time I've worn these neoprene gloves and simultaneously used the ultra-light, carbon-fiber paddle—for some reason the combination gives me no grip on the paddle, and little purchase on the ocean. Taking our first strokes into the ocean, I realize too that my foot pegs are badly adjusted, pushing my knees too high into the fiberglass deck, making me feel off-balance. All in all, a bad fit. I call back to Scott, as best I can given the fact that the helmet limits my ability to turn my head, and shout, "I'm not comfortable at all, let's go back and regroup." All I want to do is get out of the boat and readjust. But we are already beyond the surf zone, out of the danger area where Scott Kerr had been swamped yesterday. Going back in would be a risk. We paddle alongside Barry and Sean, but they are against any kind of reverse. "It doesn't get any better than this as a test," says Barry, a strong wind whipping water off his paddle.

"That sounds good," I agree, "but I can't even get a grip on my paddle much less feel like I'm getting anywhere." Obviously he's not interested in my whining, since he and Sean motor away into the fog.

We are still in the lee of the island, protected from the bigger winds we can see scouring the top of the waves in the middle of the pass. From sea level we can see better just how fast the current is moving. From this vantage it looks like a fast, wide river cruising between the islands. A few sailors had described the currents out here as dangerous, treacherous, unpredictable. Now we can see for ourselves what they were talking about.

Paddling in rhythm, Scott and I began to cut through the sea and the fog with our big, yellow-topped kayak. Within 10 minutes Kagamil disappears behind us. Uliaga, which we know is straight in front of us somewhere, is also invisible. Finally, we are truly at sea. For the next 30 minutes we pull hard, without conversation, without stopping to sip from our water bottles or to admire the fog-shrouded scene. The current pushes from the west at six miles an hour. The tide is out, which we'd estimated from tables picked up in Dutch Harbor.

Soon the low green hills of Uliaga become visible through the fog. Puffins and murres fly overhead, greeting us. Pulling up alongside the other boat, we make a quick decision on whether to fight west against the current up the island's shoreline to a small beach we can see from the water, or to paddle east, with the current, around a corner where we spotted a rocky beach yesterday. The second route requires that we skirt a series of sizable tidal rips that were marked on the map, which we can see just off our starboard. My left arm is worn ragged from our shot-from-a-rocket sprint pace. This is a good test because this is exactly the pace we'll maintain every time we're on the water. This is not Baja, no place for leisurely paddling. As we paddle out and around the long line of tidal rips—created where waves and current wash over a shallow ledge, creating standing waves five, six feet tall—I shout back into the wind, toward Scott.

"Paddle for your life," I yell, somewhat in jest. He relays it to the other boat, and it's quickly adopted as yet another motto of the expedition.

Rounding the eastern edge of Uliaga, we find the smooth-rocked beach exactly as we'd spied it through binoculars. Long, glassy swells wash onto the shore, and the small bay is filled with kelp floating on the surface, a good sign meaning this is not a place typically visited by heavy seas. It appears to be a good, safe place to pull ashore for the day. As we paddle into the calm water, a half-dozen sneaker seals pop their heads above the surface to check us out.

Despite the relief in having made our first crossing successfully, our arrival is marred by the surfacing of some team tensions. I'd been anticipating some kind of minor blow-up, simply because we are four persons who'd just spent an arduous few weeks—and more—getting out here. I sensed some small, budding anxieties—

mostly between Barry and Scott—and was hoping they would have some kind of confrontation sooner rather than later in order to get whatever complaints were building out in the open. Like the valve on an over-inflated air mattress, some hot air needed to be released. I was surprised it happened here, though, on the heels of our first crossing.

One difficulty we will face throughout this trip is that our light-weight, somewhat fragile boats cannot be dragged over the rocks. Though tough, the last thing we want to risk is spending a day or more fixing avoidable cracks in the fiberglass. Most of the beaches are going to be rocky, and working out a system for carrying the boats up onto the beach is one of our first tasks. With both boats idling just off the beach I jump out to help Sean and Barry gently pull the red Necky up onto the rocks. Loaded, it's far too heavy to simply pick up. The three of us stand knee-deep in the cold water, waves pushing us gently, contemplating exactly which step to take next.

Our hesitation leads to a shout from Scott, who is just off-shore, back paddling to keep the second kayak from being pushed into the rocks. Commandingly, he yells over the calm, kelp-filled cove, "Just empty the boat and then carry it up!"

Barry frowns not at the suggestion of what to do, but at the tone of Scott's voice. Of all of us Barry has probably been in the toughest spots. He has spent 20-plus years outdoors in an adventuresome life, and so far he has always figured his way out of tight spots. Once, for example, in China, we were on a bus with a bad axle that threatened to throw it—and us—down a steep ravine. After a brief inspection he crawled under the decrepit machine with a piece of hoopie and tied off the axle, enabling us to plod the final ten miles into Lijang. Getting this kayak safely ashore is going to happen, and safely, but given the pile of sharp and slippery rocks all around, it deserves some study.

I can see him pondering how to respond to being yelled at.

The next thing we know, Scott is slamming his boat ashore, jumping out, and beginning to heave bags out of it and onto the beach, obviously in a huff.

This brewing anxiety went back to that night in Kernville, more than two months before, when we all had that talk about Scott's not using this trip to practice his chops as a photographer. What is going on here is nothing more than a simple display of simmering jealousy. Barry—and his life as adventurer, photographer, husband, father, respected character in his various fields—is a model for Scott, 12 years his junior. But rather than respect Barry's superior experience, Scott seems hell-bent on proving that he is an equal, on all levels. He wants it all, right now, to be accomplished at everything. Basically what is taking place on this rocky beach in the middle of the Bering Sea is a display of a couple of big, man-dogs trying to mark their respective territories.

"If you don't want to listen to what I have to say, based on my years working for Necky and my travels in Baja, then I'm not going to say anything for the rest of the trip," Scott fumed.

That prompts Barry to respond with something I am sure he's been itching to get off his chest for a while. Heatedly, surprising Sean and I, since Barry is the most laid-back of us all, he says, "It's not what you're saying, Scott. It's how you're saying it."

The tension continues, as both boats are silently unloaded and carried high up onto the rocks. When that chore is complete, Barry—definitely the bigger dog here, in all definitions—

calls Scott over for a log-side sit-down, to try and get over, just the two of them, what is threatening to become a sizable personnel problem.

As nominal leader, I appreciate Barry taking charge here. It is far better for the two of them to sort this out than for a third person to mediate. The last thing we need out here in the middle of nowhere is a rift.

Perhaps the hardest factor for me to juggle is one that is common to any expedition. When you're out in the middle of nowhere, in potentially life-threatening situations for an extended period, everyone arrives with slightly different expectations. Here, we shared one general desire: to paddle to each of the islands safely and get back home. That may be where our visions of the trip ceased being identical. For Barry and I, we have income at stake. If we don't return with great pictures and a compelling story, we are out of luck financially and professionally. For Sean, his motivation is that he loves the challenges of being far from his daily grind at Rutan & Tucker.

As for Scott, his expectations are mixed. At one point on the ferry ride out here he'd told me that once he realized he wasn't going to be spending his extra minutes making photographs, the trip became more like a job to him. And we all know that on any job there are bad days, and good. Today, he was having a very bad day at the office.

As Scott and Barry try to work out their clash, Sean and I busy ourselves preparing for our exploration of Uliaga.

"That's all we need," says Sean, as he crams our sole climbing rope into his backpack, "these guys not speaking to each other. We've only been out here two days!"

"Worse," I added, "would be to have them get into some kind of back-stabbing relationship in a place where the most important thing we have to do each day is watch out for each other's back."

NINE

"In the number of things indispensable to the baidarka, formerly belonged the bladder, i.e. the cleaned stomach of a seal or sea lion, which was needed for the occasion when a rider overturned. In such a situation, to emerge from the baidarka and set it on its keel again without shipping water, and, even if water pours in, to bail it out, is not very difficult. But to get into the baidarka without any other point of support is completely impossible. An inflated bladder on such an occasion was extremely useful, because with its assistance the rider could maintain himself on the water and get into the baidarka."—Ivan Veniaminov

It is the cold water that is our biggest concern. Unlike much sea kayaking, done on much warmer water, we have absolutely no room for error. Spending more than 10 or 15 minutes in this 34° water promises only one result. Though we are acutely aware of the risk, we rarely mention it.

Although kayaking as a sport first became popular in the

1860s, it was not until the 1920s that the value of learning to roll began to be fully realized. There are at least 30 different ways to roll, but many skillful kayakers cannot roll and sometimes a highly skilled roller will fail to recover. Aleuts began experimenting with rolling as boys and were not allowed to go to sea to hunt if they had not mastered the skill. If seas turned threatening while they were out hunting, the Aleuts would raft their baidarkas together, tying two or three together to ride out the storm. Like us, they knew that if they were separated from their boats, they were most likely lost.

Men and women have crossed big bodies of water in small boats going back at least several centuries, in rowboats, sailboats, kayaks, and canoes. Many of them have ended up in the water. Their stories of loss, or survival, are legion. Spike Walker, an Alaskan crab fishermen turned writer, detailed both in his books about fishing on these very waters, including the nearly unbelievable tale of a first-day crewman who ended up in the Bering Sea wearing a leaking survival suit, only to survive 36 hours bobbing in big waves before managing to swim to a rocky island beach.

During the months prior to our arrival in the Aleutians, I kept a copy of Robert Hendrickson's *The Ocean Almanac: Being a Copious Compendium on Sea Creatures, Nautical Lore & Legend, Master Mariners, Naval Disasters, and Myriad Mysteries of the Deep,* on my desk. I'd turned down several pages, highlighting such records as "Longest Survival at Sea—With and Without Life Rafts," "The Remotest Place in the World to Be Shipwrecked" and a long excerpt from *Survival on Land and Sea,* which I read over and over for its tips on surviving a shipwreck. It could have been these readings that contributed to my recurring nightmares.

Longest with a life raft? On November 23, 1942, the S.S. *Ben Lomond* of the U.K. Merchant Navy was torpedoed in the Atlantic some 565 miles west of St. Paul's Rocks, England. Second Steward Poon Lin—25 years old—abandoned ship alone on a life raft. Using the spring from a flashlight for a hook, Lin managed to catch fish, and occasionally he was able to catch a seabird with his bare hands. He wasn't rescued for 133 days. Awarded the British Empire medal for his extraordinary record, he was quoted as saying "I hope no one will ever have to break it."

Without a raft? There is an apocryphal story of a man overboard who seized and choked to death an albatross that had repeatedly attacked him and used its buoyant body as a life preserver until he was rescued some 20 hours later. On Christmas Eve in 1955, a Norwegian seaman fell from a freighter in the Gulf of Mexico and spent 30 hours in the water before a tanker rescued him, probably the longest survival record without any life preserver or PFD. In 1978, strong currents prevented a trio of scuba divers from reaching their boat after ascending from a dive and they stayed afloat in the Gulf of Mexico for 48 hours, 50 hours, and 25 hours respectively, before being rescued.

Remotest place in the world to be shipwrecked? The worst possible place would be in the South Pacific, at roughly 48°30'S, 125°30'W. This is the farthest spot from land in the world, being approximately 1,660 miles from Pitcairn's Island, also known as Ducie Island, to Cape Dart in Antarctica. A person shipwrecked at this point would be a far from land as anyone in history save a handful of astronauts.

One thing we have in common with the Aleut kayakers—like them we know that no one is going to come roaring to the rescue from over the horizon if we somehow get in trouble, whether on land or especially on sea.

At various times, in different corners of the world, certain peoples have developed an incredible tolerance to cold and cold water. Charles Darwin described women of Tierra del Fuego nursing their babies in open boats while snow fell on their bare breasts. The aboriginies of central Australia are renowned for their tolerance of cold. They can remain asleep after their core body temperature has begun to fall, which allows them to sleep on cold ground. Eskimos can expose bare fingers to subzero temperatures for hours without suffering frostbite.

We are not those people.

In simplest terms hypothermia means a lower than normal temperature (from the Greek *hypo* for lower and *therme* for heat). We have long been taught that the normal human body temperature is 98.6°F. This is actually an average of oral temperatures in healthy persons. Normal temperature can be as low as 96.5°F. or as high as 100°F. You are suffering from mild hypothermia when your body temperature is between 90° and 95°. What we feared most out on the Bering Sea was the next step, what is known as "profound hypothermia," when your core body temperature drops below 90°.

People most exposed to hypothermia are outdoorsmen (ice fishermen, hunters, sea kayakers, sailors), but it also takes its toll on elderly folks whose heat has been turned off, people in their cars dressed to arrive not survive, as well as drunks and druggies too numb to come in from the cold. Falling into cold water, though, is the major cause of death.

"Anyone in water colder than 60° to 70° is a prime candidate for hypothermia," warns cold-weather expert Dr. Cameron Bangs, of Oregon City, Oregon. "Prolonged immersion in water as warm as 77° cools the body. However, though falling into icy water must be among the world's most miserable experiences, even ice water takes about 15 minutes to cool the body to a level at which the individual is physically impaired. Panicky overreactions are unjustifiable and must be avoided." Typically, hypothermic conditions are aided and abetted by water in the lungs, i.e. drowning.

There is no exact science on how many minutes you can live in the 35° water we are paddling across in the Bering Sea. If you were to drop 100 people simultaneously into the middle of such waters, survival times would differ, depending on previous experience in cold conditions, aerobic fitness (being one time when obesity might come in handy), ability to eat and/or drink without swallowing seawater and psychological stability—the will not to give up since panic wastes energy and promotes heat loss. It's believed that the Aleut who first populated these islands could survive up to 45 minutes in the water; we gave ourselves half that.

TEN

Peace made between Barry and Scott, at least for the time being—why was I feeling like Jimmy Carter at Camp David here, trying to broker peace between a pair of *enfant terribles?*— we have a celebratory lunch of dried salmon, nuts, and hot tea. Our first crossing was a success. Stripping out of our dry suits provokes some good, tension-relieving laughs. It is Sean's turn today at center stage; the damn rubber gaskets are so tight around your neck, it's nearly impossible to pull them off over your head without nearly sucking your head off at the same time. Combine that inelegant struggle with simultaneously trying to keep your balance on huge beach rocks, well, it can be a pretty funny sight. Unless, of course, you're the one with your head and hair caught in the grip of the way-too-tight head condom.

As well as exploring each of the islands by sea we intend to climb and hike as much of their interiors as we can. From the beach we climb straight up a steep, grassy wall and emerge onto a large, sloping meadow rising toward the 2,500-foot volcano.

Summer is just arriving here—it lasts less than two months—and the fields are beginning to bloom with buttercups and marigolds. The fog has lifted slightly and with clearer skies we have a magnificent view back at Kagamil. Multicolored layers of rock make up its steep cliff side before grassy hills lead to its volcanic peak. Its jagged peak is still hidden from sight, though, and we wonder out loud if we'll ever see it.

The absence of trees is mysterious. Forests grew on some of the Aleutian Islands at one point, proven by unearthed fossilized tree trunks. Yet but for a few thickets of undersized willow and alder on the easternmost islands, there are no trees these days, although the climate is relatively mild with plenty of rain and good soil. The only logical explanation is the constant wind, which has over centuries simply worn them out.

It is the first time we are really able to get a glimpse of the islands scattered in front of us, to the south and west, even though they are barely exposed. Even masked, the hint of their beauty is so stunning we stop talking and keep walking toward the southern cliffs of Uliaga. We can just make out a shoulder of the towering 5,300-foot volcano on Carlisle. Straight ahead, over the shoulder of Kagamil, are insinuations of the two big, snow-capped mountains that anchor Chuginadak. Prior to coming here we saw only a few photos of the impressive Mount Cleveland, black-and-white snapshots taken by pilots during flyovers. They were our only image of what this place could look like on a clear day. As our view gives hints of its potential magnificence, we cross our fingers that eventually the clouds will lift entirely and give us at least one good blue-sky day.

We hike with our backs to the other islands, peeking over our shoulders, hoping the clouds will eventually lift. An Aleut village would have been atop the cliff where we landed. As we walk through the fast-growing tundra grasses, we look for hints of where they might have built their half-underground homes. Sod-covered humps of stacked rock are the only signs that suggest this was once a village. The Aleut had no temples or idols, but there were sacred or forbidden places on each island, usually on a small hillock or prominent cliff. We find many dried white shells of sea urchins in the thick grass, plucked from the beaches and dropped here by seabirds.

At a thousand feet we discover a long meadow lake and then patches of soft snow. It was the snowiest winter in the region in the past 25 years, and the peak above is white beneath a layer of deep snow. Sean and I take shelter from the wind, which is picking up the higher we hike. Through binoculars we scout the western coastline of Kagamil, plotting the route we will take in the next day or so as we work our way to its southern tip. We can see nothing but tall cliffs lining the eight-mile coast, certainly no place to pull our kayaks in. Whenever we make that sprint, it will be with the knowledge that stopping along the way is not an option. On our maps we can see an inlet at the southern tip. Once we leave North Cove we have to reach that beach or retreat.

At 1,500 feet we rest and watch a half-dozen bald eagles soaring overhead. Scott continues climbing, his red jacket bobbing up the steep, grass-covered hill like a beacon. When he reached the snow's edge he stops and signals for us to join him. We are staying on Uliaga only for the day, awaiting low tide, which we estimate will arrive at about 7:00 p.m. With four hours to kill, we keep climbing higher under a thickening sky.

Late in the day, from the south side of Uliaga, we are offered our first real glimpses of the big volcanoes on Carlisle and Chuginadak. Just glimpses, though, as the clouds continue to hover low despite that a steady wind is blowing at 15 miles an hour. While their nearly 6,000-foot height may not sound like much in contrast to Everest, the fact that these snowcapped beauties rise literally straight up from the sea makes them impressive.

The 1,200-mile Aleutian chain is little more than a long line of blowing, sparking, fireworks-creating volcanoes, more than 80 in all, ranging from 1,000 to 10,000 feet high. The arc forms one of the most spectacular chains of volcanoes around the Pacific Basin and is this continent's major link in the basin's "Ring of Fire."

An oral and written record of eruptions out here goes back to the first Russians to arrive. Since 1760, 40 different Aleutian volcanoes have gone off, registering 225 recorded eruptions in all. Due to the islands' remoteness, and the difficulty monitoring eruptions, we can assume there have been many, many more. Some of the eruptions are mostly smoke, others full-blown eruptions, still others catastrophes like Mount Katmai in 1912. The most active today are Shishaldin on Unimak and Makushin on Unalaska. Perhaps the most famous is Bogoslof, which has seemed to rise and sink several times since 1796. It is apparently the top of a nearly submerged volcano rising 5,000 feet off the ocean floor. Eight miles in diameter at its base, each time it erupts a new peak is created, only to be quickly knocked down by wind and waves.

Some kind of volcanic activity occurs along this belt every year. With more than ten percent of the world's identified volcanoes within its boundary, Alaska has become a laboratory for scientists who are trying to unravel details of the mystery of earth processes.

I researched what causes a volcano to erupt as well as the signals it gives off just beforehand. Obviously we can't do anything if one of those big suckers starts to tremble while we are camped at its foot, but better to proceed with as much intelligence as possible. In the Aleutians, the process begins when the tectonic plates that are the ocean floor grind against each other. The plates are pushed apart along belts marked by submarine volcanoes and earthquakes; volcanoes are produced when parts of the upper plate are melted, and the molten material makes it way to the surface. In southern Alaska, a plate that underlies much of the Pacific Ocean is being pushed beneath the North American plate, along the 25,000-foot-deep Aleutian Trench.

I carry in one of my dry bags several recent printouts from the National Earthquake Information Center. They record a 5.6 level earthquake that happened just a couple weeks before we got out here, 130 miles southwest of Anchorage. It is merely one example of tremblors that are recorded virtually every week. This one had been felt in Anchorage, Homer, Kenai, Wasilla, and other parts of south central Alaska. It failed to make anyone's news reports.

In Anchorage I had a couple long talks with Tom Miller, director of the Alaska Volcano Observatory. He'd been very helpful and sent me exact data on the eruption histories of the Islands of Four Mountains. He admitted his team didn't know much of anything about Cleveland and Carlisle, Kagamil and Herbert. "It's expensive to put monitoring systems on all those big guys out there, so we haven't," he said. He asked that I call him from Dutch Harbor and let him know when we were heading out, so that if something did go off during the weeks we were gone, he'd remember to tell someone that we were in the vicinity. He also requested that I call him when we returned "because you'll know more about those islands than we do."

That statement points up the difficulty and expense of monitoring every last volcano in the region. Sometimes confusion is recorded as science. Condensation is often confused with "smoke." Many of these volcanoes "steam" as meltwater from summit snow falls on internal hot spots, an event that does not presage new activity but can appear like something's about to blow. Eruptions of Mount Cleveland and Carlisle have been confused more than once. What has helped Miller and his team is the increase in commercial air traffic over the islands since 1980. Pilots are often his best sources.

It must be something to see these particular volcanoes blow, the way they are situated, surrounded by deep blue ocean. G. D. Robinson, a geologist with the U.S. Geological survey, watched Okmok on Umnak Island explode early in the century. "There was a steady roar, like that of a railroad locomotive at the far end of a long tunnel, punctuated every 10 to 15 seconds by a violent explosion which threw red-hot blobs of lava more than a thousand feet above the cone.... About once a minute there was a particularly violent explosion in which bombs several feet long were thrown far out on the caldera floor. The temperature at the top was nearly 2000°F."

On June 6, 1912, the snow-covered, seemingly dormant Mount Katmai blew up in a series of violent explosions, throwing more than 5.5 cubic miles of debris into the air. For hundreds of square miles around, the eruptions destroyed the country. The city of Kodiak, 100 miles away, was plunged into total darkness for 60 hours while volcanic ash covered everything to a depth of several feet. The accompanying thunder and lightning convinced the terrified residents that the end of the world had come. The explosive sounds were heard in Juneau, about 750 miles away. In Seattle and Port Townsend, over 2,000 miles from Katmai, cloth fabrics disintegrated from the effects of sulfuric acid rain, which fell for days.

An Aleut fisherman observed the explosion up close and wrote in his journal from beneath an overturned boat on the shore: "We are waiting for death at any moment. A mountain has burst near here. We are covered with ashes, in some places 10 feet and six feet deep. All this began June 6. Night and day we light lanterns. We cannot see daylight. We have no water; the rivers are just ashes mixed with water. Here are darkness and hello, thunder and noise. I do not know whether it is day or night. The earth is trembling, it lightens every minute. It is terrible. We are praying."

The biggest concentration of volcanic action in the Aleutian chain occurred not so long ago, in 1986. Pavlov, Shishaldin, Akutan, Cleveland, Makushin, and Okmok all exploded that year. Most spectacular was the eruption of Augustine in late March, early April, which sent smoke and ash 4,000 feet into the air for several days blanketing communities on the Kenai peninsula and sending ash as far as Anchorage.

The 2,700-foot tall volcano on Kagamil last blew in December 1929, for only the second time since records began being kept in 1700. Carlisle—5,300 feet—went off last in November 1987, for the third time since 1700. The 3,600 foot Chuginadak East, the second, smaller volcano on that island, has no record of eruptions. The volcano on Herbert blew so dramatically some centuries before that its peak is completely gone.

Where we are, there should only be one active volcano to keep our eye on. Chuginadak's Mount Cleveland is the most active, having blown 11 times between 1893 and 1994, and still smoking constantly. It last exploded in 1994 and has a pattern of blowing about every six years, putting us nearly on target for the next one. When a volcano is about to erupt, many physical and chemical changes take place within it. Most shake, swell, and contract during the hours and days just before. If Cleveland blew while we were out here, thick ash would bury us under a heavy, suffocating blanket several feet thick. Everything within ten miles would be killed.

From our vantage, climbing the steepening side of Uliaga's volcano and looking out over the still foggy Bering Sea, heading for the snowpack, those not-so-far away peaks on Carlisle and Cleveland look wickedly beautiful and slightly intimidating. It would be an incredible experience to watch them blow. I wonder if we'd survive such an intimate look.

Our plan had been to wait a few hours more for the slack tide before trying to beat it back to Kagamil. From up high, looking out over the relatively calm seas, we worry that maybe we should just go now instead of waiting until 7:00 p.m. We're still novices out here regarding the weather, and we're going to kick ourselves if we hang out and wait for low tide only to discover it's accompanied by hurricane winds. Temperatures are in the mid-40s, and the wind has dropped to five miles an hour.

A bit earlier than planned, we squeeze back into our dry suits and get the kayaks launched. Our aim is to catch the wind blowing steadily out of the northeast. That would be a nice kick, helping to push us back toward North Cove. We paddle straight east, out to sea, heading away from all the islands in order to miss the big whitecaps created just offshore as they rebound off the cliffs. Three to four foot swells push us from the side. "Now you see 'em, now you don't," Scott yells from the back of the boat as we watch the other kayak disappear, then reappear, in the deepening troughs.

I can barely hear him for the Australian surfing helmet I've still got pulled down tight. Until situations grow far worse I'll probably abandon the thing after today. It's heavy and limits my peripheral vision. Granted, it will be nice to have if we ever look like we're in a position to tumble through the surf to get to a beach. But the whole feel of the return trip gives us all increased confidence. The boat seems to fit better now. I've abandoned my slippery gloves, glued a rubber grip on my paddle and correctly adjusted the foot pegs. Plus—and this is a major plus—when we paddle off the rocky beach, the opposite shoreline is in full view, green and glowing in the near distance.

The wind is at our backs and that feels good, too. Swamping waves come from the west, and Scott later reports that on several occasions the back end of the boat was completely submerged. By this time we are even with Candlestick Point to the east, a pair of conical spires climbing up at the point marking the west edge of North Cove. The big swells are still behind us, pushing us toward shore.

Landing even on a sand beach is tenuous with this kind of surf at our backs. Barry and Sean go first, and it's dramatic to watch their heavily loaded boat nearly submarine. Ours is an even more dramatic surf landing. We begin to back-paddle hard a 100 yards offshore as six-foot-tall trailing waves threaten to shove us sideways. With a sprinting burst we break through a series of three big waves, and the nose pushes into the sand. Sean is waiting to help us pull the boat up onto the beach. Once out of the boat, I am filled with noticeable relief. The first two crossings are now behind us.

Despite the personality clash and the ensuing conflict earlier in the day, Barry seems particularly exuberant. Wringing out his drenched ball cap, he stands by my side as we pull the boats higher onto the sand. "It felt so good to just be in the boats, paddling. That's what this trip was supposed to be all about, remember? For a while I thought we'd never actually get onto the ocean. Especially during these last few weeks. Now, no more talking. Finally, we're doing. What a relief!"

Looking up at a clearing sky, he adds, "Is it my imagination, or is it getting greener around here?"

ELEVEN

I t is the coldest morning yet. Though the air temperature is a moderate 42°, there is a stiff wind and rain out there. After peeking outside, taking my readings in a thick blanket of fog, we opt to stay in our tent another half hour. When Scott and I finally straggle down onto the beach from our camp on the bluff, we find Sean heating water for oatmeal and coffee. Everyone's wearing stocking caps and gloves, hoods cinched up tight to keep out the rain, which is blowing horizontally. Yet another expedition motto emerges as we shuffle silently in the cold, wet sand, wishing it would rain just a little harder to justify ducking back into our still warm tents and sleeping bags. "Definitely not Baja," I say to Sean.

After loading backpacks with lunch and a climbing rope, we spend the late morning literally lost in the fog. We decide not to paddle today but to hike the north end of Kagamil, for two reasons. We hope to climb its 3,000-foot volcano eventually and though the easiest access seems to be from the southern end of the island, it was possible we may be able to find a less steep route right above us. We are also curious about a "stone shack" marked on our maps. It should be just over the ridge above somewhere. It would have been built nearly two centuries ago, by Russians, and would be a good discovery for us, if it hasn't been blown down long ago by the relentless winds.

Thanks to the fog, and the fact someone neglected to pack a map when we left the beach, we end up traversing the steep, tundra-clumped hillside from east to west and back again, looking for a slot in the ridge that will take us to its far side. We stumble across the steep-sided hill, 2,000 feet above the beach, stymied by a sheer cliff rising above us. Yesterday we were able to see the route clearly from below. Now, up here, lost in the fog, all sense of direction has disappeared. We go this way, that way, up, down, at first traveling by instinct, then just starting to guess at which is the best way. I become convinced we are hiking in a giant circle and will soon end up back at our tents.

"Where is that map?" Barry jokes, knowing it was his friend and tentmate Sean who left it behind.

Not one to let even a slight dig pass without comment, Sean responds quickly, "Well, given how big that pack is that you're carrying, I was sure you had it with you. I mean, what all do you have in that thing?" One of the curses of Barry's occupation is that whenever we hike he humps a 50-pound backpack filled with camera bodies, lenses, a tripod, and much more.

It is not easy climbing. These island walls are a complex configuration of teethed summits, gnarled ridges with precipitous ravines, rock walls that thrust upward overshadowing glacial lakes, everywhere intersected by valleys. All around us centuries of ice, water, and wind have devoured what was made by fire. Above the multitude of ancient eroded peaks rise the deceptively placid slopes of more recent volcanoes.

After three hours we finally find the saddle between the peaks, leading us to a sweeping green valley and access to the island's northwest corner. Below the volcanic peaks, the southern portions of the islands ripple from the sea like elevated plateaus. I spy round grassy bluffs, broken grass-capped pinnacles, eroded cliffs laced with waterfalls, sea caves palming the crested tide, rock ledges crowded with crustaceans, and great boulder-strewn beaches. The precipitous coasts occasionally open to stretches of finer rock or sand, into protected bays.

Looking out over the steep valley before us, leading to the eastern edge of the island, we glimpse a view down the flat green coastline heading south. Trudging through the tundra, we keep our eyes on the earth around us, looking for any sign of men who preceded us long ago. Behind every rock on a hillside we envision a cave filled with mummies, in every shallow the foundation of one of their sod-and-driftwood homes. The few archaeologists and anthropologists who have seen the Islands of Four Mountains regard them a special find. Few grave-and-pot robbers have ventured out here, thanks to the islands' remoteness. I had to make repeated promises to archaeologists and historians in Alaska, particularly in Dutch Harbor, that we were not coming to search for mummies and loot any cave we might find. The reality is that most of the mummy caves have either already been found, or have disappeared forever behind rockfalls of a long-ago volcano or earthquake.

"This is the most prehistoric place I've ever seen," mutters Barry. It is the kind of desolate landscape in which you can

easily envision tyrannosaurs galloping by, pterodactyls wing-
ing overhead.

Using our amateur archaeological skills, we think we can make
out traces of where an Aleut village was built, based on changes in
the vegetation and the fact that the spot is protected from the
wind. We find a few thick, tablet-like rocks sticking straight up and
down in the tundra, which we guess could have been landmarks
for kayakers to use as a compass when they were returning from
a sea hunt. Sean picks up a smooth white, well-rounded beach rock
from the middle of a dried mud flat. It is far too heavy for any bird
to carry and is several miles from the beach. Some man carried it
here and dropped it, perhaps thousands of years before.

As surreal as the landscape around us is, more unusual is the
weather. We've been here a few days, and we are still acclima-
tizing to its constant shifts. On the north side of the island,
before we found the saddle through the ridge, we were enveloped
in a fog so thick we lost sight of each other within steps. Once
we crossed into the valley, the sun was out, high above. Once we
descended into the valley, we could see the thick fog lingering
in the crevices that lead back down the hills to the sea, poised
as if it were ready to sneak out and envelop the valley floor any
minute. But it did not, happy to linger there all day, waiting for
our return.

We descend 500 feet onto the grassy floor, getting beneath the
wind, and the temperatures rise from 35° to 65°. We strip off a
top layer of fleece and unzip the side vents of our pants, sweating beneath our backpacks. Sitting in the shade of a boulder,
protected from the wind, we eat salmon and a couple of energy
bars before taking a ten-minute siesta. To the west we look across

Samalga Pass, toward Nikolski. In the haze above where Umnak Island lies we can see the outline of the volcano named Mount Vsevidof. It is 45 miles away. Sean carried one of our VHF radios along for experiment's sake, and we try to raise Scott and Agrafina Kerr in Nikolski. We get a response—Agrafina picks up at their end, shouting, "Hello, Hello, Hello" into the receiver—but they cannot hear us, have no idea who is trying to reach them. It is not exactly a reassuring experiment, except that we now know for sure that the radios will be of little help.

After we hike for six hours, the heaviest fog around the fringes of the valley lifts. Though the sky remains gray and cloudy, the wind has dropped. We scout the ridgeline where the stone shack should be, but find no evidence of it. As we hike back to the ridge overlooking our camp, the sea spreads out before us, appearing glassy, calm. Without the fog, the route back to the other side of the ridge is easy to find. As soon as we crest the ridge, the air temperature drops by 20°. Now we see that when we were lost this morning we were way too far to the west. It was a good lesson in just how easy it is to get confused when trying to navigate through a thick fog, whether on land or sea. I was happy we had the lesson on land, rather than in the middle of one of the ocean passes.

The eight-hour hike is good exercise, and we are happy to be back down on what we dub Paradise Beach. "It won't get any better than this," Barry jokes about our long, sandy beach. A giant sneaker seal has been coming around each night just before dark—about 11:00 p.m.—to spy on us. He is back tonight, poking his head above the surface, eyeing us, then disappearing and reappearing 100 feet down the beach.

Back in our "kitchen"—a small gas stove set up on the empty oil barrel—I ask if anyone else felt any kind of "presence" during the day. Though far from spiritual, I had an inkling all day long that someone was following us. I actually stopped and peeked back over my shoulder several times. It almost felt as if we were being pushed along, guided, as we hiked the island.

I think of the ghostly figures the Aleut called the *asxaadax,* or the Outside Man. Spectral figures, they were said to haunt the perimeter of the small villages. In fact, they were not ghosts at all, but small bands of Aleuts who refused to submit to the stringent regimes of the early Russian fur hunters, choosing to live alone on the outskirts of civilization. Veniaminov had heard about them when he arrived in Dutch Harbor, and in one case he imposed a penance on any Aleut who fatally shot one of the "nomadic Aleut," even if in alleged self-defense.

In some ways that's how I am beginning to feel about our presence here. As definite outsiders, if not intruders. Though it has been centuries since anyone lived on Kagamil, it still feels—thanks to the remoteness and isolation of the place and the mystery that still enwrapped the lives, and deaths, of those long-absent Aleuts—as if we are trespassing.

It would be a mistake to remember the Aleut only in spiritual or ghostlike references. They had a very long and concrete life here. Though most evidence of their lives, their villages, is long gone, we have accounts from a variety of Russians and other early explorers to suggest just how the Aleut lived on these islands.

Their entire culture was shaped by living in one of the dreariest, stormiest places on earth. When not being assailed by gale-force winds, they were smothered by fog. Sunlight was a rare visitor. Wind howled over the islands with no obstructions—the birds learned to fly low, the wings of some insects atrophied from under-use, even the people chose to live underground. According to Ken Brower, the Aleut mistakenly thought trees grew in undersea forests like kelp. They modeled the frames of their homes after the skeletons of whales.

Typically, a small Aleutian island would have been home to 100-200 people. A large village might have as many as four of the underground dwellings—known as barbaras—and everyone in the village would have been related.

These multi-family longhouses varied in size. In a large settlement they could be from 70 to over 200 feet long and up to 30 feet wide. Rectangular, oriented on an east-west axis, they sometimes built extensions on either end that ran north to south. There were as many as ten individual rooftop entry hatches, which also served for ventilation and to let in light.

Inside, the houses were divided into compartments, occupied by separate households. These usually included a man and his wife or wives, older married sons and their families, and sometimes a younger brother and his family. The adolescent sons of the household head were sent to their mother's village to be reared by her older brother or brothers. Although anthropologists have been unable to determine the Aleuts' rule of descent, many assume matrilineal descent. They were permissive about sexual relations and marriage, but incest was well defined—and prohibited. It's believed that each wife had a separate compartment in the house. Each compartment was marked by a post on which was fixed an oil lamp, its rounded bottom fitted into a hollow at the top of the post. Twined grass mats separated one compartment from another.

The villages were most often built on the northern side of the island, near the slightly calmer seas where the majority of fish were. On this side too were larger supplies of driftwood washed up on the sand or rock beaches. They also built seasonal dwellings, closer to the sea, used in the short summer months.

Almost everything they had, from clothing to food, heating fuel to building materials, came from the sea. They hunted seals, otters, and whales and fished for cod and halibut with hooks and line. They fastened bone hooks to braided strips of stalks of giant kelp and caught salmon in nets or traps. Women, children, and old men gathered food along the shoreline, including clams and a variety of green spiny sea urchins (they rubbed off the spines, gathered at low tide, then broke the shells for the clumps of bright-yellow eggs inside, which they ate raw or steamed). They also ate several species of kelp and seaweed, and birds and their eggs. During the summer they hunted cormorants, murres, ducks, geese, loons, ptarmigans, and gulls. They gathered grass baskets full of salmonberries, blueberries, crowberries, and roots.

Men's clothing was made mostly from puffin, murre and cormorant skins. Cormorant clothing was particularly prestigious, and was most often held for the best hunters. Women's garments were of sea mammal skins, mostly sea otter and fur seals, with the skin side out. They were elaborately decorated at the neck, cuffs, hem, and along the seams with embroidery of feathers, human hair, and ocher-colored skin strips. After the Russians arrived, they learned to use unraveled wool, dyed red or green, as a seam decoration.

They were a tough people. When they bathed, they did it in the sea to harden themselves against the climate. They did not speak unless something needed to be said—reminding me a little of Sean, actually. Men often kept silent for hours on end during lookout vigils, keeping an eye out for attacking tribes or whales, then retired without saying a word to anyone. If animosity developed, men dueled verbally. The test was each man listening to his antagonist without showing anger. When near the end of life, some Aleut men went out in their kayaks never to return again.

TWELVE

It is seven o'clock on the fifth night of our adventure and the end of our first truly wild, "real Aleutian" day.

Outside the sea is pounding, the wind gusting and howling. Inside our tent—now reset on the sandy beach—it is warm but tenuous. Inexplicably the winds seem to arrive from all directions at once, in big gusts from the sea in front of us, then hammering down from the hills behind, flattening our tents with each blow. Thanks to their incredible suspension—these are the same Mountain Hardwear tents that the best expeditions carry up Mount Everest—they bounce back up. Yet instinctively each time it is knocked down, we throw up our hands and arms to prop it up. The tail winds of williwaws— fast-moving, seaborne mini-hurricanes—swirl around the foot of the tent, threatening to lift it off the sand. Zipping up my rain gear, I crawl outside and struggle to stand in the growing winds. My anemometer registers gusts of 20, then 25, 30, up to 50 miles an hour.

We've been camped at North Cove for four days. Our intention was to leave Paradise Beach today. Our goal was to paddle down the west side of Kagamil, roughly ten miles, to the next cove. The plan was to leave the beach around 11 this morning, hoping to catch the tail end of the outgoing tide and allow it to help pull us around the corner of Candlestick Point and to the south.

By 1:30 the boats are still not packed and ready, primarily due to the fact that Barry and Sean simply have way too much stuff to cram easily into their boat. Though we attempted to pack minimally, with each two-man team bringing essentially the same amount of gear, somehow they ended up with a lot more, mostly extra personal gear. They are seemingly blind to it, can't quite figure out why those extra pieces of fleece and long underwear, a Walkman, shoes, various tools as well as a mountain of camera gear will not quite fit in their already stuffed dry bags. The biggest danger is that the extra weight—they'll have to tie dry bags, tripods, rubber boots, etc., on top of the deck—makes their boat dangerously slow. If we get caught out there in bad weather, we need the boats to be as quick, as responsive as possible, not dragging along like Jed Clampett's pickup truck.

One result is that the boat-loading process drags on and on. We also have too much food at the moment. In our original plan, we hoped Scott Kerr would drop a food cache for us on Chuginadak, meaning we'd be 50 pounds lighter. Now we must divvy up the contents of the sizable yellow dry bag filled with big bags of rice, pasta, and 16 days worth of freeze-dried. Fifty pounds may not seem like much except that we are at our heaviest early in the trip, with not a square inch of extra storage space to spare.

On top of all that, Barry's carrying a voluminous dry bag stuffed with camera gear, which he's having a hard time finding a home for inside the boat. We can't start chucking lenses into the sea. Not yet. Once again, not stopping at Nikolski is haunting us. We'd planned to use the couple days there to reorganize and pack out the boats for a first time. If we had, we would have realized we had too much stuff.

As the minutes ticked by, morning turning to afternoon, and the boat cramming continued even as the winds began to slowly pick up. Scott and I have less gear, and by noon our boat was packed, cinched down, ready to go. I could see my boat partner growing increasingly impatient and frustrated with Barry and Sean's slow pace. They are spending a fair amount of time scratching their heads and joking about how they are ever going to make this work. One of Sean's solutions is to take a few jars of peanut butter and jelly which he gauged as unnecessary and heave them into the Bering Sea. Admittedly, it looks like fun so, at his invitation I chuck a couple in myself. Meanwhile, we watched the pass separating Kagamil and Uliaga grow rougher, first with the naked eye, then through binoculars. Whitecaps grow as we watch.

The danger of the delay is that we have no idea what the seas are doing around Candlestick Point, on the far side of Kagamil, which we cannot scout from here. Our goal is to round Candlestick Point and then slide down the west side of the island, staying within 150 feet of the shoreline, if possible. We figure it will take three to four hours in our heavily loaded boats to poke our way down the coastline. The best-case scenario is that we round the corner and find the wind at our backs. That would match what we saw the previous three days, prevailing winds blowing out of the north. Our fear is that if the winds are blowing from east to west—as they are in the middle of the pass—they will push us away from shore, toward Carlisle, and Kamchatka.

Another option—not a promising one—is that we round the point, start heading south, and find the wind blowing hard out of the south, off the Pacific Ocean, making forward progress difficult to impossible. Given that we know there is little chance we'd find anywhere to pull in on the west side of Kagamil, that would most likely mean we'd have to retreat. In our heavily loaded boats—especially the red boat, overloaded as it was with fishing rods, pelican boxes, stuff sacks, dry bags, and Extra Tuffs bungeed to its deck—we might not even be able to get back to Paradise Beach but end up sleeping in our boats afloat a kelp bed or being pummeled against tall cliffs and rocks.

Scott and I kneel at the edge of the spray-whipped beach and study the sea.

"I think we've missed our window of opportunity," he says as we watch a williwaw blow a horizontal band of sea spray in a quarter-mile line, just a half-mile offshore.

"The window has actually just been slammed shut," I add a few minutes later after a gust nearly picked our loaded, 500-pound kayak off the sand.

I walk over to Barry and Sean, who were tying down the last of their load. They are disappointed when I suggest we missed our chance, especially now that their boat, finally, was packed, with tents, stoves, and food stuffed deep inside. But caution and patience are the final arbiters. This is our first real glimpse of the

Aleutian weather we fully expected, our first opportunity to make a decision about whether to move or not. We opt for caution. None of us want to round that corner and be swept out to sea, unable to paddle back to Kagamil.

Picking up the binoculars, I see the very definition of ominous through the lens. The Bering Sea in front of me is black and bleak, wind-whipped, and cold. Onshore the wind chill drops to near 20°. This is exactly the kind of dangerous day that the locals out here warned us about. Clear days like we'd been having meant accompanying winds, winds big enough to turn the Bering Sea into a frosty, smoky cauldron.

"Good call," Barry says as we watched one williwaw after another chase through the pass. Uliaga became invisible. Then it begins to pour, a cold, blinding rain.

Hustling, we manage to get our tents back up, both of them on the beach, planning to try again tomorrow as we dug in the sand to place sand-and-snow anchors as well as driftwood deadmen buried two feet down. As soon as we jump inside, a string of 35 mile an hour gusts blew down the hills, flattening the tents, giving them their first real test as well. Our jaws drop as guy lines sagged, then snap rigid as the tents spring back up.

I stick my anemometer out the tent door. It registers gusts up to 50 miles an hour. I would not want to be on the water during this.

I remember the word *anima* from my high school Latin classes as meaning "soul." The root of the tool I'm using actually comes from the Greek *anemos*, for wind. One of the reasons the wind is so fierce out here is thanks to the large basin of water we're floating on. When wind travels over land it encounters friction, which acts in the opposite direction to the wind and slows its progress. Since land creates more friction than water, surface wind can attain far greater sustained velocities over large bodies of water than it can over land.

It is the right call to stay put. As Scott balances a pot of tea water atop the stove in the vestibule, I write up the day's action.

I'm not bothered by the bad weather. We knew that would arrive sooner or later. What is bugging me is the cliquishness I observed today between Barry and Sean. I know from previous travels that it is something to avoid on any expedition, leading as it can to splitting a team into two.

Barry and Sean are old friends. On one hand, that's a benefit, because they have traveled and worked together before, which means there is a certain unspoken communication between them. I'm fully in favor of combining adventure with a good time, as long as it doesn't endanger anyone. No one said this had to be a funereal experience. The downside is that too much levity— too much joke cracking, too much light-hearted frivolity—can limit efficiency. Once again, this ain't Baja. My concerns, so far unvoiced, arose today while we were packing up. I think if they'd taken the chore a little more seriously, we'd have been on the water close to 11 as planned and—hopefully—down island before the winds and storm arrived.

If it were a bigger team, or a longer trip, I would encourage us to switch tent and kayak partners. My concern is that their incestuous humor and inside jokes will soon open a chasm between the four of us, potentially turning the team into an us and a them. I'll survive it, sure, because it's relatively a short trip. But I'm more than a little concerned what toll it might take on Scott. I can sense he is just anal enough—everything in its place, everything has an order, habits most likely refined during his stint in the Marines—that I'm sure their *laissez faire* attitude has him boiling. For the moment, it's being internalized. It's a big question how long that will last.

Bad weather brings on gloomy thoughts like this. I watch the storm grow as dinner cooks, from inside the protection of our tent. We'd thrown them up in a hurry and dived inside even as the winds grew fiercer. Both were now erected in the sand, within a paddle's length of each other. Where the Sea Breaks Its Back. The Birthplace of the Winds. Cradle of the Storms. All these monikers are earned, given the wild thrashing going on outside our tent door.

Waiting out our first real storm gives me reason to wonder if we will ever get off this beach. We have known since before we arrived that a combination of wind, storms, and currents could prevent us from reaching all the islands. If we are stuck on this beach, or another, until Don Graves returns, what will be our reward? Our experience? Our excuse? How do you measure success, or failure, in such a venture in this day and age? Is just getting out here enough?

All of this stormy, fast-changing weather makes reading the sea, especially its strong currents and tides, one of the most difficult parts of our journey. That it is nearly impossible to read the waters we can see just offshore makes the start of each crossing—and often the middle—extremely tense. Scott passes me a bowl of pasta and without sharing a word, our shared look begs the same question: Will we be able to continue? Or have we already reached the end of the route?

THIRTEEN

B y morning the tent has stopped flapping in the wind. A cool breeze greets us on the beach, and our best guess at the weather is that the existing wind will help clear the skies. Tents are taken down quickly and the two boats readied, as if my unspoken concerns of yesterday's tedious pace of loading had been spread by osmosis. We all realize now that when the weather is good, the time to move is immediately.

Despite the improved weather the mood in camp is tense as we stuff dry bags into the kayaks' big storage compartments. We still cannot see—and cannot predict—the conditions we'll find when we round Candlestick Point. All looks tranquil from here, but yesterday proved how quickly those williwaws and violent rains can come from around the corner, out of the literal blue.

If we round Candlestick Point and the wind is sweeping down off the western hills of Kagamil's volcano at 20 miles an hour, it will be a struggle for us to stay close to the shoreline, our desire. It's possible we could allow them to push us out to sea a bit, toward Carlisle, but not so much that it would be a fight to get back into shore on Kagamil's southern tip. Optimistically, the current wind out of the northeast could last at our backs all day, which would push us straight down the coast. But to the north, on the far side of Uliaga, the island shining under a nearly blue sky, we can see heavy clouds gathering. Most often the weather here changes from the south. Depending on how quickly they come our way, if they do at all, those clouds could greatly influence our paddling.

It is said that the Aleuts memorized the various skies. The most reliable indications by which they could foretell the weather for the next day were the sunset and the dawn, by which those who knew were able to tell without error what sort of day was to follow. They observed changes in the sky with such an intensity that their expression for it, was "talking with the sun and sky."

We again go through our private dances as we struggle with our forever-tight dry suits. Thankfully, I can't see myself as I fight to pull the rubber gasket down over my head. The others look damned foolish—like big, blue, drunken penguins stumbling blind in the black volcanic sand with the suits pulled halfway over their heads, stuck. We'd tried to stretch the rubber neck gaskets before we came, oiling them and snugging them around salad bowls to give the tight sheath some give. But the only way to loosen them up was use, which meant a lot more time on the cold water. Now, even when you pull them down successfully, the gasket is so tight around your neck, it threatens to cut off all circulation to your head, making me a bit dizzy for the first ten minutes after I'm finally encased. I find the only way to talk is to put two fingers in the choking collar and pull it away from my larynx. The only thing that makes all this daily staggering worthwhile is knowing that in cold water the expensive Kokatat suits would give us a few more minutes to live.

Our bigger struggle this morning as we launch is with another piece of tight equipment. The neoprene spray skirts we'd brought are the best made, utilizing Kevlar in their rims to create an incredibly tight fit over the coaming of the cockpit. The goal is to keep that cold Bering Sea out. And they work tremendously, once you manage to cinch them tight over the kayaks' cowling. That, like pulling the dry suits on, will remain an arm-wrenching chore until they are successfully broken in, which in this case could take several months longer than we are out here. This morning as we push our heavily laden boat into the surf, trying to time our departure between the four-foot waves breaking on the beach, the launch is hurried and Scott makes the final push without checking to see if my skirt is snugged down—which it isn't. My cockpit is swamped by the first wave we hit, and much cursing ensues. I wrestle to pull the bilge pump out of the cockpit, which is crammed full thanks to a 20-pound mesh bag filled with freeze-dried food resting between my legs. Scott curses because, in his judgment, I didn't snug fast enough.

Any grumbling tensions are relieved within 30 minutes when we make the turn around the two tall rock spires that mark the northwest corner of Kagamil. The wind is not blowing from the south against us, or blowing off the hills threatening to push us farther out to sea. Just as we round the corner, the skies, which had been dotted by big, darkish clouds, begin to clear. As we turn our boats back toward where we'd come, for the first time the entirety of Uliaga exposes itself to us. Its snowcap glitters under the sunlight, and its steep, moss-covered cliffs glow a verdant emerald.

The western coastline of Kagamil, as expected, is devoid of pull-ins. This would have been a dangerous paddle on rough seas, no matter where the winds originated. The walls are steep, rising 500 feet straight up from the ocean. No small bay, inlets, nothing. The tall crags are covered in thick moss, and the coastline resembles parts of Hawaii I've seen, or those of Ireland or Newfoundland. The first real sunshine we've seen in days lights up the shoreline and turns the surface of the Bering Sea shiny blue. All of a sudden we feel like boys on vacation in a breathtaking paradise. It's funny how all that's needed to change a mood is a little blue sky.

Another first is the appearance of literally thousands of birds. Though devoid of mammals, these otherwise uninhabited islands are rich aviaries. As soon as we round the point we are greeted by a small fleet of pigeon guillemots, easily identified by their intensely red legs and feet, swooping out from shore and diving toward us, like advance scouts for some kind of feathered military. As we continue down the coastline, we spy evidence of their hideouts. The cliffs are guano-stained where the murres and ptarmigans, gulls, and puffins make their homes in the steep walls. Our presence, though we are 150 yards offshore, scatters them from their nests with a grand ruckus. Within minutes of our arrival the air is filled with hundreds of the birds, swooping around our heads. Their approach makes me wish my helmet was within easier reach, rather than strapped on the deck behind me.

The approach of the puffins made us laugh out loud. Built and colored like miniature penguins, they lurch through the air—

seemingly the least efficient flying contraptions I've ever seen—just feet above the sea's surface. Some brake to fish for a little lunch, but the bulk continues straight toward us, dive-bombing as they near, from all sides at once. They head straight for the boats, as if they are about to land on our bright red-and-yellow decks, then put on the brakes and pull up just short, exposing their fat white bellies and short legs as they veer away at the last second. It seems a defensive attack, intended to keep us a good distance from their cliff homes.

The farther south we paddle, the more dazzling the day grows. Toward the southern end of the steep cliffs a steady breeze blowing off the Pacific Ocean grows stronger, forcing us to pick up what had been a steady, almost lazy pace. Fighting into the wind, we cross wide kelp beds surrounding the southern corner. The thick kelp slows our efforts, for each stroke snags in the underwater growth. The only way to make progress is to take shallow, less efficient strokes. We hope to round this point and find a small, big-rock cove, one of the few specific hints Scott Kerr had shared during our midnight run. He claimed one reason very few people have landed on these islands in the past century is because there are so few places to land, even for rubber Zodiacs or metal skiffs. We, on the other hand, will be more likely to find spots others could never consider because our kayaks are, relatively speaking, easy to pull into the narrowest rocky inlets and roughest shores. Though fragile, especially if dropped on sharp volcanic rock, our boats are tough enough and far lighter to carry ashore than Kerr's 18-foot Lund with its 40-horsepower Mercury outboard, for example. The downside to our advantage, of course, is that if a big storm comes up, having a 40-horse Merc might not be a bad thing.

Sure enough, just as Kerr had described, a narrow spit of rocks flanked by tall rock walls appears. The V-shaped inlet is perfect for us. I dub the previously unnamed cove Eagle Camp, for the pair of bald eagles—mom and dad—who greet us as we pull in. From the water we spy their nest high on a cliff above; two eaglets rest in an elaborate aerie. Big, sea-smoothed boulders and a thick blanket of pungent kelp stud the cove. We nose our boats toward shore one at a time through a labyrinth of obstacles. The beach is a 100-foot-wide heap of immense rocks. On the right side is a sliver of sand, not much wider than our boats, which we use to pull in. Once the boats are unloaded and onshore, we fan out among the beach rocks, wrangling, pulling, and tossing the giant pink and yellow buoys we find into a pile. They have been washed ashore from various of the Bering Sea fishing fleet, off boats from as far as Russia, Japan, and San Diego. Scott proposes that we build "beds" for our kayaks out of the buoys, as a way to protect them from grinding against the rocks during the night, especially if the winds grow fierce. Lining the soft buoys up two by two, we nestle the kayaks on top of them, then strap them to heavy boulders to eliminate the chance they might blow over—or out to sea.

As we construct the kayak beds, I lay my thermometer on the beach rocks. It climbs as high as 71°F, partly caused by the reflection off the white rocks. We take advantage of the unexpected sun and heat by spreading all of our gear—wet and damp already, though we've been out here less than a week—on the rocks, a giant Aleutian Island yard sale.

Sean and I explore the cove, scampering over big rocks and shinnying up and over small walls. When we reach a dead end near the entrance to the cove, unable to go forward and not wanting to fight back the way we'd come, we jump off the cliff into the sea, still wearing our dry suits and booties, and swim-walk 30 yards into shore. Despite the warm air, the cool of the ocean takes our breath away the instant we hit the water. It is the first and last time a dip in the Bering Sea will actually feel refreshing.

We decide to pitch camp high above the shore, 300 feet up a steep, slippery, grassy cliff. Once we've scouted it and made several sweating, cursing trips lugging various bags precariously balanced on our shoulders, we linger on the warm rocks of the beach, stripping to our T-shirts. It is an early June day, and we feel as if we've just pulled our boats off some California river. As the sun lowers, we unsheathe the trio of folding fishing poles we brought and spread out along the cliff wall, attempting to snag the kelp bass we can see wiggling just beneath the clear surface. "If you'd told me a month ago that we'd be fishing in T-shirts on the Bering Sea, I'd have said you were missing an important element of your brain," says Sean as we dangle lines. Unfortunately, fishing amongst the thick kelp proves impossible.

Scott and I end the day with a paddle along the perimeter of the cove, checking out the dozen of caves that line its shore. A trio of seals, like big brown monks, watches us from atop seaside rocks until we get close, then slip off into the sea. Cormorants nest on ledges high inside the caves, and white-bellied ducks lift off from their resting spots on the sea in front of us. Just beyond the shoreline, as we paddle through the cooling, calm seas, we spy the spray of a pair of minke whales making their way east through Kagamil Pass. Pulling the boat ashore, we climb back out to near the edge of the cove, strip and shower under a waterfall of near freezing snowmelt. Only the last rays of the setting sun make it possible; drying off and redressing is very fast.

From our campsite we watch the eagles feeding their chicks. The male's seven-foot wing span creates haunting shadows as he launches from the cliff in search of food, then returns, swooping and soaring overhead, cawing at our presence.

Sean studies the nurslings through binoculars. "Why don't you just crawl over there with your camera and see how close you can get?" he suggests to Barry. "See just how many seconds it takes for mom and dad to come down and take a piece out of you."

We don't cook dinner until 10:30. The stove is lit outside in the grass, and we prepare minestrone soup, pasta, and bread. Night has arrived, and it grows colder as we cook. The air temperature has dropped 30° and is now accompanied by a steady, ten-mile-an-hour wind. Pulling on layers of Gore-Tex® and Windstopper, snugging fleece hats down over our ears, we eat dinner quickly, our exposed fingers numbing as we empty our bowls with plastic spoons.

"Just when I think I'm starting to get a feel for a weather pattern, everything changes," laughs Barry, checking the barometer on his watch. "Judging by this reading, we should have this weather for at least another 24 hours."

"The only thing we know for sure about this place," I remind him with a smile, "is how much we don't know."

FOURTEEN

What a difference a day makes. Twenty-four hours before, we lolled on the rocks in T-shirts. Today we climb to 2,500 feet buffeted by 40-mile-an-hour gusts, drenched by sleet, choking on heavy wafts of sulfur emanating from vents in the volcano's side, loose rock raining down on us from above. It is hell compared to yesterday's paradise.

When morning arrives, heavy fog and mist have buried the island. As soon as I leave the tent, I walk to the edge of the cliff to peer over and see how our boats have weathered the night. Thanks to the fog I can't even see the beach a few hundred feet below.

The climb is otherworldly. The sleeping volcano consists of two cones, one oval in shape. Reports of a "flaming" Kagamil go back to 1840, but no explosion has been registered here since December 1929. Instead, Kagamil is known for the "noisy steam jets issuing from a rocky bluff and rumblings heard from under the boulder beach."

The ground beneath our feet, beginning at 1,500 feet, is a mix of loose sand, volcanic ash, centuries-old lava, and rock scree. Two-thirds of the way up Kagamil's 3,000-foot volcano we find deep, wet patches of snow. We scramble over the loose rock, then kick-step our way up through steep, soft snow. Sulfur vents dot the mountainside, surrounded by rock stained a shiny, brilliant green by the heavy metal residue blowing from deep inside the island's interior. Shafts of hot, putrid fumes blast into the air. We investigate each vent, sticking our heads over them, nearly gagging. Strong gusts rolling down off the peak nearly blow us back down the slippery hill. Three steps forward, aided by an ice ax or hiking stick, are required to gain one. My right foot slips, and I'm almost carried downhill in the accompanying slide of rock and gravel. When a softball-size chunk of volcanic rock misses Barry's head by a few feet near the summit, we take cover on a barely stable slab of granite anchored behind a 10-foot boulder, protected from the sliding scree and falling rock, and hold a conference over dried salmon and chocolate.

"That was too close," says Barry, shouting to be heard over the roar of a nearby sulfur vent. "If that had hit any part of my body, I'd have slid all the way down."

We agree to take two different routes and see if we can't find a safe way to the top, which is only about 400 feet above us. After another 15 minutes of sliding and dodging falling rock, though, we gather again and decide to head back down rather than continue.

"This is no place to take a digger, diving out of the way, or a rock to the head," says Sean. "It's a long way to the emergency room if somebody falls and ends up bleeding at the bottom of the hill." The truth is, out here, on these small mountains, we are farther from help than someone climbing Mount Everest. The nearest helicopter, if we could contact it, is in Dutch Harbor, 150 miles away. Chances are, if we needed that kind of rescue, the weather conditions would most likely thwart a helicopter coming anyway. Before descending, we make a toast to the volcano Kagamil. Then we make our way gingerly down the loose rock, skiing on our boots through the soft snow until we reach the fogged-in grass below.

Though the worry remains unspoken, these conditions make us very concerned about our hope of climbing the big volcanoes on Chuginadak and Carlisle, each rising nearly 6,000 feet straight out of the sea. Twice as high, covered with 100 feet of new snow, they are far steeper, far riskier than Kagamil. Will we be able to climb them? Today, with winds gusting upwards of 40 miles an hour, it is a troubling notion.

Swirling winds unload on the tents throughout the night, with a clatter of full metal garbage cans being thrown on top of us. Even in the pitch dark I can see the thin nylon twisting, arching, buckling. A torrential rain accompanies the winds. We set our tent in a flat streambed protected from the wind, assuming there was no way enough water could accumulate fast enough to flood us out. But it rained so hard I struggle out of the tent at 4:00 a.m., half-asleep, checking to make sure that the long-dry streambed is not filling with a torrent that will carry us and our tent over the cliff in a flood of rainwater. Throughout the long night I have kept the back vestibule unzipped so that I could touch my hand to the ground to make sure it wasn't soaking, sponge-like.

It rains and blows for 12 straight hours, continuing late into the morning. It requires minimal communication—just a few shared words when Sean arrives to borrow the lone coffee filter we share each morning—to agree we will spend the morning in our sleeping bags. Along with the hard rain that pounds the tent wall, it is a cold 18°. The end result is a good reading day, not an uncomfortable way to spend a wet, cold day, zipped inside sleeping bag and tent. Thankfully, we brought along a sufficient library. I spend the day whipping through the bulk of Martin Cruz Smith's *Polar Star*, which is partially set in the Aleutians and Dutch Harbor.

By mid-afternoon the rain and wind let up enough to allow us to emerge from our tents. Restless, we set off across the southern end of Kagamil on foot, in search of the thermal caves Scott Kerr said we might find in the cliffs there. Stuffing a bar of soap and a pack towel in our pockets, we hope to have a bath. A warm one.

Hiking along the southern rim of the island, we trace the cliffs that drop straight down 200 feet to rock-congested shores below. The clouds and fog lift enough to give us a sighting of the lower tier of Chuganadik's coastline. The pass separating Kagamil from Chuginadak will be our longest crossing and most likely our most difficult. Through binoculars we can see the sea whipped into a frenzy in the middle of the pass, despite the fact that the water at the bottom of the cliffs below seems to be calm—another indicator of just how tricky it can be to read these seas from a distance. We can just make out a 150-foot waterfall pouring over the edge of a cliff on Chuginadak directly across from where we stand. It's marked on the maps, and we decide to make it our primary target when we make the crossing, hopefully tomorrow.

The shoulders and peak of Mount Cleveland are buried in thick clouds, but to the west we catch occasional glimpses of the snow-capped summit of Carlisle. Just a peek, though. Sometimes it feels like these volcanoes are purposefully playing a game with us, exposing just slivers of themselves through the clouds, then quickly closing up again, like sly, flirtatious dowagers. The closer we get to Carlisle—we are probably 15 miles away as the crow flies—the more impressive, and more daunting, the big peaks become. We're not sure we have the right "stuff" to climb them—meaning ropes, axes, and safety gear.

Our goal this afternoon is the southeast corner of Kagamil, where the Aleut had a large village known as "The Village That Is Always Warm." The name is due to the sulfuric volcanic activity that literally burns through the surface, turning the tundra into browned and blackened patches of raw, hot, smoking marl. Though dormant—meaning they don't explode—all of these islands remain seething hotspots, bubbling just below the surface. These burned plains are probably the best landmarks of the early Aleut life we'll see; they used this warm place for drying, cooking, heating. We pace back and forth through the grass, trying to guess where the Aleut would have built their communal underground homes. Any sign of a foundation has been buried long ago by weather, wind, explosions and tall grass.

Climbing high onto the plateau, we overlook the valley and study the flat meadow below. It would have been the perfect building site: out of the wind, near the warmth. We try to imagine the shape and feel of a village. Just below where we stand, down the edge of the cliff, is where mummy-filled caves have been found.

"It makes sense. That would be the perfect place to build a house," suggests Barry as we plod through the tall grass. "This would be the place to hide from the winds."

"Can you imagine what winters were like here? Remember Rex, Scott Kerr's buddy? Just before he nearly died from hypothermia, he was comparing this place to Florida. I know one thing for certain, this sure ain't Florida!" Sean jokes.

"What the hell did they eat all winter long?" echoes Barry. We know they had a penchant for eating most of their food raw. In the winter, low on fuel from blubber, they survived on whatever they had caught, killed and prepared the year before.

"It's no wonder they left these islands, eventually," says Sean. "I mean, can you imagine a place where life was tougher? Consider the conditions—the wind, the rain, the gray. I guess the only thing going for them was that it would be easy to hide from your enemies— –or bill collectors. You could see them coming from a long ways off."

Most of the Aleutian islands had two "villages," the second a seasonal camp. This site we're observing would have been a permanent one, a winter home, given its distance from shore. Winter villages, used year-round, were generally in protected locations along the shoreline with a good beach nearby, freshwater, a headland for observation, and close proximity to marine mammals, fish, and intertidal resources. Most of the settlements were located on the north side to avoid the prevailing southwest wind. This one is a rarity, given its southern exposure, but the heated tundra and protected bowl would have made it a perfect home site.

We spend a fun afternoon of amateur sleuthing, trudging back and forth, up and down through the thickening tundra, which is getting greener by the day. It's mid-summer in the Aleutians, and we've arrived smack in the middle of the short, two-month-long growing season. The vegetation grows wildly almost in front of our eyes. Each day there are new, and more, flowers—buttercups, knee-high lupine, blue and white and bleeding with purple, pale-blue Geraniums, monkshood, yarrow. If we had come a month later we'd likely need a machete to hack our way through the tundra.

FIFTEEN

The most famous mummy caves in the Aleutians were discovered on Kagamil—234 mummies dating back to the late 1800s, some beautifully preserved, found and taken, divvied up among various museums around the globe.

Once thought to be the particular cultural tradition of desert peoples—in Egypt, plus southern Peru, and northern Chile—how and why the Aleut came to use the sophisticated manner of preserving their dead here in this cold, wet, remote place remains a mystery still, even to those who have studied them for decades.

Not all ancient Aleuts were mummified. Only a few individuals in an entire generation may have been artificially preserved, though they could be famous hunters, chieftains, or children. Each island had a burial ground. Burial practices suggest they had a complex cosmology, a belief in the afterlife, an elaborate set of rituals about death and relations between the living and the dead. Aleuts believed that contact with the mummified bodies granted special powers, but that such contact was extremely dangerous. The best whale hunters, however, were expected to engage in such contact and to rub pieces cut from corpses on their weapons and kayaks. It was still believed to be dangerous by some, and that those who visited the caves could eventually suffer from insanity, severe sickness, and early death.

According to Corey Ford, whose book *Where the Sea Breaks Its Back* recounts a post-World War II visit to Kagamil, scientific studies have revealed that the Aleut had a detailed understanding of human anatomy. Mummification depends on two factors: deactivating tissue-destroying enzymes in the body and halting invasion of the body by microorganisms that decompose flesh and soft tissue. Both are best accomplished by warmth and dryness as found in the arid dryness of Egypt and Chile. The Aleut controlled these processes by extracting the viscera from the body, inserting dry grass into the cavity, and constantly drying the body for up to a month after death. The body was kept in a flexed position bent at the knees. Prior to entombment, the body was wrapped first with multiple layers of seal or sea-lion intestine, then with clothing, and finally with skins or mats. It was often placed in a wooden cradle or upon a raised platform in the cave. The success in preserving the mummies stemmed from their choice of warm, dry caves. Subsurface heat escaping through cracks to the surface in the chosen caves ensured that the mummies had optimal conditions for preservation.

Dr. Alex Hrdlicka, who led Smithsonian Institution searches for mummies in the 1940s, provides the simplest rationale for how this sophisticated habit arrived here in the middle of nowhere. By comparing photographs of mummies taken from the Aleutians and Peru, he pointed out specific similarities. In each, a feather is thrust through the left earlobe. In another example, a Peruvian wooden doll and a splintered portion of one from the Aleutians are almost identical. Whatever the exact route the immigrants to the Americas took, it is evident that the knowledge practiced here in the Aleutians eventually made its way south through North America, across Mexico, to the high deserts of South America. Most interesting to me is why that knowledge didn't stop off along the way. Why didn't American Indians, for example, learn to mummify? Or the sophisticated indigenous populations that occupied Central America, the Mayas, or the Incas?

"The Aleuts had an intense respect for the dead," wrote Hrdlicka. "Curiously, their nearest neighbors and closest tribal relatives, the Eskimos, have an almost diametrically opposite attitude. In fact, it makes them stand singularly alone among the various races and tribes of the earth." Whereas the Diomede Eskimos would complacently carry the bodies of deceased relatives out to be torn to pieces and devoured by their own dogs, an Aleut mother often would not bury her dead infant for months but carry it continually about upon her back. Mothers sometimes placed the body of a deceased infant in a carefully carved wooden box. This was often kept for months near them in the cave-like homes, where the mother would watch it with the greatest tenderness, wiping away the mold and adorning it with such ornaments as she could procure. Occasionally a wooden dish, a *kantag*, containing food, was placed beside it for the spirit to feast upon. Often a dead baby would be kept and treated in this fashion until another one was born to take its place.

Wives would also keep the bodies of their dead husbands in their homes, offering them food, conversing with them, and in other respects treating them as though they were still alive. Occasionally, when the time for necessary burial arrived, the interment was even made inside the compartment of the dwelling where the family lived. A bereaved lover would often commit suicide just to be able to lie in peace beside the body of the beloved one.

During the past 150 years numerous parties, most of them legitimately trained and sponsored archaeologists, have attempted to find mummy caves, most without success. A key reason is that they are evidently hidden with great care in the most inaccessible locations among the sea-pounded cliffs. The frequent earthquakes and eruptions of the many active volcanoes of the district contributed to completing their obscurity.

Waldemar Jochelson followed Veniaminov to Dutch Harbor and spent 20 years in the islands. Along the way he found a few of the burial caves. "Two types were used as burial-places: one with deep grotto-like passages with a large opening, the other in the form of small hollows in the rock," he writes. "Mummified corpses of distinguished people were hung up chiefly in the bottom of the grotto-like caves, while in the small caves, which evidently were regarded as village cemeteries, all the less distinguished people were placed. According to Veniaminov, common people and slaves were buried in such small caves, while chiefs and other eminent people were hung up in high, square, wooden boxes with slanting roofs, or were buried in separate earth lodges. However, it should be stated that we nowhere found traces of burials above the ground in boxes."

According to Aleut legend, the mummies of great *togas*, or skilled whale hunters, retained the prowess of the original individuals, and those who possessed them were blessed with the same ability. If the mummies were stolen their prowess went with them. This legend confused laymen, i.e., white men, who'd heard about the supposed curses, which were the penalty for desecrating their sacred ground. Such is the peculiar psychology of a native mind that living with a curse could sometimes be a good thing.

SIXTEEN

The summer solstice, the longest day of the year, dawns in a fog. We can't see the cove below our camp, and the temperature, with the wind chill, is below freezing. Chuginadak, 11 miles across the ocean, is invisible. All in all, the weather is probably as good as it will get for what we expect to be our longest crossing.

The conditions bring the knot in my stomach up to my throat. It was comforting yesterday to be able to see Chuginadak, and the waterfall we'd be aiming for. Now, with everything wrapped in low clouds, the place again wears the bad side of mystery, seeming more daunting than spiritual.

As we break camp, packing and sliding everything down the steep, wet slope of grass and mud to the rocky beach below, there is little conversation due to the unspoken anxiety. Launching our boats in this kind of dense fog requires a fair amount of trust. In ourselves and in each other. While I had buckets full of faith in these other guys, I do have a niggling concern about myself.

How would I react if we get out there between islands and start being blown east, back toward Alaska's mainland, unable to reach land? What if it requires five, six, seven straight hours of paddling—or more—to reach land? What if we don't reach land at all, but end up in our boats for two, three, four days? Though 11 miles aren't that far, if the currents or winds are too strong, no matter our collective skills, we are in a world of trouble, truly paddling for our lives. How long do I think I can paddle and keep a straight head? It's the kind of test impossible to administer until we're out in the middle of it—so that's the plan. To give ourselves an ultimate test this longest day of summer.

As we load the boats, our small talk steers clear of such potentials and focuses mostly on how good it's going to feel to reach the other side. I sense a certain false bravado in Barry's claim: "It will just feel good to be out there, paddling hard. I need a good workout. That's why we came out here, isn't it?"

His old buddy Sean shoots him a look of wonder mixed with slight mocking. "Good, just keep that motor of yours cranked up. I don't want to get halfway across and have you run out of gas." The irony, of course, is that of anyone in the world I know, Barry would never run out of gas.

"It ain't Baja out there," I remind from the edge of the sea, pulling my fleece hat down tight over my ears. The wind carries a cold spray off the uncalm bay. On previous days this little harbor had been perfectly calm, no matter what the weather was out on the pass. That the wind is whipping in close to shore is not a particularly good omen.

Packed and loaded by noon, we push off just as high tide is peaking. We've done this on purpose, hoping to catch a bit of the ebbing tide as it recedes. When we push off, Barry and Sean's boat still dangerously overloaded, we sit side by side in the windy harbor for a few minutes adjusting last-minute strappings and tightening lines. The plan, arrived at after walking on the shoreline yesterday, is to paddle along the southern shoreline of Kagamil until we reach some steam jets sending a hot spray into the air. That point is the closest piece of land to Chuginadak and the most direct route straight across the pass. From there we'll put our heads down and begin sprinting.

Our compass course is 170°S, almost directly due south. With no wind we would be able to paddle in a straight line. But even inside the relative protection of the harbor at Eagle Camp we can see the wind whipping across the pass and know there are currents out there up to ten knots. The more likely scenario is that we'll have to paddle hard toward the west for 20 to 30 minutes before we can afford to head south. If we try to sprint directly across, we'll most likely be pushed by winds and currents so far that we'll end up to the east of Chuginadak and miss the island completely.

We'd agreed beforehand to head along the coast of Kagamil, but as soon as we clear the corner of the harbor, Barry and Sean make the decision to head straight out to sea. When Scott and I reach that last protective point of land, it instantly becomes clear why. The wind is whipping with such turbulence along the coastline, into our face, that we are gaining nothing by hugging the shoreline. As we quickly pull up alongside, Barry shouts over the wind, "Better to just get started."

Before us is only wild, gray sea. Within ten minutes Kagamil disappears behind us. Not for the first time a feeling of eerie desolation settles over me. Alone at sea, in a small boat, no land in sight. This is where Sean's experience in sailing across the Atlantic using only a sextant comes in handy. He's done it more than once, crossing from the Panama Canal to Europe, then south to Africa and back to Brazil. If he could guide a big sailboat through similar conditions, I am convinced, why not our little Kevlar-and-fiberglass boats?

Soon the fog grows so thick we lose sight of the other kayak, just 20 feet ahead of us. I remember Veniaminov telling of the Aleut that sometimes, though not often, when they lost sight of land they would "employ whitened sea-lion bladders…to which they tied on a long rope a stone, dropping them so far apart that they could see from one to the other." Sometimes they did the same with whitened kelp bulbs. Why hadn't we thought of that?

My wind and temperature gauge is tucked in the front pocket of my Skanorak, and I slip it out of its case once we are at sea, free of any wind-influencing point of land. Winds gust to 17 miles per hour, dropping the temperature, with the wind chill, to 25 degrees. As we predicted, when the outgoing tide meets the steady wind blowing from the west, we are forced to turn our boats perpendicular to our goal—Chuginadak—and bear due west into the open ocean, paddling as hard as we can.

All along we have been sprinting, knowing that we have to keep up the same pace for a minimum of two hours. If the wind shifts slightly, to the south, the headwind could keep us out here more than three hours.

A mile off Kagamil the sea is a cold, wave-rocked soup. We are cutting at an angle into the southwest, and wind-driven four-foot swells bang on our starboard. Even as we try to head into them, a combination of current and tide pushes us sideways. I can feel Scott in the steering position, struggling to keep the boat headed at least partially into the waves. In front of us the blurry, orange-jacketed figures of Barry and Sean zigzag as they try to match Sean's predetermined compass course with the reality of the conditions. We follow, after a fashion.

This is the nut out here. Despite all of Sean's carefully calculated onshore machinations, once you get out into the middle of the sea, you simply have to put your head down and paddle, relying on experience and strong shoulders to push the kayak across.

Within 20 minutes my bare right hand is numb from the cold water. We've all given up on gloves, preferring the better grip of skin on paddle, despite the constant cold. Each time I take a stroke on my right side, my hand dips into the water, thanks to the waves coming from the west. I overcompensate, shifting my body weight to the left in order to get a stronger pull on the weak side. But every time I do this, Scott has to throw his body weight to the right to keep us upright. This lurching paddle effort is diminishing his powerful stroke.

"When you paddle on your left, lean hard on your right butt cheek," Scott shouts over the wind. "We've got to lean into the waves. I almost lost us a couple sets back." I try to turn my head to respond, but decide the energy is better spent paddling instead.

An Aleut kayaker could spend 24 hours at sea, in his boat, without putting his feet on ground. In the morning before such journeys he ate nothing, believing "there will be no shortage of air and I will not be tormented by thirst." It sounds a bit apocryphal; I've been sucking on the tube that runs to the water pack strapped to the back of my PFD since we left land in order to stay hydrated.

Not until an hour has passed can I manage to check my watch. My arms are flagging from the nonstop pace, and my feet are numb from the cold. A badly packed camera mount sticks through the back of my seat, causing me to sit forward awkwardly. We are halfway and still no land in sight. The wind and waves grow even as our paddling rhythm loses its unison. This is the most exposed we've been in yet. In the middle of the pass, in cold, weather-whipped seas. It is far too late to go back. Any mistake here and we are dead. It's hard to imagine a more isolated, menacing spot on the map to kayak.

Ahead two orange-hooded Skanoraks bob in and out of the waves. Paddling hard, we catch up and I shout to Barry, "How's the weather?"

"Dangerous," is his simple response.

Two-thirds of the way across the pass, the mass of western Chuginadak begins to block some of the wind out of the west and the seas calm into longer, more rolling waves. An hour and a half after leaving Kagamil we can, for the first time, make out a green coastline in front of us, followed by the cleft in the cliff that holds the giant waterfall we'd spied the day before. In just under two hours we pull into the calmer seas that lead to the ravine. A 150-foot waterfall sprays a cold-water greeting as it pounds into the sea. Despite the cold it couldn't be more welcome.

Paddling back out to sea, we head a mile east toward a rocky beach known as Skiff Cove, which we'd also spied through the binoculars from Kagamil. The seas are trailing us now, pushing us, and though it is still gray and growing colder, we are all breathing easier. Our longest crossing is over. Then, as we are unloading the boats in the big surf at Skiff Cove, the sun and blue skies arrive. We've never expected such a scene out here—magnificent waterfalls, blue skies filled with puffy white clouds. By the end of the afternoon even Kagamil unveils herself completely. Looking back across at the tall brown-and-white mountain, we can pick out the scree we climbed a couple days before and see just how close— or far—we were from the top of the volcano.

In the middle of the crossing I found myself searching for something to take my mind off the rather dire conditions. I imagined what it must have been like for those early Aleuts out in these same conditions in their skin boats. Few humans have ever lived as amphibious an existence as the Aleut. No man has ever engaged in hunting as difficult as chasing whales on the open ocean armed only with a simple harpoon. The demands of this open-water hunting led to a cycle of physical and intellectual development that, in the words of anthropologist William S. Laughlin, allowed the Aleut "to shuffle a whole lot faster through the [evolutionary] deck."

For the how-tos of Aleut hunting I am carrying along a trio of books, Dyson's *Baidarka,* Ken Brower's *The Starship and the Canoe,* and Laughlin's *The Aleuts, Survivors of the Bering Land Bridge.*

Since no mammals lived on the islands the Aleuts were solely dependent on the nutrient-rich sea. They ventured out in their superlight, fragile boats armed with a small artillery: sinew-backed bows, bone-tipped arrows, spear throwers, bolos, harpoons, bird spears, and lances. They carried an inflated bladder or skin both to buoy the harpoon line and to tire the game. The Aleut perfected the art of the throwing stick, or atlatl, to increase the range and force of their spears and darts. It is a long, narrow board with one end carved to fit the hand and with a small peg inserted at the other end to hold the butt of the spear shaft. The throwing spear or dart was laid on the board and then thrown. The device extended the length of the arm, thereby giving more power and distance to the cast.

On land, the Aleut captured birds in nets with snares and in flight with bolas—four to six strings about three feet long and tied together at one end, with small stones attached to the free ends for weight. As a bird flew over the hunters, they twirled the bola and threw it upward, each string swinging out like a spoke on a wheel. Lines wrapped around the bird and brought it down. On the sea they stalked seals, sea lions, sea otter, sea cows, and whales. They fished for giant halibut and cod with 150-fathom lines braided from the stalks of giant kelp, and they caught flounder with small hooks made from shells.

According to Brower, the sea otter hunts were cooperative efforts involving four to 20 kayaks, some with one manhole, some with two, fanned out in a semicircle. When a hunter saw an otter surfacing for air, he pointed with his paddle and the kayaks converged on the spot. When the otter surfaced again, a barrage of stone darts greeted it. These were cast with the added leverage of a throwing stick, and each was connected by a line to a seal-bladder float, which impeded the wounded otter's escape and marked its position. The kayaks kept pace easily with the fleeing float. The pursuit added interest to the otter's oxygen debt, and it had to come to the surface to pay off. When it did, the kayaks were gathered in a tight circle around the float, and the throwing sticks were cocked once again.

Once the animal was tired out, they brought their clubs into play. They clobbered it until it was dead, then loaded it into the hatch in the center of the two-man boats. That required a delicate balancing act as the man in back stood in the boat and dragged the lifeless animal aboard while the man in the bow steadied the boat.

By comparison, hunting a whale was highly ritualized. To prepare for the hunt the best kayakers in the village abstained from sex for weeks. First they prepared their souls through the arduous rituals that always preceded Native American whaling. Then they smeared their lances with a deadly extract from the roots of the monkshood, a dark-cowled flower common in the Aleutians. Venimaniov reports that they sometimes greased the speartip with human fat or pieces of mummified corpses.

At least two canoes went out. If a whale's flukes smashed one, the other could come to the rescue. The hunters approached the whale cautiously from the rear. They threw their lances, blew on their hands in superstition, and paddled like hell in the other direction. Once wounded, the whale could live several days to a week while, as they believed, the poison slowly worked. (In fact, it's been proven that the plant wasn't actually poisonous. It just took that long for the whales to succumb.) Each hunter's harpoon blades bore his own distinguishing mark, and no matter where the dead whale washed up, it was credited to the owner.

Hieromonk Gedeon, Alaska's first campaigner for Native American rights, witnessed a whale hunt in 1804 and wrote this description:

The harpoonist go out in their one-man baidarkas and select migrating whales whose meat and fat are softer and more tasty. When such a whale is sighted the approach it to within a distance of nor more than three sazhens (21 feet), trying to hit it with the harpoon below the side fin, here known as the last, and then turning away from the beast very carefully and skillfully so that they do not get crushed when the whale dives or that their baidarka does not get capsized by the disturbance. If they can not hit the side fin they try for the back fin or tail. When it is wounded the whale dives to the bottom. If the harpoon has hit home accurately then the whale is bound to come to the surface dead after three days; if the wound is away from the side fin towards the tail then the whale will take five or six days before it floats to the surface—and if the harpoon is in the tail then it will be at least eight or nine days before the whale appears.

During the time the whale was dying, the hunter who successfully harpooned the whale would seclude himself in his house and pretend to be sick, hoping the whale would feel likewise and die. Other hunters would watch the whale, nudging it toward shore when possible. If the whale died nearby, it was hauled to the beach. Unfortunately for the hunters, wounded whales were often lost when they floated to other islands. They were lucky to recover as many as they did; more than half were lost.

Even the best of the whale hunters failed more often than they succeeded. Ferdinand Wrangell watched a hunt of Kodiak Island in 1831:

It sometimes happens that an incautious marksman is unable to put a sufficient distance between himself and the wounded whale, which throws itself from side to side in anguish, lashing its tail; this either tosses the baidar into the air like a ball or sinks it deep into the ocean.

The reason whale hunters were so celebrated was for the simple fact that a 20-ton whale could feed a village for a year. The whales were well used. The ribs and mandibles were used in the framework of their homes. Intestines of larger animals such as those of sea-lions or larger seals were inflated with air, allowed to cure, and then split lengthwise into strips of membrane as much as several hundred feet in length. As waterproof as any material today the intestine was used to make kamleikas or rain coats. The smaller vertebrae became seats, the shoulder-blades a table or desk. The epiphyses became plates, the sinew used as threads and cords. Fat was burned for light and heat and chunks of ribs were employed to cover the dead in a burial. The rest of the big animal was burned like incense during cremations.

SEVENTEEN

W e decide to take this sunny day off, moving slowly around camp, which we'd set alongside a fast-moving stream flowing from a magnificent, wide waterfall a half-mile up the inland hill. A high wall rises to the west of camp, dotted with thin waterfalls and rock faces. We spend the day hiking into the snow that covers the smaller of the two volcanoes on Chuginadak and exploring the coastline.

Physically we are in good shape. One of the great things about traveling into such an isolated, little-visited place is that there's no possibility of bacteria or related diseases. Despite the constant cold—"It's like living inside a refrigerator," is how Sean sums up the conditions—we're all healthy. Despite the on-the-water exertion, we've come prepared.

The rest day is more for our mental fatigue. The anxiety leading up to yesterday's crossing took its toll. I could see a weariness in the eyes of the others when we arrived, more from the expenditure of tension rather than physical energy. On top of that are continuing tensions between Scott and, well, everyone. In what should be a noncompetitive endeavor, he seems to want to compete with each of us, on different levels. He doesn't like decisions to be made—even on where a tent should be placed—without his say-so. Last night as I put up our tent, he suggested I move it two or three times before it ended up exactly where I'd begun. That said, our tent life together is fine. He volunteers to take care of most of the chores, from gathering water to cooking. But I have found myself wishing on several occasions that I'd followed my friend Will Steger's counsel that on expeditions you should travel only with people over 40. That way you're—hopefully—traveling with people that have "found" themselves, aren't still trying to figure out who they are, what they want out of life. There are, of course, many exceptions to this rule; Sean couldn't be more solid and he is only 31.

As we hike Chuginadak today, we spread out, each of us choosing without words to spend the day mostly alone. I head east, up the hills along the coast. I am starting to appreciate the real beauty of these islands. Each day different facets of the volcanoes expose themselves to us, in the constantly changing light, giving us new perspectives on their grandeur and the rugged remoteness of this place.

Chuginadak was the most special island of all to the Aleut. They called it *Tanax angunax*, the great island. Tradition held that their ancestors originated here. Until 1764 more than a hundred Aleut lived on the island, but in that year Stepan Glotov, the Russian credited with "discovering" the Islands of Four Mountains, killed most of the men living here during small battles. Following that, many of the island's women died of starvation, and the survivors were resettled on Umnak.

Late in the afternoon I take refuge from the sun and wind on a high ridge with a full-on view of Kagamil completely exposed. Long belts of beach grass and beach pea spread eastward, a sight few men have witnessed during the past few centuries. I am overwhelmed by how incredibly beautiful—and mysterious and enchanted—this place can be. Before we arrived, I envisioned these islands only as windswept rocks set in the middle of a cold, gray sea. I did not imagine what jewels they are, at least when the sun is out.

Chuginadak was once two islands, each with its own imposing volcano. Mount Cleveland was named for the 22nd and 24th President of the United States, Grover Cleveland and was formerly known as *Goriashchaia Sopka*. It forms the western edge, rising 6,000 feet straight out of the sea. The smaller, unnamed volcano rises just above where I've taken refuge from the breeze. Sometime before the Russians arrived, an explosion of Mount Cleveland rained down rocks and lava, filling the narrow strait that separated the two islands. The Aleut lived in the corner of the island where we are camped in part because of its sizable sea otter population.

I am nearly dozing under a warm sun. The smell of fresh growing grass and damp spungeon moss filled my nostrils. There are only two sounds: the pulsing streams filled with early summer snowmelt and the chatter of bird life, many of which are startled by our presence, having never before had their days interrupted by the footsteps of a man.

I make a mental list of the birds we've seen so far: Layson albatross, with their six-and-a-half-foot wingspans. Red-faced cormorants in the caves along Kagamil. Bufflehead ducks diving off Skiff Cove. The bald eagles that soared over Eagle Camp. Fox sparrows hiding in the bush behind our Eagle Camp tents. Willow ptarmigan and rock ptarmigan running all around where I am lying right now. Black oyster catchers. Puffins, horned and tufted. Red-necked phalarope, with the short, deep, quack when we come up on them by surprise. Mew gulls. Black-legged kittiwake that flew over us when we rounded Candlestick Point. Thick-billed common murres. Pigeon guillemots and their shiny red legs. Lapland longspurs and semi-palmrated plovers.

Opening my eyes, I stare out at the open sea east of Kagamil. The color is Caribbean blue. Gone is the gray and black sky and silver flash of whitecaps. It feels like today, the day after the solstice, summer has finally arrived in the Aleutians. I twist my head far from one side to the other, trying to take in as many of the five islands as I can. Uliaga is out of sight, behind Kagamil. Tall cliffs block my sightline from Carlisle and Herbert, even Mount Cleveland. I hope, from one unique place, we'll be able to see all of the islands at once. I find myself wondering too what these mountain ranges must look like just below the surface, how many more once proud peaks are buried by the oceans.

The very few people who've sailed past these islands in recent years told us they possessed a spiritual essence, making them feel different than the other Aleutian Islands. Only after seeing them on a day like this, can I begin to understand what they meant. That the Aleut regarded this place as their birthplace—not the Birthplace of the Winds, but the Birthplace of the Aleut—gives Chuginadak even greater weight. That we are walking through grassy fields last walked by the Aleut lends an extra layer of mystery to the place.

At 8:16 p.m., our eleventh day on the Bering Sea, we witness another first, something we haven't experienced since boarding the ferry boat back in Homer. At that exact minute—I was so startled I looked at my watch and made a note—the wind died. Completely.

Just like that out come the gnats, and the putrid smell of sea kelp at low tide overwhelms us. Bird songs explode, as do the great, gentle wash of the sea dropping onto the rounded beach rocks. For the first time in days we no longer have to shout to be heard. The tents stop flapping, hats are pulled off revealing badly matted hair, jackets unzipped. It is 52°, and the temperature with wind chill is…52°.

Dragging stoves out of the vestibules, we cook a communal dinner of pasta, even throwing in an extra bag to celebrate the calm state of affairs. It lasts for just more than an hour, when a light breeze begins to pick up from the east. We agree the Birthplace of the Winds without winds does not feel right.

We should have known that the wind's dying was not a good sign.

The storm begins at three in the morning, with a ferocity we've not yet seen. Our tent is set just west of the foot of a small hill, and the winds arrive hard out of the east. Our tent's placement is lucky. If we'd put it up with any more exposure, just a few feet farther from the hill, this roaring new wind would have picked it up like a piece of Styrofoam and tumbled it into the sea…with us in it.

Through the nights big rains dump and 50-mile-an-hour gusts pound down on us like a heavyweight's fist, flattening the walls around our sleeping bags over and over. The wind sounds like a busy carpenter's shop, sawing, hammering, and drilling on our thin nylon membrane of protection. Unable to sleep, I sit up, turn on my headlamp and try to write in my leather-bound journal. All around me the thin gray-and-orange shell quivers and rattles, while ultimately staying put, protecting. Though we are warm and dry inside, Barry and Sean made a slight miscalculation, placing their tent in a slight depression. At 7:00 a.m. I hear them scramble of their tent, in the torrential rain, moving their tent to get it out of the small lake that has spread around their vestibule. Peeking out, I can see Sean drag timbers of driftwood up from the beach to help weight down the sides of the tent for extra security.

This is the most serious storm we've seen, and it continues through the morning and into the afternoon. Emerging from the tent around 8:00 p.m., in full Gore-Tex® rain gear, I shore up the tent's guylines, desperate after nearly 24 straight hours in the tent for any kind of fresh air, even if it is cold and wet.

I stand on the knoll overlooking the beach where we landed, bracing myself against the wind, which arrives from two, three, then four different directions at the same time. This is what Veniaminov was referring to when he dubbed the place "the empire of the winds." The bay in front of us has turned charcoal, whipped by menacing whitecaps. Out in the pass we can see monstrous waves being whipped by a wind from the east blowing a ferocious 40 miles an hour. It is cold, too, in mid-20s. All the beautiful waterfalls we'd seen draining the snow melt from up high the day before are blowing horizontally across the rock faces. We can see water pouring out of narrow chutes, falling over the lip of rocks, then being blown back uphill by the winds. The sea crashes onto the shore in steady, frightening roars.

The strongest winds whip down the valley from behind me, south off the Pacific Ocean, gathering momentum as they whoosh over the stubby volcano and literally dance across the bay and out to sea. This wind turns the water from a gently whipped sea close to shore and churns it into five, then six, then ten foot waves just beyond, where it meets tidal rips and currents. Yesterday when I'd napped in the heat of the sun the same scene was so calm. Now it was back to itself, the seething, raging, cold Bering Sea.

The gusting wind threatens to blow me off the bluff, a reminder that this is no entertainment I am watching. This is serious, and dangerous, weather in the making. Our biggest hope is that it won't last for a week, or longer, as it is wont out here.

I suppose it could be worse. Here's a report on Aleutian weather from the *Baltimore Sun*, November 12, 1961. "The wind has been known to play the dangerous game of round-robin, with the island as the center, coming from successive quarters of the compass in rapid sequence. The velocity during this whimsical mood is frequently 60 to 70 miles per hour, near hurricane speeds, it tests buildings while playfully twisting them. Winds like this arrive in the late autumn but they are small compared with those which charge out of the dark tempestuous Bering Sea when it is in its most violent winter mood. The sea, aided and abetted by Arctic storms, brews the wind, which then beats the sea into a black froth. In this mood the storm rages, sometimes for days. The waves hit the shore in walls of water estimated at 40 to 60 feet high. Observers claim that stout wooden piling has been uprooted and slammed onto the beach."

Back inside the now warm tent, I content myself with those things you do when stuck inside a tent during such a storm:

drinking, reading, napping, picking the lint out of your Velcro, then starting all over again—drinking, reading, napping, picking the lint out of your Velcro. Our menu for what would turn into nearly 60 hours stuck inside our tent was quite good: oatmeal, halibut jerky, French chocolates, potato soup, hot Gatorade, coffee, fresh blueberry cornbread, and pasta, though not in that particular order. Ventures outside are limited since it means returning completely soaked and frozen. Each time out I carry my measuring gauge—winds range from 15 to 40, wind chill temperatures are down to 15° above zero.

We end up stuck inside our tents from Tuesday evening until Friday morning. Throughout, the skies over the Bering Sea remain black, and winds and rain pummel the tent without pause. The wind shifts constantly, whipping the sea into a froth, creating ugly boating conditions no matter the size of craft. We never once consider kayaking in this storm.

Late in the afternoon of our second full tent day, Sean pounds on our tent wall. Suffering from a combination of claustrophobia, tent fever, and listening to Barry snore, he's taken a solo hike despite the wet and cold. He shouts his excitement over the wind, "I found an airplane!"

Scott and I hurry to pull on boots and rain jackets, dressing for the cold and wet in four layers, including Gore-Tex® pants and jacket, mittens, and shells, squeezing heavy socks into our Extra Tuffs, we pile out of the tents. Barry packs his cameras and, motioned by Sean, we follow. It is a steep hike directly up the grassy hills. The terrain is difficult, elbow-high sea grass covering a maze of slippery tussocks and wide, bony mats of rocks punctuated by deep holes. Forty-five-mile-an-hour winds threaten to blow us over backwards. Our path is somewhat dictated by the winds as we weave back and forth across the ridgeline. Fast-running streams-turning-to-rivers are forded carefully—slip into one of them and next thing you know you'll be headed out to the sea. The temperature is 8°.

As we follow, hoods cinched up tight, making conversation difficult, Sean tries to explain what he's found.

"I came up over this hill and in the distance saw something I thought was a beached whale. Big, white, glistening. But it didn't make sense, since it was a couple miles from the shore, high on the hill. I didn't have my binoculars with me, so I just had to keep walking, trying as I approached to figure out what it was. I was probably 200 yards away when it dawned on me— it wasn't the white belly of a whale but the silver fuselage of a small plane."

Sean's right—from a distance it looks like the shiny pale underbelly of a large animal. As we draw closer, we can see a propeller cast to one side, a piece of wing to the other, an unexploded bomb with grass growing around it.

The main fuselage lies upside down, its two-passenger cockpit smashed into the spongy moss. Its front landing wheel still spins on its axle, the rubber surprisingly intact, considering this plane has lain here for more than 55 years. A big, red U.S. Air Force star, the color worn thin by years of rain and wind, is barely visible on its tail.

We get down on our hands and knees, crawl underneath and peer up into the cockpit. Everything—gauges, seats, controls— seem perfectly preserved. Canvas, khaki-colored seat belts are unbuckled. Bullet holes ripped through one side and out the other. There's no sign of man—no skeleton, no blood. No one could have survived this kind of upside-down crash, so we guess that the pilot and gunner bailed out somewhere before the plane crashed. We remark on how well preserved it is. Stainless-steel screws and hose clamps—even the black rubber hoses in its crushed engine—are shiny. On the fuselage I find a metal plaque indicating the plane was last inspected in September 1943, on Kodiak Island. The plane is a King Fisher fighter, used as an observation patrol plane—most likely it was on one of its two daily spotting runs out of Dutch Harbor when it was shot down. We would later discover that it was one of only five or six in the world.

"This raises more questions than it resolves, doesn't it?" poses Sean as we tread carefully around the perimeter of the unexploded bomb buried in the nearby tall grass. "I mean, now we've found it. That was easy. But where did it come from? A ship? Land? Shot down by the Japanese, that's a certainty, but where were they? On a big boat offshore?"

"And what happened to the two guys inside?" Scott throws out. "Maybe somebody's been here before us and scavenged their bodies."

"Or maybe they parachuted out, landed on shore, and are still living here on the islands, septuagenarians making a home in caves, surviving off berries and birds," I suggest.

We are back in camp by eight, energized by the discovery, not knowing what—if anything—we can possibly do with the information. We wonder if anyone else knows this plane is out here. Can it be that we are the first to find it? We've brought back the plane's registration number and vow to find out what we can about it and its occupants when we return to civilization.

Still windy, the darkest clouds seem to be lifting, allowing us a vision of the persistently wild and cold sea, as well as the lower half of Kagamil's volcano.

"I'm glad our first days out here weren't like these," says Barry. "Otherwise we might have gotten so depressed we wouldn't want to ever leave the tent."

EIGHTEEN

Finding this plane, with bullet holes ripped through the side, its occupants most likely drowned in the Bering Sea, probably wounded, their parachutes dragging them down to a horrific death in the cold waters, is a sobering example of the role the Aleutians played in World War II. At one point more than 15,000 Japanese soldiers were spread out through the chain. More than 600 Americans died during the fighting here, most due to exposure to the harsh conditions rather than enemy bullets.

At the time the Aleutians' strategic location made it a key factor in America's defense strategy. The fortification of the Aleutians began soon after war broke out in Europe. Japanese spies had been surveying the chain, just 650 miles from their home bases. Both countries recognized the islands as potentially strategic North Pacific holdings. As thousands of troops were rushed north, Navy and Army bases were constructed on islands ranging from Unalaska to Kodiak, as well as in Sitka, Anchorage, and Fairbanks.

In 1940, military crews and civilian workers arrived in Unalaska/Dutch Harbor, filling the small town with thousands of workers and troops and constructing the Dutch Harbor Naval Station, a football-field-sized dock at Chernofski Harbor, and secret airfields. When Japan bombed Pearl Harbor in December 1941, the U.S. became fully engaged in the war, and Navy weather stations were opened on Kiska and Kanaga islands. After Pearl Harbor, the wives and children of military personnel or civilian workers were sent away from Unalaska.

The fear, accurate in hindsight, was that the Japanese would mount attacks in the Aleutians to draw attention, and military might, away from the naval station in Midway, its true objective. More American troops and ships spread through the Aleutians meant fewer near Pearl Harbor.

On June 3 and 4, 1942, Dutch Harbor was attacked by Japanese planes flying off the carriers *Ryujo* and *Junyo*. At 5:50 a.m. on June 3, four waves of Japanese bombs struck Army barracks in Margaret Bay, killing 25 men. During the second attack on June 4, 22,000 barrels of fuel ignited. At 4:30 p.m. a giant PBY transport plane was flying from Cold Bay to Unalaska carrying mail and a crew of seven. Thirty-one Japanese Zeros were skirting the southern side of Unalaska island, and a handful peeled off and shot down the PBY off Egg Island. The crew scrambled into life rafts, only to be shot by more strafing Zeros.

Two days later—on June 6, 1942—500 Japanese troops waded ashore on Kiska Island and quickly captured the small U.S. Navy aereological unit stationed there. A day latter Attu was taken, securing the Japanese foothold on the western Aleutians.

The bombing of Dutch Harbor was the last action the troops stationed on Umnak and Unalaska saw. When the Japanese realized their diversion wasn't working—it turned out America had enough boats and troops to man both Pearl Harbor and the Aleutians simultaneously—their focus shifted. Their last challenge in the Aleutians was getting out those 15,000-plus troops they'd already landed.

On May 11, 1943, 16,000 U.S. troops stormed ashore at Attu's Massacre Bay in an effort to recapture the westernmost Aleutian Island from 2,600 Japanese. This followed a prolonged aerial bombing of the island from U.S. positions hastily erected on Amchitka and Adak. In 18 days of savage fighting in horrific conditions, 549 Americans and 2,350 Japanese were killed. They were defeated more by weather than anything else; 2,100 more Americans suffered from sickness and non-battle injuries thanks to biting winds, frozen feet, frostbite, and trenchfoot. After stopping a banzai counterattack, the surviving Japanese committed suicide. That basically brought the war in the Aleutians to a close.

As for the Aleut, the war was the proverbial last nail in the coffin. When the Japanese invaded Attu, Aleut villagers were evacuated by U.S. forces from their homes across the Aleutians and the Pribilof Islands to the north. Given just 24 hours to pack, each person was allowed only one suitcase of belongings. Mothers dressed their children in several layers of clothes. Every family was forced to leave behind heirlooms, including icons, samovars, photographic albums. Doors were shut and locked. By July 26, 1942, the 881 Aleuts who had lived in the villages west of Unimak Island had left the Aleutians. Except for a small group of Aleut volunteers in the military still in the islands, the Aleut inhabitation of the islands—continuous for more than 8,000 years—had effectively ended.

In crowded, unsanitary conditions they were sailed across the Gulf of Alaska and into southeast Alaska, where they disembarked at abandoned canneries and old CCC camps at Funter Bay on Admiralty Island and nearby Kilisnoo Island. Conditions were deplorable at each site, with lousy housing, little sanitation or medical facilities, no hunting or fishing gear, boats, and other of their cultural tools. One of every 10 Aleuts died, mostly from disease, in the internment camps. Conditions varied from bad to worse, with few jobs, little government help. Many died from malnutrition and lack of good medical attention.

Survivors returned to find their homes had been looted, vandalized, occupied. Soldiers had carried furniture to their foxholes and the unforgivingly harsh weather had taken its toll on the buildings. The U.S. government paid each Aleut $35 "for loss of personal property."

The press, neither during the war nor after, took little notice. Before our trip I'd picked up a 500-page, newly published book of Alaska history and found two sentences about the war in the Aleutians and no mention of the Aleut people. Few people knew anything about this mess until the late 1980s, when Congress took up the issue of compensating Japanese Americans for their World War II internment. The evacuation and resettlement of the Aleut population became part of the hearing. In 1988 Congress authorized $27 million in reparation payments to the surviving Aleuts. Some of the 400 living survivors received $12,000, about $16 for each day they'd spent in the camps. Today a trust fund established with $5 million of the reparation pays out $500 a year in nontaxable distributions to Aleut senior-citizen camp survivors.

The impact of military activities irrevocably altered the pace and tenor of life across mainland Alaska. In addition to the influx of well over $1 billion between 1941 and 1945, Alaskans also benefited from the modernization of the Alaska Railroad and the expansion of airfields and the construction of roads.

In the Aleutians the military legacy dragged on. As the U.S.'s relationship with the Soviet Union declined, the Aleutians were used more and more to hide spy planes, submarine chasers, and secret intelligence listening posts. The U.S. military kept bases open on Adak and Shemya, used for air and sea patrols as well as intelligence gathering into the 1990s. A long-range navigation station is still based on Attu, though just barely—in 1995, winds clocking 170 miles an hour blew the stations's wind meter off its post.

During the 1960s and 1970s, the islands proved perfect test sites for weapons developers working on nuclear warheads. In 1971, the most powerful nuclear device ever detonated on American soil shook Amchitka, the result of the testing of a five-megaton warhead. Despite that the island was 200 miles from the closest inhabited island, protestors swarmed to the Aleutians concerned about the potential radioactivity and tidal waves.

What is perhaps the biggest postwar change throughout the Aleutian Islands? Afterward the few Aleuts that remained used only motor-powered boats. Kayaks were now a thing of the past.

NINETEEN

W e kayak away from Skiff Cove, finally, with the weather gods smiling on us. It is gray and cool, but the rain and strong winds have dissipated. We are sorry to leave this great camp, with the waterfall pounding down just behind and the fast-running, clear stream at its side, but 72 hours in one place is sufficient. We have to keep moving if we are to get to all of the islands. Our biggest concern remains getting pinned down in a storm, unable to keep moving. Our confidence is growing with each day we are out here despite this last big storm. The crossings to come no longer seem quite as intimidating, although this could be a bad thing. The last thing we need is to start taking this place for granted.

The goal is to paddle roughly ten miles along the northern coastline of Chudinadak to Applegate Cove. Reaching Applegate has been an objective since we arrived, for a few reasons. Its four-mile sand beach is centrally located, giving us good access to Carlisle Island or Kagamil (if for some reason we have to get back there, to North Cove, for example). We have also talked about downloading some of Barry and Sean's extra gear there, maybe even leaving some food behind, to truly lighten the boats for the last sprints we will make between Carlisle and Herbert. Eventually, our hope is to return to Applegate Cove because it is the pickup point spot we agreed to with Don Graves. We expect him to look for us there during the week of July 7.

In a soft gray mid-morning light we push the boats out onto the calm bay and paddle back onto the Bering Sea. The east-west coastline continues to turn green. We duck back into the deep ravine containing the 150-foot waterfall we'd targeted when we first came to the island. The spray created when it pounds down onto the rounded sea rocks is translucent in the muted light, turning the narrow slot into a splendid shower of cold blue and white mist.

Next to it we find a similarly tight cleft in the rock, with walls rising even taller, to 200 feet. The pool inside is calm and clear, and thick green moss climbs the wall. This is Otter Cove, I decide, thanks to the appearance of our first such creature. We surprise him as we poke the nose of our kayak into the final corner of the crack, and he slips off the rock where he'd been asleep into the clear jade-blue waters. I try to follow him with my eyes as he swims deep, tracing the volcanic rock as it disappears down below. Watching him makes me wonder what these mountains must have looked like when the sea level was 350 feet lower. And what must this place have been like when colonies in the thousands of sea otters populated these islands?

The paddling is easy, through long, glassy waves. Quickly the two boats get separated. Sean and Barry choose a route a half-mile off shore while Scott and I poke along the coastline. It's potentially dangerous to be separated by such a distance—they are easily a mile ahead of us after 45 minutes. Accidents can happen on even the calmest water, and this is still cold water—I measured it this morning at 35°. But given our years of paddling experience and a growing confidence, I make no big deal of the separation.

The offshore is lined by a series of dramatic rock fingers jutting straight out of the sea, moss-covered outcroppings standing solitary guard. Scott sees in them pirates watching over the channel. Though I see where he's coming from, I can't get over the fact that a pair of them look distinctly like Fred Flintsone and Barney Rubble. So much for any romantic visions of nature created by God's hand....

Scott wants to find more caves. He is addicted to kayak cave exploring. The first time we met, he took Barry and me out to Santa Cruz Island off the coast of southern California. Using sit-atop kayaks, which are easier to remount if you're knocked off inside a cave, we explored several deep caverns accessible only from the sea. At one point we "parked" our boats on a narrow sandy beach at the end of a quarter-mile cave deep inside the island and, following Scott's lead, dived underwater into a neighboring smooth-walled cavern. Using another underwater channel as an exit, we arrived back in the main channel just as our kayaks were being sucked off the beach and out to sea. Inside another cave we visited, the ocean waves rocked so hard that all three of us were knocked first into the ceiling overhead, then off our boats.

Here we're not on sit-atops anymore. If for some reason we stick our nose in too deep and get in trouble—we can't back out, can't turn around, or the boat flips—it's obviously a more serious situation than off the coast of California. Still, we nudge into cave after cave as we work our way down the coastline, going deeper and deeper into the pitch-black, dripping, water-swelling chambers carved into the side of Chuginadak's cliffs, with me—of course—the point man.

Near the point where we will turn south and head into Applegate Cove we find the biggest cave yet. The color of the sea at its entrance is a startling aquamarine. The surface is broken by "plinking" drips of water from the ceiling 30 feet above. Once the kayak is completely inside, we find two branches. To the right we can make out a longer arm and hear it lapping onto some kind of beach at its end. As our eyes adjust to the dim light we can see down the shaft and make out soft swells falling onto a rocky beach.

Scott would love to pull the boat up on the shore and go explore. He wants to see if the "beach" might lead to another cavern or tunnel.

I'm not so interested. I've been here with him before, and I'm not sure I trust his youthful adventuresome side, knowing that he is hardly risk-adverse. This is still no place to be fooling around.

"I say we back up while we can," I suggest, "before we get pushed onto the beach."

"Let's just keep nosing ahead," is the reply. I can't control the kayak; he's in the back and still paddling forward.

Before we have to make a decision, it's made for us when a puffin hits me in the head.

Apparently the poor guy, startled by our appearance in his domicile, attempted to fly off his rock ledge. Unfortunately for

Sean puts his hand close to a hot vent on the southern end of Kagamil, near the place the Aleuts called "The Village Where It is Always Warm."

Our kayaks are in many ways similar to the early boats created by the Aleuts. Though the materials are different—they used seal skins and whalebones, ours are made of fiberglass and Kevlar®—the shape and design are nearly identical.

PHOTOS BY BARRY TESSMAN

Scott McGuire and I paddle the 22-foot-long kayak off the shore of Chuginadak in a typical surf.

The World War II King Fisher plane found near Skiff Cove, on Chuginadak, was shot down by Japanese destroyers in 1942. It remains in surprisingly good condition. Note that the rubber on the landing wheel is still black and solid.

Scott and I share a moment of calm beauty—exploring a 150-foot waterfall—just after finishing the longest crossing we would make, between Kagamil and Chuginadak.

When the sun set at camp at Applegate Cove, it lit up the big volcanic peaks—here, Mounts Cleveland and Carlisle—like diamonds.

ILLUSTRATION BY FRIEDRICH H. VON KITTLITZ, COURTESY OF BEINECKE LIBRARY, YALE UNIVERSITY

We were not the first to kayak among these islands; the Aleuts preceded us by many thousands of years. Incredible hunters, they lived off the nutrient- and animal-rich seas, their kayaks the most important of their many tools.

Sean warms his feet
over a driftwood fire
on Applegate Cove.
Each day we load
and unload our
boats while standing
in the 35°F ocean,
resulting in cold feet
all day long.

Long, dry drainages surround our tents on Carlisle Island. Despite the biggest snowfalls in years, we find no freshwater here, thanks to the super-hot volcanic activity just below the surface of the island that drinks up all the snowmelt before it can reach the sea.

Scott McGuire and I reach Herbert Island at the end of a long, cold day's paddle.

We climbed Mount Cleveland on a beautiful July 4th; the higher we climbed, the more exposed the islands around us became. By the time we reached its 6,000-foot peak, we could see all of the Islands of Four Mountains at the same time.

Scott, Sean, myself, and Barry
stand atop Mount Cleveland.

The world of the
towering volcanic
mountains dwarfs
our kayak as Scott
and I paddle in front
of Mount Cleveland.

both of us, he badly misjudged the required length of the run-way—remember, puffins are not the smoothest of birds in flight. Before he can gain the necessary altitude, he swoops low and smacks into the right side of my head, knocking my Oobe cap into the still waters and scaring the bejesus out of me.

I have no idea what hit me—some Aleut ghost, pissed off that we are disturbing his grave, a piece of volcanic rock loosened by our paddles striking the wall—though Scott saw the whole thing happen from behind, in slow motion. I will ask him what happened, once he stops laughing.

Backing out of the cave, we paddle into a small army of pigeon guillemots, easily identified by their bright red legs and feet, come to check out the commotion. A fleet of brother puffins, fishing for lunch, follows them. The latter take great pleasure in dive-bombing our kayak, heading straight for the boats, looking as if they are about to land on our bright yellow deck, then pulling up just short, exposing white bellies and short legs as they veer away at the last moment.

Once we round the final point and can see the four-mile black sand beach spread before us, we still have a two-mile slog into the wind. Scott voices aggravation that Sean and Barry will get to the beach before us, and thus choose the campsite. This is by now a typical complaint of his. I can't understand why this bothers him; I'm happy, given their collective wisdom, that they take the responsibility. It seems Scott is bothered if he's not involved in every such decision. We've chosen to take our time—what's the hurry, we agree, we'll never pass these cliffs again—and it's a relatively nice day for a paddle (air temperatures 42°, water warming to 40°, with just a light wind). But Barry's not much for sightseeing. It's a gray day, not great for photos, and as Sean says, Barry has two paddling speeds—Olympic pace and 90 percent Olympic pace, so they arrive at the beach a good half hour before we do.

When we land, Sean helps pull us up onto the sandy beach. It's a luxury to land again on the sand, despite having to negotiate a steep surf to reach the beach upright, because it means we don't have to stand in the cold water to unload the boats. That's a good thing today since we are all colder than usual, from the feet up. The last couple miles, with the wind blowing in our face dropping wind chills into the 30s, didn't help. We are carrying a couple pint bottles of Southern Comfort with us, intended as bribes for boat captains but never dispersed. Sean bought them in Dutch Harbor, thinking the motto on the bottles—"The Grand Old Drink from the South"—would be an ironic gift. Today we judge is an appropriate time to unseal their screw caps, and a couple quick shots help take off the chill long enough to get a driftwood fire started on the far eastern edge of the beach.

It's good to be back in a place where a beach fire is even an option. At neither Eagle Camp nor Skiff Cove was there sufficient driftwood to build a fire. As we gather wood, Barry and I talk about his frustration with not yet being able to see the big volcanoes on Chuginadak and Carlisle, in all their snow-capped glory, fully exposed.

When we come back, Sean has his bare feet suspended directly over the flames. "My feet are so cold, they're like fricking bricks," he says. "Makes it kind of hard to walk, even in the sand."

Heat was a precious resource for the Aleut as well. When the first Russians arrived in these islands, the Aleuts who received them with a smile—rather than a spear—were polite enough to offer to share any warmth they had. They understood what it was like to be cold. They lighted their best oil lamp and encouraged the guest to put it under his own shirt first, to warm himself.

Waldener Jochelson, one of few outsiders to learn the Aleuts' language, described the inventive warming system he discovered: "People stood over the burning lamp or sat over it in a squatting position, covering it with their shirt-like coats. The ancient Aleut wore footwear only or a breechcloth and footwear under their coats, so the naked body could easily be warmed. Before getting in their skin boats the Aleuts took off their footwear. Sick people were also seated over the *a'nux* to make them perspire. Generally the warming lamp served in place of the sweat-bath, which was unknown to the Aleut before the coming of the Russians. As was in later days the case with the sweat-bath, visitors were always offered the use of a warming lamp first."

Similarly, whenever the Aleut went on a hunting trip, one of the first items packed in their skin boat was a little stone lamp. Fuel was gotten from the fat of the animal they killed. Dinner, though usually eaten raw, could be also be warmed over the stove.

From Applegate we must choose a route taking us either first to Herbert and then back to Carlisle or vice versa. Much will depend on the weather tomorrow. If the wind is in our favor, I vote for heading directly across to Carlisle. If not, it might be worthwhile to work our way to the far western end of Chuginadak, then sprint across to Herbert. Those are the kinds of decisions we are most preoccupied with out here, which is a great luxury really. No concerns about "Did I pay the telephone bill?"

or "The car's got to go in for a tune-up," or "Where's the revision you promised me two weeks ago?" Only, should we go here today…or there.

Interestingly, the beach is named after a guy we've actually heard of. A New Jersey native, Samuel Applegate came to Alaska in 1881 as a weather observer with the U.S. Signal Service. Joining the Alaska Commercial Company, he made a career out of sea otter hunting, then fox farming. The latter is his great claim to fame in the Aleutians. He is credited with founding the fox farming industry that was rampant throughout the Aleutians in the late 1800s and early 1900s.

"I never saw Samuel Applegate with working clothes on," was the report of longtime Dutch Harbor resident Henry Swanson, who raised and hunted foxes alongside the patron on various islands. "He always wore starched white shirts, the kind they wore in those days with high collars. He wore a coat that was round in front and came down low, not a Prince Albert." That's not to suggest he couldn't handle these Aleutian conditions. When his crew sailed aboard his boat, the *Everett Hays*, he sailed with his men and was regarded a solid navigator.

We probably wouldn't have gotten along with Applegate, though. He fought hard against government policy attempting to curtail sea otter hunting. Losing that fight was what pushed him into fox farming, as a way to help him recover from losses when government cut sea otter hunting. He won permission to transplant foxes from the more northern Pribilof Islands to the islands closer to Unalaska, and fox farming became a stable economy here for decades, before it was eliminated due to its disastrous effects on the native bird populations. Applegate also built sulfur mines and traded with Russia, dividing his year between Dutch Harbor and Berkeley, California.

I walk the black sand beach named for the entrepreneur. Massive, ghostlike piles of driftwood and plastic debris from the Bering Sea fishing fleet litter the long, foggy shoreline. It's easy to see where all this crap comes from; big seas break on the shore, pounding out of the north and east. Deep onshore I find a pile of sea-weathered logs filling a half-mile square of sand.

Exploring the giant pile, I also find samples of plastic from around the globe. An orange box of Japanese parachute rocket flares (empty), a red Sapporo case (empty, alas), various booze bottles of a variety of nationalities (all empty), paint brushes, dozens of orange buoys, white and blue bumpers from fishing boats, mounds of thick white and orange netting, metal gas containers, heavy round metal buoys (how do those things float?), and a wooden sign painted yellow and red in Japanese, saying something like, "Be careful out there."

The boys join me, and we scour this seaside dump for additions to our Applegate camp. We have set up elaborate tent sites, using the abundant driftwood to build front and back porches as well as deadmen buried deep in the sand, in case the big winds return. Plastic beer cases become tables and chairs. Scott and Barry find glass balls from Japanese fishing nets, which we use as glowing sculptures around the campfire. I hang the Japanese sign on the rocks overlooking our tents, as a reminder. "Be careful out there."

TWENTY

The Aleuts referred to springtime as "The Time for Eating Thongs." After a long, harsh winter their stored food would be running out, the big fish and mammals they depended on for everything wouldn't have returned yet, and still fierce storms made it impossible for them to get out and hunt.

It's not quite that bad for us, but we do have our first discussions about whether or not our food supplies will last. We guess that we are halfway through the trip, and a little more than halfway through the food. Our only problem would be if bad storms in mid-July pinned us down and Graves was delayed for an extra week or longer.

Minor—and sometimes major—food and fuel balancing acts are part of any expedition and always subject to much campfire debate. While we've tried to split the food equally between the two boats, Scott and I now have more. During the weeks before we left California, Barry and Scott packed all of the food into equal packages and baggies, divvying the 200-pound mass into equal A and B quantities. (The A team, for Scott and I, of course—his choosing.) Plus, we bought another 50 pounds of salmon when we passed through Haines.

Scott and I are carrying plenty for ourselves to last another two weeks. Barry and Sean are starting to run low, for several reasons. During the first few days at North Cove we cooked dinner communally out of their dinner bags. Then, to lessen their load, they tossed a bunch of peanut butter and odds and ends. As a team we left behind a 50-pound bag of pasta and rice at North Cove as well, which we hopefully won't regret. Lastly, Barry has a big appetite. It takes a lot of fuel to keep his highly energized body going full-blast. The result is that they have plowed through their salmon, fruit, oatmeal, energy bars, etc. Barry's spoken-out-loud thinking since we arrived has been: "Lighten the boat, eat more food." His theory made some sense, in that it was certainly cheaper in the long run than tossing any of his valuable camera gear into the Bering Sea. The situation is not serious yet. I'm not imagining "The Time for Chewing on Polypropylene" anytime soon. But it is definitely time to start counting.

"We wouldn't be having this conversation if Scott Kerr had come through for us," Sean points out. "Remember we were going to ask him to drive that extra bag of food over to Applegate before he went back to Nikolski. How much did we leave behind exactly?"

"A dry bag stuffed with 50 pounds of pasta and rice," says Scott angrily. "It's in a dry bag under a cliff ledge so we should tell somebody about it. Who knows who might need it one day?"

Scott has all of our food counted and memorized, and though it's hard for me to believe, he is starting to hoard things, like the salmon we have remaining. I know it irks him whenever I share my salmon with Barry, who finished off the last of his share days ago. While I understand the necessity of a disciplined approach to food in a place where there is no corner supermarket, I feel confident that we will finish with plenty of food.

To lighten the boats we decide to leave a few dry bags hidden under the cliff wall adjoining our camp here at Applegate, loaded mostly with food, extra camera gear, exposed film and some clothing. This should be the spot where we are picked up, but if for some reason we can't get back here from Herbert—if the weather really turns bad—we'll try to get a message to Graves to pick us up there. We assume if he doesn't find us at Applegate, he'll look on the other islands. We will carry plenty of freeze-dried foods with us—the Kathmandu curry, Mexican rice and beans, etc.

Last night, over a roaring campfire, we talked about our options for today. Scott wants us to make an immediate attack on Mount Cleveland, thinking that if we don't make an effort to climb it now—and then don't get back to Chuginadak—the option would be lost. I want a day of exploring on foot the wild, south side of Chuginadak. Barry and Sean are noncommittal, but they are ready to keep paddling if conditions are right.

The morning dawns in what we now recognize as typical fashion. The camp is socked in by fog, it is drizzling and the temperature is 42°F. I get out of the tent early and take a long walk down to the other end of the beach, hoping to get a feel for the crossing we will have to make to reach Carlisle. During my two-hour hike the fog thins and by the time I get back to camp, I see the tents are coming down. The boys have made the call, since the weather is cooperating, to head for Carlisle.

It is a seven-mile sprint from our camp at the eastern edge of Carlisle. It will be our shortest crossing if we cheat west along the coastline of Chuginadak, then sprint across from the nearest point of land. But we gamble that the currents might be flowing in our direction and opt for an angled route, straight from our beach to a point midway on the south side of Carlisle. On the map we saw a landmark—Hunter's Cabin—dating back to the days of fox hunting, and Sean begins to work on waypoints that will deliver us there.

As we pack the boats I realize that the lump that has previously risen to my throat before every crossing seems much smaller. My bigger worry is the diminishing of camaraderie between Sean, Barry, and Scott. I sense them both pulling back from Scott, sharing less conversation each day, certainly less joking around. In these potentially dangerous conditions it's imperative that we watch out for each other's backs constantly. Instead, I'm hearing more private back-stabbing. I wouldn't make an issue of what is basically a personality clash except that out here we have to be able to rely on each other—not diss each other. If Scott, or anyone else, for that matter, falls into this cold sea, there cannot be any hesitation to act. That these guys are barely speaking doesn't give me much confidence.

Barry is tired of Scott's constant, even finicky, attention to every minute detail—maps and tents folded just so, dry bags rolled exactly like this, boats loaded in the same order each time. All of this strikes Barry, decidedly more of a last-minute kind of guy, as too much attention for too little return. Efficiency is good; it's great to know where everything is at any given moment. But that's different from the way Barry is used to traveling. He tends to dump everything out of his dry bag to find whatever he's looking for at its bottom. The real problem here is Scott's inability to adapt to the systems of others, or to cede responsibility.

When we depart Applegate, under an afternoon sun, the red kayak is finally floating free. Just before we leave the beach, Barry finally admits that maybe, just maybe, he brought some unnecessary gear, but such are the feelings of the moment that he has a tendency to blame Scott for everything, even his own overloaded boat.

"He was supposed to be the expert on what these boats could carry. I thought he'd be able to tell me way in advance what would fit…and what would not fit," Barry grumbles as he loads. I chide him a bit. How can he claim to be more experienced but then grouse that he depended on Scott to tell him what he should or should not bring along?

"What can I say?" He grins sheepishly. "My only excuse for bringing all this camera gear is that I have a demanding client. Me."

Despite the sun, a strong wind is blowing from the north, directly into our faces. That means we'll basically have to double our paddling efforts, taking two strokes to gain one. Today is the calendar day when the disparity between low tide at its lowest and high tide at its highest should be the least all month, so it shouldn't affect us either way. Still, until we get out into the open sea, we can't judge the strength of the current we can see moving fast through this section of Carlisle Pass.

Given the force of the wind, we pursue an indirect course, heading upwind, halfway between Kagamil and Carlisle, ostensibly away from the point of land we've picked as our landmark.

The current is fast, from west to east. If it pushes us too hard to the east, i.e., backward, we'll be forced to dig in and head back to Chuginadak. If it's really fierce, the extreme worst-case scenario is that we'll be pushed back as far as Skiff Cove, the last decent campsite.

Putting a mile between ourselves and Chuginadak on our left, we paddle into a choppy sea. We can see the heart of the pass, and we are staying parallel to it for the moment. We don't want to jump into its fast-moving center until we have to. Within a half hour we've set up a perfect ferry angle for hitting Carlisle just where we want. Still, the paddling is going to be strenuous.

"Set your most comfortable pace," Scott yells from the back of the boat. "I'm following you. But I need to know if this is a pace you can keep up for another hour, hour and a half. The worst thing would be if we burnt out halfway across the channel."

I don't know how to respond to that. I feel good, but how can I guarantee that my pace won't drop? "Don't worry," I shout, straight ahead, wondering if he can hear me.

"Are you going to be able to keep up this pace or not? I need to know now."

"I think so. I'm doing my best." Now he is undermining my self-confidence. Everything feels fine to me, we are plowing ahead, I feel strong, arms not overly tired. One big difference in this paddle is that we have left the shore late in the afternoon, about 4:30. I think Scott's concerned that my energy might drag since it's later in the day. I suggest to him, again, not to worry.

He has a legitimate concern, I guess. As Barry said, what seemed months ago back in Chugnik, this kind of sea kayaking is not the lawn-chair kind off the shore of some luxury resort. The boom created by the notion that anyone can sea kayak is great—for those who do it, for those who sell the boats and gear, for those who organize sea kayaking trips. I'm the first to advocate that anyone who can swim can sea kayak. I think it's a great leisure-time activity. But make no mistake. What we are doing each time we hit the water is fast and furious. There's no screwing around. We're paddling for our lives because we're in the middle of the frigid Bering Sea.

Before entering the fastest current—which we can now see whizzing by—we stop briefly to suck water out of the hydration packs rigged to the back of our PFDs. The next 20 minutes of sprinting will be furious, paddling into a mile-and-a-half-wide strip of fast current, battling a wind that has grown to a steady ten miles an hour. We can make out slack water just on the far side, but we can also see gulls playing tag in and around a set of nasty, whitecap-tipped tide rips that runs nearly the length of the far side of the current. They are big, permanent waves—so permanent they are marked on our map—caused by a combination of tides and current moving over a low shelf of rock. If we are pushed somehow into those tide rips, it will be like whitewater kayaking through Class V waves.

I'm as strong as I thought. We manage the current with no problem, other than my arms are wearing out by the end. Our only trouble comes when we slide into the calmer seas on the far side, just on the edge of the tide rips. The big boat is rocked by the mishmashed sea, which requires us to brace hard—slapping our paddles and leaning into the waves so that they don't spin the boat out of control.

Quickly we pass into slack, kelp-filled, and lake-calm water leading us all the way to the coastal cliffs of Carlisle. We are aiming for the site of where our 1940s-era maps (the best available) indicate we should find the remains of that 100-year-old trapper's cabin. Our main criterion for a camp is accessibility and fresh water. Judging by the long gullies lining the flanks of Carlisle, we're sure the latter won't be a problem. Harder to find is a beach that is easy to land on. All we see are steep cliffs and beaches of big, jumbled rocks.

Even fresh water proves scarce. We paddle along the shoreline for a half mile each way, looking for a stream roaring with snowmelt. After another mile of one dry drainage after another we would be happy with a trickle. Apparently this volcanic mountain absorbs its snowmelt faster than it can join into a stream and reach the sea. We paddle down the coast, then back up. It's getting late now, nearly seven, and we're going to have to settle soon. The sun is getting low, the evening cool.

"Maybe it's still too cold and the snow's not melting," guesses Scott.

"Or it's what we've read, that these volcanoes are so porous that they drink up the water before it descends," counters Sean.

We finally choose a rocky landing site near where we'd first come to shore. Big boulders lead to camp, a small, nearly flat meadow with plenty of soft, mossy tundra for our tents.

TWENTY-ONE

S itting on the sea-rounded rock beach on Carlisle, at the end of a sunny, windy afternoon, I can for the first time see four of the five islands from one spot. Despite the preponderance of gray skies, these select few moments of unadulterated sunshine remind us that we are among a very small, select crowd to have sat in this particular seat of nature. I flash back to that brief moment we had with Bob Adams, on the dock in Dutch Harbor just before we pulled away. He had visited Carlisle ten years before, picking up an archaeological team. His last words were that we would find these islands "magical." I am looking straight across at the low green hills of Chuginadak that lead to the snows of Mount Cleveland. Behind me towers the 5,300-foot peak of Carlisle. Turning my head to the right, I can just make out beneath the white billowy clouds Herbert Island. Twisting my neck back to the left, I can see the corner of Kagamil that hides Eagle Cove. The blue sky turns the kelp-filled waters just feet in front of me shiny,

mirror-like, and I can—also for the first time—truly under
stand what so inspired Adams.

It's this sense of magic that has most surprised me. I anticipated
the cold, rain, and fog. We've had that, certainly. But we've also
had incredible blue skies, a constantly changing cloud cover,
sunlight dappling green coastlines, mysterious hints of the cloud-
and-sun-draped volcanoes, although they still somehow manage
to mostly hide from us. Even the fog has not always been ominous.
It has opened and closed over the mountains like gossamer shut-
ters, allowing just enough soft sunlight in to occasionally set the
whole sea aglow. Sitting here, stripping out of perspiration-soaked
fleece, I understand Scott Kerr's last words to me, whispered on
the beach before he motored his metal skiff back to the *Miss Pepper.* "You guys are going have a great time." At that moment, a cold
wind whipping, our last connection to the world about to depart,
I was not sure I agreed. But then, I couldn't have imagined an
evening like this one, good-tired from a late afternoon paddle, sitting on sun-warmed rocks, watching the sky evolve around us, a
360° view of nothing but nature's finest.

Carlisle's single, symmetrical cone behind us is impressive for
the way it climbs straight up out of the sea. Its steep upper slopes
are covered by snow year-round. Veniaminov described it as
"hardly more than an almost completely round *sopka* [peak],
terminating on all sides, except the north, in low-lands and
possessing neither bays nor streams. Its northern extremity is
crumbling cliff whereon birds nest, while sea lions, seals and
occasionally sea otters are found. This island was never inhabited but the people of neighboring islands spent some time there
in summer to lay in a supply of sea fish." The last time its cone

exploded was in November 1987, though the volcano experts admit there has historically been confusion between its eruptions and those of Mount Cleveland, which rises just a few miles across Carlisle Pass.

Harold McCracken's 1930 *God's Frozen Children*—about his three expeditions to Alaska—was one of the few historical narratives I'd found that even mentioned the Islands of Four Mountains. He had landed near where we sat, nearly 80 years before, in search of mummies: "Despite the storm that was building up about a hundred miles behind us, we decided to go ashore briefly on Carlisle.... Within a few minutes we located a rock shelter high above the cobble beach and George and I climbed up to it. Inside it was dry, despite the wet conditions on the face of the rock cliff, and we found an assortment of bird bones, seal bones and fragments of some kind of fur.... But the most exciting find was matting; woven grass matting of the type Andrew Snigaroff had said was used to wrap mummies. There were only a few shreds of it left, and those almost fell apart in my fingers as I gathered them from the dust.

"'Look!'" shouted George excitedly, and he picked up a human thigh bone. There were others lying in the rubble, but no skulls and no other signs of burials. Apparently we were in the right place, however, The Aleut had said that there were many rock shelters along this shore. But there were hundreds of places to look for them, and it would take us all afternoon just to cover a few hundred yards. Outside the wind was picking up and the surf was growing."

There was no surf off Carlisle today. Instead, a trio of big, playful sea lions romp and snort in the kelp in front of us.

Until we return to Applegate Cove, in another week or so, dinners will be from our freeze-dried rations. Tonight's spicy curry is a nice change from several weeks of pasta, even though it's shaken from an aluminum bag. We lounge in the soft tundra and spoon directly from the bag, tired, nearly falling asleep mid-spoonful.

When we finally crawl it into the tents, we read for half an hour (*Heart of Darkness,* for Scott, *Blue Highways,* for me). It's 11:30 and just starting to get dark. The calm, kelp-heavy sea rolls softly in front of us, filling the view through the plastic window of the vestibule. We are lured back outside by a new sound: the blowing of a pair of minke whales swimming through the channel just offshore, directly in front of our tents.

The next day, our 15th in the islands, we spread out and spend six hours searching the island for fresh water. Scott ranges east toward the hunter's cabin marked on the map. Barry and Sean head up the mountain, toward the snow. I try to reach Dragon Point, where McCracken came ashore. Despite a record snowfall the previous winter and the warmer days of summer, the inner heat of this volcanic island absorbs the snow into the earth as soon as it melts. The result is that the numerous ravines we saw from the sea, which we assumed would be filled with flowing fresh water, are all bone dry. Toward the end of the day we regroup and agree that we can't stay here long. Though we have several bags of fresh water we'd carried from a stream near Applegate Cove, it won't last long, especially considering the quantities we use each day for cooking and our thermoses. Snow is a good mile hike uphill. Tomorrow, we decide, we'll make our move for Herbert, so that we don't get stuck here in a storm without water.

Our disappointment turns into contention. Planning the approach to Herbert from Carlisle turns into a logistical wrestling match. Scott carries the tide tables and consults them before each crossing. He spent many days working on fishing boats and in kayaks off the coast of California, and from the beginning of the trip he assumed the responsibility of predicting the tides.

"I'd like us to leave early tomorrow with the outgoing, the ebb tide," Scott says. The four of us are sitting in the grass overlooking the sea, studying the map. "It would be great to take advantage of the tide as it pulls away from Carlisle."

"I think we'd be better off going a little later, during slack water," suggests Barry. Slack water is the period of relative calm between high and low tide. It can last from a few minutes to an hour.

"No," argues Scott, "I don't think we should pass up anything that might give us a little boost, like the tide moving away from the island. What's wrong with using nature like that?"

"My concern is that it might pull us away too fast," Barry shot back. "But I'll let you make the call." The tone of their disagreement is harsh, not friendly, and Scott walks away and sulks the rest of the day. Ah, the naïve joy, and thin skin, of youth!

We are anxious because Chuginadak Pass, running from south to north, boasts the strongest current we've seen yet. Though excited by our plans overall, Scott Kerr strongly suggested we not attempt to cross to Herbert. He thought the currents too fast, too unpredictable, with no chance to bail out if we get halfway across and realize the conditions are overpowering. If we head for Herbert but are blown south and can't get to land, literally the next stop is Midway.

Late in the day, while dinner is boiling, we get out the maps again, trying to make a final decision on what time we should leave the next morning. Scott sticks by his earlier suggestion, that we leave very early, pushing off before 9, to take advantage of what he predicts will be a strong outgoing tide. With its help, he is convinced, we should be pulled easily across to Chuginadak.

"We should definitely consider stopping on Chuginadak and either setting up another camp or at least scouting for one, just in case we can't cross right away to Herbert," I say.

The map spread across his lap, Scott is concerned that he doesn't see good camping options on the map at the west end of Chuginadak. "I don't see anything that looks like we'll even be able to pull ashore," he says, tracing the shoreline with his finger.

"But, Scott, most of the places we've landed haven't looked like good camps on the map," says Sean, interjecting strongly. "That can't be a reason not to try. This place we are right now, for example. On the map it looks like cliffs. In fact, it's an okay camp."

The debate lasts an hour. The argument against leaving too early is that we don't want to be sucked by a fast-moving tide into what we suspect will prove to be a dangerous current, without at least the option of pulling back and landing on Chuginadak.

"I'm ready to try," concludes Sean for all of us, "if you're convinced that tide sucking out of here won't be too strong."

"I think we should take advantage of it," says Scott. "Plus, it will help us preserve our strength for the crossing to Herbert, especially if we decide to do it right away. I don't see any downside."

We agree to get up at six, pack up, and see how it feels in the morning.

When the alarm goes off at 6:15, a cold rain is pounding the tent fly. Silently, I pray it will rain just a little harder. That way I can justify our staying inside our warm tents rather than going out into what I can already sense will be a day that never gets much above the freezing mark.

It turns out that Barry and Sean accidentally set their alarm an hour early and already packed up their tent, so staying put is not an option. We gather on the shore, where 36 hours before it had been sunny and warm, to hash out the logistics of the crossing. The temperature is 34° and it is sleeting.

We agreed to launch between 9 and 10 o'clock, which should put us on schedule to catch the fast-moving, outgoing tide. The northwestern corner of Chuginadak is about four miles away. We figure that if we can get to that point, we can then judge better the current separating us from Herbert. If it looks doable, we'll go. Otherwise we should still be in range of pulling into Chuginadak and trying for Herbert tomorrow.

Bundled up so heavily we can barely twist our shoulders, in a thick layer of Polartec 200, Gore-Tex dry suits, Gore-Tex anoraks, fleece-lined neoprene skull caps and neoprene Pogies protecting bare hands, we push off. It is just before ten—early for us, given that we usually take two to three hours to completely break camp, cook breakfast, and load the boats.

Sure enough, just as Scott predicted, once we clear the kelp beds we are caught immediately in a fast-moving tide pulling toward the corner of Chuginadak. We take off like kayak rockets. The wind at our backs also drives the rain, slipping inside our hoods and running around our necks.

It's a fast ride, almost like an invisible hand is pushing us from behind. While the push—or pull, which is what the tide is doing—feels welcome, I'm a little concerned by the speed. On the far side of the current I can see—and I have to assume Scott and Barry see what I'm seeing—standing rip tides, those permanent waves we are always trying to avoid, some of the biggest we've seen. And we're being propelled straight toward them. Despite the tide we are forced to paddle as hard as we can, through growing wind- and tide-borne waves in order to stay out of the maw of the tide rips.

Forty-five minutes after leaving Carlisle we clear the strongest current separating Carlisle and Chuginadak and float, fatigued, into flat water just a quarter-mile off Chuginadak. Now, from sea level, we need to gauge the speed of the current that separates us from Herbert.

First we check out several rocky beaches on Chuginadak as potential retreats. Paddling west, toward the current and Herbert, we are still riding the tail end of the tide, heading to the swirling edge of the choppy current we can now see clearly. It's running east and north, neither directions we want to go. Once we venture into the current, it promises to be a fast, bumpy, swamping ride, demanding all of the skills of Barry and Scott, who—seated in the back of the boats—man the rudders. We are on course—due west—and it will be very difficult forging straight across amidst all the tumult.

It's our coldest day on the water. It's not the sleet that causes the particularly bone-numbing cold. The body parts that are covered up are okay. In fact, I'm sweating beneath my multi-layers, thanks to the sprint from Carlisle. It's the extremities, the hands and feet, that are numb. Pogies protect our hands from the rain, but not from the dip into the cold ocean they get with each paddle. Cold feet have been our biggest problem throughout the trip. We'd planned a system of fleece-lined rubber socks, a sealing sock, and neoprene zip-up booties, which we thought would provide plenty of warmth. We hadn't foreseen the problem of starting each day standing in the water loading the boat. With this system, as soon as we step into water much above our ankles, the short neoprene boots flood and cold water soaks the underlayers.

We realize a couple of options that probably would have worked better. Having neoprene booties sewn directly to the ankles of our dry suits is one we considered, but passed on because we foresaw having to struggle into yet another tight gasket. We each carry a pair of tall, rubber Extra Tuff boots that we wear onshore, but wearing them in the boat would be dangerous if we were dumped. You wouldn't want to spend the first five minutes upside down trying to take your boots off before they filled with ocean and dragged you to the bottom. Chota mukluks might have worked. We consider duct-taping the bottoms of our drysuits to our booties each morning, which might help but seems a mighty, and messy, daily challenge.

As it is, by the end of the day we are usually suffering from numb, nearly frostbitten toes. Inside the boat I spend an exorbitant amount of time trying to keep my feet awake—wiggling, shaking, curling my toes—thanks to the combination of cold and being stuffed into the tiny compartment for hours on end.

The cold plays a role in our decision to try the crossing. We really want to get to the other side, get out of these boats, and get warm again. As we approach the channel, though, it sounds like a thundering white-water river. Once we head in, it quickly feels like we're on a river, too. A chaos of waves, from behind (east) and our right (north) swamps the boat, burying it under cold seawater even as we continue to paddle. With every other stroke the boat disappears under a flood of cold sea. I can't see Scott, focused as I am on paddling straight ahead, not breaking stride, but I can feel the drag on the boat whenever we are smacked sideways, suggesting he is doing everything he can just to keep the boat upright, not putting his energy into propelling the boat forward. We are instantly pushed off our compass setting, heading now 20° farther south.

Midway across, the opposite shore comes into focus. We need to pick a landmark, some concrete feature of nature to target. That is the primary advantage of paddling without fog. If you can see what you're aiming for, you can far easier judge progress, or lack of same. "How about that V to our right?" shouts Barry. Only ten feet apart, we are on the verge of being out of communication, thanks to the roar of wind and sea.

"Or that washed-out cliff farther south?" Scott shouts back. We split the difference, choosing a rocky spit we can make out between the two sites. We pick up the pace of paddling, anxious to clear the mile-wide rage of the current.

When we hit the line of kelp on its far side, suggesting we are out of the biggest currents and wind, I breathe a sigh of relief.

We will reach Herbert, the fifth of our five islands. Though only another step in the journey—we still have to kayak back to Chuginadak and return to Applegate Cove and climb Mount Cleveland—at least we've achieved one of our primary goals, to step foot on each of the islands.

"To the best secretary of the Navy this country ever had," I toast from the boat, "Hilary Abner Herbert." We'd made the last four to five miles in just 45 minutes, or about six miles an hour—damn speedy for these big, heavy boats. As we near shore, a pair of great sea lions are basking on a rock, the first we've seen in a region that was once home to hundreds of thousands of them. They respond to my toast with mating calls that sound very much like dogs barking. Once assured we'll be able to land beyond the rocky spit, we decide to head south along the coast and scout the shore from the boats. Within a half hour a 20-mile-an-hour wind has kicked up at our back, dropping the wind chill into the teens, and ensuring that what we'd hoped would be a relaxing little end-of-the-day excursion will turn into a fight just to get into camp.

After we've pulled the boats high up onto a narrow, rocky beach, Scott and Sean clamber up Herbert's cliffs to scope out possible camps. As always, setting camp will involve a half-dozen trips up and down lugging all the various necessities.

Barry pulls me aside, visibly angered, anxious to vent something though I can only guess at the subject matter. "We were boomeranged out there, you know, when we left Carlisle. I was doing everything I could to keep our boat upright but we were nearly out of control. Crossing that channel, 'using' the tide, coming so close to those tide rips, it was like running Class IV rapids in a 700-pound boat. I don't know about you, but I don't want to surf rapids in the middle of the Bering Sea."

He's convinced we should have waited for the tide to pull out a bit before trying to jump on its back. I remind him of Scott's argument that the strong outgoing tide would "pull" us across. He was correct, in that we flew across both crossings.

"But if we hadn't made that eddy at the corner of Chuginadak, then where would we have ended up? It was definitely sketchy."

As we tie the kayaks off to big rocks, he continues to fume. "Before we got out here everyone told us, 'Be patient, wait for the slack tides, stay out of the currents because they are impossible to judge from a distance.' And here we are getting slingshot across the pass, straight through big tide rips.

"And between Chuginadak and Herbert, for a while there I was getting pushed around a lot by the fast current. Same thing: If that current had been just a little stronger, carrying us either farther north or south, where would we have ended up? I want to get out there and be able to paddle, to be able to control our direction, not have our fate tied to currents we can't judge in advance."

Yet another small pissing match between the pair of big dogs.

Scott himself admits later that night, in our tent, that the tide tables he's been using are from Dutch Harbor. We are one time zone farther west, meaning throughout the trip he's been assessing the tides using slightly out-of-kilter information. I'm glad he admits this to me privately. I choose not to share it with Sean and Barry.

TWENTY-TWO

A t one point today, halfway across the second pass of the day, we came within a simple paddle brace of going over. Capsizing is not the kind of thing you talk about, especially when you're in danger. In tandem boats it is a shared moment of panic that most often passes without comment. Given how cold we already were, going over between Chuginadak and Herbert would have been a death warrant. The primary reason is hypothermia, which during this trip is lurking before, during, and after virtually every paddle stroke.

It is not a pleasant way to die. In the short term, the effects on the body of cold water are an increased heartbeat, rising blood pressure, and hyperventilation. The first few seconds of immersion are characterized by huge, involuntary gasps, followed by a minute or more of rapid, deep breaths, which increase breathing volume to about five times that of levels at rest. The victim feels he cannot catch his breath. If the water is rough, most likely he will be swallowing lots of water. If it is windy, heat lost is the square of the wind's velocity—not in proportion to the velocity. In other words, a wind of eight miles an hour removes four times as much heat—not twice as much—as a wind of four miles an hour.

Long-term immersion in cold water—which experts define as anything less than 70°F—equals slow death. *Seventy degrees!* After 10 to 15 minutes in the water, shivering becomes conspicuous and continuous. Psychologically the victim despairs, and begins saying to himself, "I can't last much longer." After 15 to 20 minutes the body's core temperature begins to drop. Swimming to safety is an option, as long as safety is less than a half mile away. Available data suggests the average person is unlikely to be able to swim more than that in 50° water. If you're more than a half mile from shore, you're pretty much dependent on someone rescuing you. (There are stories of fishermen in full-blown survival suits surviving in the Bering Sea for more than 24 hours, but we are not able to wear those bulky suits in our kayaks.)

Imagine if one or both of our 22-foot carbon-fiber-and-Kevlar kayaks flip. We are unable to successfully roll the boat back over, clinging to it (or not), afloat in 36° water. After 15 minutes our organ systems will begin to fail, one at a time. Cold does not affect all organ systems uniformly but it will cause one system to fail, followed by another until you're dead.

This is how your body responds to cold water (thanks to Dr. Cameron Bangs):

Muscles: The cold causes a decrease in the rate at which nerve impulses are conducted to the muscles, which means the muscles are unable to contract effectively. The result is jerky, uncoordinated movements, the inability to perform even simple tasks, such as zipping up a jacket. Victims of prolonged cold water immersion in most cases are incapable of helping in their own rescue.

Brain: With just mild cooling, thinking processes and decision-making become slower. With profound hypothermia, mental function is impaired to a far greater extent, leading to confusion, apathy, disorientation, and erroneous decision-making. The desire or ability to obtain protection from the cold is progressively lost, leading to more rapid loss of body heat. On land, victims of profound hypothermia commonly take off their clothing (*paradoxical disrobing*). Lethargy, somnolence, slurred speech, and loss of vision are said to occur just prior to terminal coma.

Circulatory system: One of the most devastating effects of profound hypothermia is a reduction in the volume of circulating blood. Exposure to the cold decreases blood flow and oxygen transport to a rate far below what is necessary to keep functioning normally. Vital organs like the brain and heart stop performing properly, compounding the situation. Essentially all hypothermic victims suffer dehydration and as a result have a reduced blood volume. The cold also increases fluid loss by producing "cold dieresis," the increased excretion of water by the kidneys.

Heart: At normal temperatures the heart can force viscous blood through smaller vessels by pumping harder and faster. Unfortunately, when the heart is cooled to the level of profound hypothermia, it pumps weakly and slowly. In such cold the heart muscle becomes stiff and weak, and the volume of blood pumped decreases with each beat. Some evidence suggests that when an individual dies of hypothermia before he is found—alongside the road in a snowbank, for example—his heart simply beats slower and slower…until it stops.

Lungs: Ventilation—the movement of air into and out of the lungs—functions adequately as long as the body's core temperature stays above 90°. Below that, carbon dioxide begins to accumulate in the blood. Acidosis results, thanks to an increase in the accumulation of acidic metabolites, which are normally counterbalanced by increased ventilation. Unfortunately, with profound hypothermia such respiratory compensation doesn't occur.

My favorite stories (i.e., the most frightening) from my readings on the causes, symptoms, and results of hypothermia are those of poor folks who succumbed on the verge of being rescued. We are schooled in this simple truth: The best advice for anyone afloat in cold water is to lie still—ball up like a turtle, float on your back, huddle together, anything to keep the body still, to conserve energy and warmth. On many occasions after a victim suffering from profound hypothermia has been floating and sees a rescue craft headed his way he logically begins to swim as hard as he can for the boat, waving, shouting, etc. Many die as they help hoist themselves into the rescue boat.

Here's why. When you're suffering from profound hypothermia and lying or floating still, the blood circulating to your extremities is greatly diminished. The blood already in your extremities—fingertips, toes, etc.—becomes colder and more metabolically bankrupt, with a high acid and potassium content and low oxygen. What fells the excited victim is when he starts pumping those arms and legs, after a period of immobility, and the sudden muscular action pumps blood quickly back to the heart. This organ, already compromised by the cold, is suddenly hit—wham!!—by even colder blood containing the irritating products of anaerobic metabolism. Even if he survives, ventricular fibrillation, an abnormal heart rhythm, is the common result.

To avoid this lethal complication, the victim of profound hypothermia must never exert himself. "He must not walk, climb, swim, or even move when lifted. If the victim is in cold water, he must not try to climb into the boat, but should allow himself to be carefully and gently lifted from the water," warn Dr. Bangs and comrades.

So how do you survive a dunk in cold waters like these? A full-on survival suit, as are carried on most fishing boats, would be the best choice. Huddling together in the water, two or more persons can reduce the cooling rate by about one third. I was also told to adopt a body posture that minimizes the area of exposed body surface to the water, known as HELP—Heat Escape Lessing Posture—or "downproofing," a technique of floating that minimizes the movements made, thus conserves energy. There's also a breath-holding maneuver, using minimal kicking strokes to return the victim to the surface.

The problem for us is that any of these methods are only valid in 50° water or higher. It's predicted they could keep you alive an extra one and a half hours. The bottom line, out here especially, is the boldface warning repeated over and over in texts on cold-water immersion: "Hypothermia should be avoided, not treated."

The other expert maxim is: "No one should be considered cold and dead until he has been warm and dead!" This is every doctor's final word and should be burnished into the brain of anyone considering paddling on cold water. This only counts, of course, if you're able to get a hypothermic victim out of the water and to a warm place. "The skin may feel cold and non-pliable. It may be pale and have a slightly bluish hue," writes Dr. Bangs of a typical hypothermic victim rushed to the emergency room. "Pupils of the eyes do not undergo any characteristic changes. The pulse is often weak, hard to feel. Pulse rate is typically slow and irregular. Blood pressure is difficult to measure and may be normal or low. Breathing is shallow, slow. Victim's breath has a fruity, acetone odor resulting from the incomplete metabolism of fats caused by the inadequate blood supply to the peripheral tissues. Urine-soaked clothing also indicates a serious situation. Even when brought to an ER, victims of profound hypothermia die 50 to 80 percent of the time, even when they've been brought 'back to life.'"

We are far from an emergency room. Since most likely we would all be in the same situation—swimming for our lives in the rough waves of the Bering Sea—I'm not figuring on having much opportunity to smell my buddy's "fruity breath."

TWENTY-THREE

Just after midnight a strange light fills our tent, like somebody's flashing some kind of giant demonic flashlight. Scott and I bolt up from our bags and go outside. Our first assumption is that all of a sudden we're not alone on Herbert Island. Who the hell is out there?

No one, it turns out, but something we haven't seen in more than six weeks: the moon. It is the first night since we arrived that has not been socked in with heavy clouds. As they break up, pushed to the west by a high, strong, clearing wind, they unveil a majestic moon. From the tide tables we knew this was to be the first night of the full moon, but we never expected to see it. As we watch from our high-meadow camp, it exposes itself in all its perfect roundness.

Sean and Barry come out, too, drawn by the same spectacle. We stand outside our tents, set apart from each other across a shallow furrow. The rain stopped late in the afternoon, the wind calmed and temperatures climbed into the mid-30s. In the moonlight

Mount Cleveland, six miles across Chuginadak Pass, sends a shadow reaching just onto our camp. Above, the deformed peak of Herbert gleams. It is deformed thanks to a centuries ago explosion that eliminated its perfect cone and left behind a tilted mountaintop resembling the jagged, broken neck of a beer bottle.

The night light gives the island an even more mysterious feel. The calmness of the night is unusual, as well, and we can hear the low wash of the sea below the steep cliffs. It is a perfect birthday present—for me—from some unnamed Aleut god, I suppose.

The morning arrives with yet another foreign quality: bright sunshine. No new clouds have returned, and for the first time the sky is virtually free—virtually, since because of the panoramic vision we have, under a truly gigantic sky, there are always at least some wispy clouds on the horizon. This morning they hang over the twin peaks of Cleveland and Carlisle, which pop out of the sun-splayed ocean like a pair of white-frosted ice cream cones. Thanks to the lessened wind the songs of the birds jump out, too, like somebody turned the volume to 10. We see another first: flying bugs. Thanks to the constant winds it's a place where bugs live very close to the land, if at all.

The day is spent discovering Herbert on foot. Again, we search for streams without success. With our water sacks running low— we can carry 30 gallons among the eight different bags—it looks like we'll have to resort to taking water out of the still ponds we find just over the high ridge above camp. Normally you wouldn't consider such a move, and normally we'd have a good filtering system, but the two small, simple filters we brought along crapped out within the first few uses.

Veniaminov described Herbert as "a round, craggy, cliffy peak with a cup-like crater at the summit, without bays or streams. Here were two villages in the old times and sea otters were plentiful. At the present no settlement and scarcely a sea otter exists." We find it odd that there had ever been villages here, given the lack of water. Perhaps at another time the streams were somehow able to survive the island's sucking heat.

As we explore, the day keeps getting better. Carlisle and Cleveland expose themselves completely, and magnificently. Through the afternoon, the constant plume blowing from the caldera atop Cleveland casts up pinkish-white smoke against the crystal-blue sky. I spend the afternoon wrestling with big stones on the cliff that look like they might be doors to hidden caves—mummy caves?—running deep into the island. No luck. I also take a birthday bath, using my plastic dinner bowl to pour cold sea water over my head and rinse out the soap. Except for the slippery kelp I must stand in, it feels good. Afterward I sit on a big, sun-warmed rock and admire the scenery.

At five o'clock we celebrate the day by taking the kayaks out for a pleasure paddle, something we have not often allowed ourselves. It lasts about an hour. Caught up in our excitement we've underestimated just how cold it still was on the water.

I hadn't told the boys it was my birthday, wanting to celebrate it for myself first. Just before dinner I pull out the small sack I carried from the start, with cigars, a flask of my father-in-law's homemade (i.e., bootleg) plum brandy (Lake Viry 1999) and a quartet of different tins of sardines, albeit without key—which means we open them in Aleutian Island fashion, with our saw-toothed knives.

Dinner is long (freeze-dried Kathmandu curry, Bretagne sardines, French milk chocolate). My sole presents are postcards—compliments of my French wife—featuring pictures of a dozen different kinds of fresh bread, a plethora of *saucissons* and cheeses and a solitary bottle of red, Chateau Latour. Just pictures, unfortunately.

All is chased with cigars and sips of brandy, leading to the end-game played any time guys sit around too long in the great outdoors, a version of "no shit, there I was...." Barry entertains with accounts of his visits to all the "Stans"...i.e., Kurdistan, Khazakistan, Pakistan, etc. Sean tells of his last heliskiing trip to Valdez, which basically means being dropped by a helicopter onto a sponge-size piece of mountain and skiing 2,000-feet straight down an icy glacier. Scott, who worked as a fishermen out of Ventura, California, for several years, trumps all with stories of jumping off two-man fishing boats at night under full blackness, for kicks and to practice turning the boat around in case a man went overboard for real.

I unfold a less personal story, one I read before we got out here about one way the Aleut celebrated. During unexplained ceremonies—unexplained because they left so little record of their time here on these islands—they carried weirdly carved wooden images or stuffed birds from house to house during the darkness of night. Sometimes a large congregation of women would gather in a spot from which all men were rigidly excluded, and, wearing masks, would dance naked in the moonlight. The men had similar dances in special spots of their own. For any individual of the other sex to intrude upon these occasions was punishable by death. As our night set in—clouds returning, full moon cloaked—in the post-dinner quiet I try to imagine the sounds and smells and sights of those masked, dancing, naked Aleuts parading over the hills. I make a promise to myself that every birthday to follow I will, no matter where I am, flash back to these visions of dancing natives and this very special place.

On the next day we explore two very different parts of the island. The first lies over a high ridge to the west of the long drainage basin where we've put our camp. The ridgeline draws us because of the seven tall stone cairns, seven feet tall, spaced evenly 50 feet apart, lining the seam. There's not a single rock of any size on the ground between them, suggesting these had been gathered and stacked by the hand of man. It could be a freak accident of nature, rocks blown from the exploding peak of Herbert some centuries back, but I don't think so. Now covered with grass and moss, they were most likely built as sign posts for the kayakers—markers or targets for hunters after long days, weeks, even months at sea.

Crossing the ridge, we find a series of seven small ponds on a flat overlooking the ocean. It is easy to imagine an Aleut village here, out of the wind, next to fresh water. The human spirit of this otherwise raw, untouched place rises up to grab our attention. Everywhere we go on these islands was once someone's home.

Later in the afternoon we climb the hill that leads to the top of Herbert's volcano. An eruption some centuries before had blown the tip off its peak, leaving it oddly cantilevered, several hundred feet higher in the back. Looking straight down inside the crater, we see it still boils with incendiary activity, at its deepest glows a shallow bowl of hot, ruby-colored magma.

The languid days of summer have definitely arrived in the Aleutians, though we know they will be short-lived. This morning it was sunny, almost warm. That said, whenever we are out of our tents we still wear three layers—long underwear, fleece with Windstopper, and often a down jacket, topped by a stocking cap, even gloves. Such is summer here at 53° latitude.

The wind has been calm the past 24 hours, never a good sign in our experience, and the barometer is at its highest in three weeks, suggesting we are in for a change. All we hope for is one more good day.

We've allowed a slightly lackadaisical feeling to creep in. Our next crossing takes us back to Chuginadak and Applegate Cove, from which we hope to climb Mount Cleveland, explore the rest of the island, and wait for the return of the *Miss Pepper*. We are in no big hurry to return there. The long bay is known for hosting long, low fogs. By comparison, from our camp here on Herbert, when the clouds have lifted we have magnificent views of the Fuji-like twin towers of Cleveland and Carlisle. Applegate's beach makes for soft kayak landings, but means we are living in sand, which has a tendency to get everywhere inside tents, food, and clothing. One nagging issue is the lack of fresh water. Our daily searching continues. We realize how lucky we were on the first three islands to find camps within a relatively easy walk to fresh-running streams. On Herbert we are taking water from a pair of small ponds uphill, just behind our tents.

"I can't believe I'm saying this, but I'm looking forward to getting back to Applegate and that big bag of pasta and rice," says Scott, sitting in a cool wind outside our tent. "I should be sick of both by now. But after this freeze-dried stuff, a big bowl of rice sounds as good as a juicy steak."

"I'm not in a particular hurry to go back," I say, "if only because of the view through our picture window here." Just over the pass the sun is setting behind the snowcapped peaks, and the constant wisp of smoke blowing off the top of Cleveland is turned pink in the twilight.

The sea is glassy-calm the following morning, and it is tempting to pack the boats and make the run back to Chuginadak, to have it out of the way. But we take the easier decision to stay longer on Herbert, explore the rest of the island.

It is admittedly a lazy Saturday. We stay in the tent for roughly 12 hours, from midnight to noon, reading and eating, including freshly baked whole wheat bread (Scott brought along a small convection oven that fits over the gas stove), potato cakes (made from last night's leftover powdered potatoes), freeze-dried eggs and coffee, followed by a mandatory post-breakfast siesta. We rationalize the morning off since it's the beginning of the Fourth of July weekend everywhere in the U.S., even here in the all-American Aleutians. Again this morning we heard whales feeding in the pass. It is a one-of-a-kind sound, a deep moo-like bellow, accompanied by just a rippling of surface water as the 20-ton animals make their way west.

One small mistake we made when we left Applegate was bringing along a mostly freeze-dried diet. While the stuff in bags tastes good (just add boiling water!) and its spiciness is welcome after several weeks of blandness, it is simply not filling. Eating one of the bags of Kathmandu curry or Mexican beans and rice that is supposed to "serve two" provides only 600 calories. Not nearly enough for growing boys paddling through cold seas. We are supplementing with protein-rich Gatorade and energy-laden GU, small squeeze bags of protein paste, but our supplies are running low. It will be good to be back to Applegate, where we stashed our last rations of rice, couscous, mashed potatoes, and pasta.

I spend the early afternoon on the edge of the cliff studying the fast-running water moving through the pass that separates us from Chuginadak. It's so hard it to read these waters from a distance, even from this vantage, high on a hill overlooking the sea. From the north Carlisle Pass flows perpendicularly into the big, fat, fast-running Chuginadak Pass. Depending on the time of day, thanks to tides, currents, and winds, they can be moving west to east and north to south, respectively. When they meet—again consider the varying factors of wind, current, and tides—they create one big confusion. These are exactly the kinds of waters that boats three times the size of our 22-foot kayaks carefully avoid. For us trying to assess the "best" times to cross involves a certain roll of the dice. The truth of the place, as we have learned, is that there are few rules. We've learned to mix in the barometric readings recorded on our Suunto watches, the direction of the wind on our face, the threatening of the skies. But the truth is, our every move here is best undertaken after careful study by the naked eye, by the feel of the day, your gut.

By late afternoon the sun is back and high, and we decide to paddle to the north end of Herbert. There is another "hunter's cabin" marked on the map, and since we've had little luck finding the others, we hope maybe this one still exists in some fashion. We are curious to get a feel for some other human presence on the islands, since we've been only speculating since we arrived.

Sean and Barry push off first. I wait on the rocky beach for Scott, who has taken a hike up Herbert. We'd arranged a rendezvous time, and he carried one of the Talk-About radios, so I knew he'd show up sooner or later. In the past couple days he has pretty much dropped out of any decision-making discussions, largely since he and Barry are barely speaking. The problem is mostly Barry giving him the cold shoulder, which feels unfortunate. I can't shake the feeling that this is a dangerous place to carry a grudge.

Scott arrives, with tall tales of glissading down the snowpack from Herbert's top directly to the bottom of the mountain. My attitude towards Scott in these waning days of our traveling together is as a peacekeeper. We still have some big crossings and hopefully a big climb to do together, and we need everyone in synch. Within 30 minutes we are on the water. A squeak of the radio tells us that the other kayak is already on a beach three miles to the north.

A white-skinned seal greets us as we slip through a kelp bed to the small beach. Pulling the tops of our dry suits down around our waists, we climb to the high ridge in our neoprene booties. The hill is covered with new, waist-high grass, and after a half hour of tramping we manage to find the hunter's cabin. Its foundation is covered by grass and its roof collapsed. The timber walls are gone, having apparently disintegrated. Dropping to one knee, I run my hands across the floor and find tiny bits of a porcelain teacup and a bent metal fork.

Russian fox hunters built the cabin more than 100 years ago, long before Sam Applegate. Although no mammals live on these islands today, 150 years ago foxes were introduced throughout the Aleutian Islands as a new economy. With no wild predators or humans, the islands were perfect breeding grounds for foxes—and their valuable pelts—multiplying in an isolated, protected setting.

The easternmost Aleutians actually had native foxes, which crossed over former land bridges during the last ice age. Every few years the southern edge of the Arctic ice pack reached down to the islands, and foxes, known to travel considerable distances in their search for food, could have ventured here. When Vitus Bering first arrived, he found indigenous red foxes—thus the Fox Islands. Even in more recent times one intrepid fox found along the coast of northern Alaska had been tagged along the coast of Russia the year before. Often foxes will follow a polar bear across the ice pack, feeding on the remains of seal killed by the bear.

The Russians began introducing Arctic foxes on Attu Island, in the 1750s, bringing them from the Commander Islands, where they were native. The enterprise thrived during the 1800s but boomed in the 1920s and 1930s when fur production was the third largest industry in Alaska after fishing and mining. During those years, there were fox farms on virtually all of the Aleutian Islands. After World War II the fur market collapsed and fox farmers were forced to return to subsistence hunting or travel hundreds of miles to work for wages. Federal agencies claimed 95 percent of the Aleutian chain as either wildlife refuge or for military sites.

The effect of introduced foxes was devastating to the islands, largely because hundreds of species of ground-nesting birds had evolved without any predators. Foxes decimated a phenomenally rich seabird population. As far back as 1811 the natives reported that they were forced to travel to nearby fox-free islands in order to get the birds they depended on for their clothing. Eventually, with the bird population so reduced, they would have to use fish skins in their clothing instead. The birds were good for the islands in other ways. Their waste encouraged rich soil, creating luxuriant plant growth, as well as phosphates, nitrates, and other nutrients used by phytoplanktons that, in turn, benefit organisms farther up the food chain. In the end, foxes were far more disastrous to the bird population of Alaska and the Aleutians than the Exxon Valdez oil spill, killing millions each year.

Efforts to remove foxes from the Aleutians began in 1949, on Amchitka, in order to save the endangered Aleutian Canada goose. Today foxes have been successfully eradicated. Chuginadak was once home to many, since red foxes had been introduced there in the early 1800s, joined in the 1930s by a population of Arctic foxes. We saw no sign of them.

Conditions allowing, we will leave Herbert tomorrow for Applegate Cove. It has been a good, four-day stay, a blend of exploration and rest. But it will feel good to get back out to sea.

TWENTY-FOUR

"We were still some from the harbour. Almost every wave broke right over us and we often got mouthfuls of sea water. But it was mostly our hands that suffered as they became number with the wetness and intense cold. As we plunged the paddles in one side and then the other they were almost torn from our hands. Despite this the Americans in my baidarka rowed skillfully and showed no signs of fear, and as each huge wave came up they shouted: 'koo, koo, koo!' in order, I think, to warn their colleagues of the coming danger."—an early 1800s report from one of the first non natives to paddle a baidarka, a young Russian naval officer stationed at Kodiak

If we'd known the kind of day we were in for, we might well have opted to spend the day inside the tents, waiting out another fierce blow sleeping and reading, holding out for a less wild day to cross to Chuginadak.

Maybe we'd grown a little overconfident and were taking the Bering Sea a bit too casually. We'd been out here three weeks and had made six successful crossings, and I think we naively felt we could handle a day like this one. Blowing, gray, cold. If everything went smoothly, we could. The flaw in this thinking, or lack of such, was that one false move and we'd regret ever getting out of bed. The chance for something going wrong was tipping the meter toward "Danger, Danger, Danger." Yet we never talked about the option of staying put.

In fact, when I woke, I had virtually no anxiety about the upcoming—most likely final—crossing. Rested by a good, eight-hour sleep, feeling as good as I had all trip, I was anxious to get going.

Our first clue should have been aural. From the beach at Herbert the roar coming off the pass is ominous. It isn't the sound of the wind or waves, but like a locomotive river splitting Chuginadak and Herbert. I've never heard a current so loud before. That alone should have warned us this would be a wild day. But by the time the tents are down, we are anxious to get moving. We've been camped on Herbert for four nights, and it has been almost luxurious. Now we're ready to get back to base camp, in part for that dry bag of "real" food that awaits. Plus, once we are back at Applegate, the trip will have been a true success. All five islands explored, all crossings made safely.

As soon as we push the boat onto the water, I am overwhelmed by an ominous feeling. The normally calm kelp-filled cove is wind-churned, foamy. We push out first and try to wait for Sean and Barry, which proves impossible. The wind is so strong we cannot stay in one place. We are forced to paddle full-strength, right off the bat, just to avoid being sucked out to sea. Beyond, the roar grows louder.

As soon as we emerge from the protected lee of the land, we are hammered by the winds and current. I can barely make out what Scott is shouting from the back of the boat. "Mach! Mach 1!" he's screaming, over and over, his indication of how powerful the winds are. For the first time we are paddling in a Bering Sea storm.

Our hope is to cross directly to Chuginadak, a four-mile sprint in good conditions. Even on a clear day it would be tough to hold a true line. With these winds, and an even stronger current sweeping up from the south, we'll be lucky not to have to circle Carlisle in order to reach Applegate.

A third of the way into the pass it is apparent just how big a day we'd bitten off. Unleashing my wind meter from the bungee cord in front of me, I register gusts of 20 miles an hour and wind chill at a nippy 22°. Yet it is too late to turn around now. Four- and five-foot swells march north, breaking over the bow at an angle, forcing Scott to stroke, then immediately try to reposition the boat to face into the cresting waves. We are constantly buried under assaults of icy saltwater.

My hands, which are bare and constantly in the water, are soon aching. Interestingly, they seem to be getting used to this exposure. That's what happens to cold-water fishermen, Sami and Eskimos—anyone who works all their lives in cold climates— eventually your body acclimatizes. Scott seems to be relishing these conditions. I can hear him yelling, to himself, things like "Bitchin'!", "Finally we meet the real Bering Sea!" and "These are the conditions I've been waiting for!"

This *is* exactly the weather I think we all expected to find out here, every day. The truth is, if the seas had been this wild during our first few crossings, I wonder if we would have continued. Having several successful paddles under our dry suits is the only reason we even attempted this one today.

"Jon, if it feels like we're about to go over," Scott yells after a six-foot wave submerges our boat entirely. "Just brace hard and tuck as far forward as you can. That way you'll be that much closer to kissing your ass goodbye."

"Funny guy," is all I can muster, too focused to share my thoughts.

Peeking back over my shoulder, right, then left, I keep a lookout for the pair of orange hoods of Barry and Sean, who are trailing behind. If I can see them, it means they are still upright.

When we pull within a mile and a half of towering Mount Cleveland, which rises straight above us, we are greeted by a new, even fiercer wind that races down its 6,000-foot slope to cross hatch the sea. Now, even as we are being swamped from the south, the boats nearly pitch-poling into four-foot waves, we must paddle even harder into a 20-mile-an-hour headwind.

"Still having fun?" I shout back over my shoulder, to no response.

After a perilous 75 minutes, we leave the hardest current, getting to within a half mile of Chuginadak's western shore. We had hoped its landmass might protect us from some wind, but instead we find ourselves still buffeted by a stiff wall of wind roaring down the mountainside. We turn north, paralleling the shoreline, targeting a rocky point that marks the island's corner. We hope to round it and then make our way east. The winds coming off Cleveland are ominous because we read in the *Pilot's Guide to Navigation* that in Carlisle Pass—which separates the twin volcanoes of Cleveland and Carlisle—wind speeds could be double strength, due to the narrowness of the pass and the winds coming off both volcanoes. Twice this strong, and we're sunk, literally.

When we turn the corner of Chuginadak, we are still about nine miles from Applegate Cove. This will definitely be our longest day on the water. There is a small headwind and we are paddling against the current, but the sun is trying to shine through, which helps. We stop at the corner and tread water. Looking back at Herbert is a scary sight. The island is totally consumed by fog and rain. If we'd stayed much longer this morning, we would have never left; and if those conditions last there, we would have been stuck for who knows how many days. Despite the morning's harrowing conditions, leaving was the right call. On this side of the pass the volcanoes are beginning to pop out of the clouds. Our seventh of seven crossings is nearly complete. The final stretch should take us less than two hours.

Just pick a reference point, I tell myself. Whenever I'm paddling, whether on the Walkill Creek near my house in New York State or here on the Bering Sea, I measure advancement by choosing landmarks onshore. That rock outcropping, for example, the big boulder on the hill, or the green stripe of moss running down to the cliffside. Pick it, site it, and paddle for it. When that landmark has been passed, start over. Without that small challenge I find that paddling, especially into a headwind as we are right now, can verge on the self-defeating. Accomplishing something concrete—such as passing that lone tree jutting out from the cliff—proves you are actually making progress. Here,

I recognize the point of land we have to reach before we can enter the four-mile wide bay fronting Applegate Cove. I make that point my long term landmark and pick out several others along the shoreline. At first the paddling isn't particularly difficult. My arms and shoulders feel surprisingly strong, in part because I'm convinced the hardest part of the day is behind us.

Hah!

Just as we pass the last rocky pinnacle jutting into the sea, my final landmark of the day—anxious to lay eyes on our base camp, our home away from home in this remote place—a rigid 40-mile-an-hour wind from the south smacks us hard. Its source is easily identifiable: the narrow slot separates the foot of Mount Cleveland from the rest of the island; it is the small pass that once separated Chuginadak into two islands but is now clogged by rock and sand. The wind off the Pacific Ocean is roaring relentlessly through. When we left Applegate Cove a few days before, that wind had been to our side, slightly behind us. Now it is blowing fiercely, directly into our face.

Whitecaps surround us. When I pick my extremely light, carbon-fiber paddle out of the water, the wind nearly rips it from my frozen fingers before I can plunge it in again. Bearing down, desperate to gain a few inches of forward progress, proves nearly impossible. Despite our combined strongest effort the best we can do is stand still. The bow of the boat digs into the waves at an angle, and each time one breaks across I take a bucket full of saltwater in the face. Simultaneously, each time I lift my right paddle stroke out of the water, the wind carries its load directly into Scott's face. There is so much saltwater spray in the air, it is difficult to keep your eyes open, much less focus on any landmark.

What we'd expected to be a 30-minute glide into camp turns into a two-hour slog, the hardest paddling we've done since we arrived. The good thing is we can just make out our camp at the far end of the beach. The downside is that the wind is growing stronger as we near the center of the inland slot.

Shouting at the top of my lungs, I suggest heading into the nearby kelp pads, where we might take refuge from the winds, resting atop them like the seals do during storms. Why not sit for a while and see if the winds might die?

Scott yells back, "No way. It could get much worse before it gets better, and then we'll be stuck here for the night. Let's keep paddling."

I look around for Barry and Sean and can't locate them. Then I spy their orange heads far out to sea. They've chosen a different route, opting to distance themselves from the vortex of the Pacific winds, hoping they will have diminished by the time they get farther out to sea.

Scott sees me looking towards the other kayak. "I don't like what they're doing," he shouts. "If they get blown out, if the winds are as strong out there, pretty fast they'll find themselves in the middle of the pass. If the weather really goes to shit, that's not where I'd want to be. I'd prefer to stay as close to shore as we can, in case it really goes off."

We've paddled a hard ten miles to get to this point, all of it into a headwind. Though we continue to fight, there are moments when I think we'll be blown back onto shore—or out to sea. When we reach the very heart of the slot, the winds grow stronger. There is no gusting involved, just a steady, howling gale. I can see into the canyon where the winds come from, and it is black, covered with blown dirt and filled with a heavy fog, despite the fact that otherwise we are surrounded by sunshine. The place is a suckhole for foul weather, like some kind of subarctic hell. Scott was right about one thing this morning. Finally, on day 20, we are paddling into the godawful conditions we'd been expecting since day one, straight into the Birthplace of the Winds.

Despite our different routes the two boats pull onto the sandy shore within minutes of each other. Standing up is difficult. We've been in the cockpits for nearly five hours and every joint is stiff. My hands are raw and cracked, calluses rubbed fiery red. I rummage through my cockpit for the ever present thermos and pour a congratulatory cup of hot Gatorade. Sharing it with Barry, we stand on the shore's edge, looking back at the seas, which are growing even wilder, and the two exposed volcanoes.

After recovering my land-legs and regaining feeling in my hands, numbed by a death grip on the paddle, I give a small thanks to each of the boys. Now the trip is truly a success.

"It doesn't get any better than this," Barry laughs.

"No, I suppose it doesn't. But I would never have expected when we left Herbert that we'd see all of that—gray, rain, sleet, big waves, incredible winds…followed by sunshine, big waves, and even more incredible winds. What a place! Whose idea was this anyway?" I joke. I trot this line out every time we survive some particularly arduous experience and, curiously, none of us are willing to take credit.

The rest of the day—we arrived after 5:30—is spent in an idyllic summer style. The beach sand was warm, the temperature climbing to 65°. We remake camp in our bare feet, wearing—miraculously—just a single layer of clothing. Sean takes charge of a "real food" dinner—mashed potatoes, pasta, chocolate, more hot Gatorade. (The last tastes great when you're out there in a cold place, but never quite as satisfying when you're back home, trust me.)

The views of Carlisle and Cleveland get better and better as they show themselves to us in their full glory, almost as a reward for our day. Through binoculars I eye the peak of Cleveland and can see wind violently whipping the plume of smoke that emanates from its active crater. Turning the glasses down the beach, I can see the wind still roaring through the slot, turning the sea in front of it into frothing madness. Though the sun is out and bright, the wind continues to flail land and sea unrelentingly, hour after hour after hour.

It is still light at midnight, thanks to our latitude and the date, and we enjoy another sight we haven't seen in several weeks: the setting sun. It goes down perfectly, round, clear, and orange behind and just to the right of Carlisle. At 2:00 a.m. we are still outside, silent, marveling at the after-light of dusk.

TWENTY-FIVE

With our riskiest paddles behind us—we plan to make some forays back onto the sea to explore the rest of Chuginadak—we take a rest day, sleeping until noon and treating ourselves to freeze-dried omelets. Our camp, located at the far eastern end of the four-mile black sand beach, is the best observation point for regarding Mount Cleveland, which we plan to climb in the next few days.

This afternoon Sean and I lounge comfortably in our Therma-Rest chairs and scout our options. Several fingers of lava rock climb up from the base of the mountain. They lead to several miles of deep snow covering the steep upper reaches of the perfectly shaped cone. We might be able to zigzag up one of those fingers to the top, as long as the snow is not prohibitively deep. Another option is to hike around to the other side of the mountain, which we know, since we saw it from Herbert, is less steep. But that option is ruled out pretty quickly because hiking around would take most of a day. Sean, who has the most climbing experience of the four, predicts a straight up-and-down shot in the same day should take between 12 and 15 hours.

Cleveland is definitely the wildest in this part of the Aleutians, the only volcano still active. It has exploded at least 11 times in the past century, maybe more since a few of Carlisle's eruptions may have been wrongly attributed. Since these volcanoes are not very well monitored, often the only sure sign that they have erupted is when an international flight high above detects the aftermath of an explosion. In science-speak, here is the report from March 11, 1998, during a flyover by the Alaska Volcano Observatory: "A strong sulfur smell was noticed 50 kilometers downwind of the volcano; the summit was visible but a thin cloud layer at 1700-1900 meters obscured the fumarolic areas."

Its huge blow in January 1932 lasted for days. Between June 10 and 12, 1944, continual explosions from its central crater produced lava flow combined with severe earthquakes. Clouds and steam rose to four miles into the sky, and lava flows extended reached eight miles from the central crater. Boulders "as big as automobiles" were ejected across the island and into the ocean. This eruption was significant since it was the first time any modern man had been killed by a volcano anywhere in the Aleutians (who knows the damage wreaked by volcanoes during the Aleut's days). A small detachment of the 11th Army Air Force was temporarily stationed on Chuginadak during World War II, operating a radio relay station. Apparently a curious soldier got too close to the active vent and was killed, probably by a mudslide. The Army post was immediately abandoned for the duration of the war. Remnants of the site—rusted barrels, electrical generator parts, and the rebar that held its antenna in place—were buried in the tundra above and behind our Applegate camp.

In the past half century, Cleveland has erupted roughly every six years. Eruptions were measured in June 1987, then again in August 1987, sending a plume six miles into the sky. On May 25, 1994, it blew, rocketing smoke and ash seven miles up. Since 1997 its activity has increased, suggesting it may be ready to blow again soon. Hopefully, that won't be today, though near the top we can make out sulfur deposits discoloring adjacent snow and ice.

The next morning we leave camp, carrying light packs, at exactly 7:04 a.m. on the Fourth of July. It is 26° with a steady eight-mile-an-hour wind as we head down the long beach for the hills that will hopefully lead us to Cleveland's peak. In a direct line—4.5 miles of beach, plus 6,000 feet straight up—the trip is about ten miles each way.

Thanks to the heaviest snows in the past 25 years across Alaska, we anticipate a steep uphill slog rather than a technical, vertical wall climb. The knowledge that the hot, porous volcano will make the snow very soft makes us wonder if we have the right tools. Since our carrying space was so limited, we brought only a few bare essentials—half crampons, two ice axes, four harnesses and a solitary 100-meter rope. Our concern is that we could find ourselves thwarted by soft, deep snow on the steepest part of the peak and be forced to turn back.

Once off the beach, we trudge through dew- and fog-wetted mossy grass, where our shoes pick up twice their weight in moisture, not a good beginning to a day to be spent in wind and cold. Sean and I are wearing particularly leaky shoes, and by the time we leave the tundra for the layer of black lava rock encircling the mountain, our feet are sopping wet. As soon as we are out of the wet grass for good, we sit on the sharp lava, take off our shoes and wring water out of our socks. The lava rock extends another 1,000 feet up to where the inverted V-shaped snowfields begin. Through the spotty fog and clouds we catch glimpses of a robin's egg blue sky above.

If some god looks out over the Aleutians, and by coincidence us, he or she is definitely smiling this day. Each day since leaving Herbert the area has been socked in with clouds. In fact, if we hadn't left Herbert when we did, we'd still be stuck there. Today, the one day out of 25 that we chose to climb the biggest volcano— "Why not the Fourth of July? Nothing better to do!"—the weather can't be more accommodating.

Sitting atop the exposed and hardened lava flows, putting on crampons and harnesses, we lift our eyes from our busywork and look out over the Bering Sea. It's an amazing sight. All of Uliaga and Kagamil are perfectly clear of clouds, completely exposed. We can easily make out the routes we took between the islands, even the nasty rip tides we avoided and the coves where we made camps: Eagle Cove, Skiff Cove, the western wall of Kagamil, and the rocky beach at Uliaga where we landed. Surprisingly, we spot a sizable clear blue lake not far above the waterfall at Skiff Cove; we'd had no idea it was there. Since we left Uliaga and Kagamil, thanks to the generally warmer days, much of the snow on their volcanoes has dissipated.

To the east we look down the long extension of Chuginadak. The smaller volcano, its peak at 3,400 feet, rises straight through the cloud bank that still chokes the hell's canyon we'd fought against a couple days before. The name Islands of Four Mountains makes perfect sense from this perspective. We can see the sailing route the early Russians would have followed and the views back they would have had of Herbert, Carlisle, and the two volcanoes on Chuginadak. Forty-five miles away we can see the peak of the big volcano near Nikolski named Vsevidof.

The traverse in the snow is as difficult as we expected. Wanting to avoid any risk of triggering rockfalls, we get off the rocks as soon as we can and into the snow. We choose a route that leads up the widest, snowiest shaft, and begin our zigzag up, north to south and back again, single file, gaining altitude slowly, steadily. I try not to look down—a slip in the steep, soft snow would send me glissading down 1,000 to 2,000 feet until hitting the lava rock below that would, without doubt, rip me into bloody pieces.

One step after another, using the ice axes and a pair of walking sticks as braces. Scott breaks trail, since he's the only one among us with full crampons. Barry, Sean, and I wear just half-crampons that cover the toes of our boots, handy little items we'd picked up at the last minute when we drove through Anchorage. The higher we get—I count off the gains on my altimeter by the hundreds of feet, 3,600, 3,700…4,100, 4,200…5,000, 5,100—the windier it grows. Any icy blast races downhill from the volcano's caldera, whistling past us. Dry snow ricochets off our now hooded heads. We stop to pull on snow pants and another layer of fleece, hacking a ledge into the soft snow with boots and axes. The view has grown ever more magnificent blue, crystal clear, allowing us to see 50 miles into the distance. From here we can't yet see Carlisle, or Herbert, and we hope the clouds stay away until we reach the peak.

Seated on the rudimentary ledge, struggling to pull snow pants over crampons and harnesses, we are balanced precariously. It would be a 2,000-foot slide to where the snow ends, and with 40-mile-an-hour winds ratcheting up, we do everything we can to keep our weight uphill. The gusty wind whips a thick drift of light snow down on top of us, burying us in its confetti. Within seconds everything accumulated around us—crampon bags, photo gear, bags of nuts, axes—is completely buried under the drift. I've left a zipper in my backpack open, and the light snow invades and fills the cavity immediately, like some kind of snow hurricane. As quickly as it arrives, it subsides.

The next one thousand feet are far steeper. I lean back—not too far—and can't see the peak, though it's just another thousand feet above. We're at 5,100, standing on the very thin edge of a steep climb. After another 100 feet up, as Scott and Sean forge ahead, Barry and I sneak out to the northern limit of the mountain. For the first time we can see Carlisle, straight ahead. What's amazing about the mountain, which we knew but can now see clearly, is how little flatland there is around its base. It truly rises straight out of the sea, its snowy peak surrounded by a thin blanket of sparkling green meadows. Swiveling our heads from west to east and back again, all Barry can get out is "Unbelievable." Like floating jewels, the snowcapped peaks of Kagamil, Uliaga, and Carlisle drift on the Bering Sea a mile below us.

The next traverse takes us past a smaller, secondary crater, its plume filling the air with noxious smoke. Just below the main peak we arrive at a jumble of rust-and-black-colored lava rock rimming the top of the mountain, sharp and jagged. A handful of boulders the size of Volkswagens litter the rim. Scott and Sean are waiting for us behind a big rock. The summit is just 50 feet over a scree field that lies above us.

Taking off crampons, wringing out socks—again—we sip more hot Gatorade, eat our last dried salmon and some dried fruit—and bask in the cold sun, protected from the wind, with the knowledge that we would make it to the top. We were so certain we wouldn't make it, because of the deep snow, steepness, or simply that it would take too long, that I don't think anyone considered just how good it would feel to actually stand atop Mount Cleveland.

Perhaps the hardest work of the day follows. Scrambling into 50-mile-an-hour winds over the loose scree turns out to be nearly impossible, until we drop to our knees. It is hard to get a foothold on the uneven surface while simultaneously bracing against the strong wind. It requires a motion that is half crawling and half walking to get to the summit.

I stand up first and get to the far side as quickly as I can. I want to stare down into the heart of the volcano, but first I want to see Herbert and its malformed peak. Turning in a tight circle, I can see all of the Islands of Four Mountains at once—maybe not the first person to do so, but one of very few. Crawling, again, to the side of the highest point, we peer down into the bubbling caldera, its poisonous plume green and beige, forcing us back when the wind carries it into our nostrils.

I dig my pocket wind meter out and stand, leaning into the wind. It is blowing from the west and south, up and over the crater, 35, 40, 42, 48, then 51 miles per hour. With the wind chill, the temperature is three below.

We shout congratulations to one another, take some pictures

and trade positions so we can see all of the views. I take another look down into the guts of the volcano, its caldera an oblong hole, bubbling and yellow, surrounded by hell-inspiring poisonous smoke from bubbling magma.

Once over the initial excitement of arriving, I sit, my back against a serrated tawny-colored rock and try to drink in everything I can. Simultaneously I let my mind run back over what we have accomplished during the past month.

We came to one of the most remote corners of the world, little known, little seen, with a plan to visit them in a way that had not been attempted for some centuries. Just how remote are we? In more than three weeks we've crossed paths with man three times. During our first days we spied a tanker on the far horizon, about 40 miles away. When we were camped on Carlisle, we heard a small plane overhead but never saw it. Then, from Herbert, on a cloudy day we heard a helicopter, most likely an oil company bird, but again, we didn't see it. Otherwise it's been just the four of us. Plus the small Sony shortwave radio I listen to nightly. It's a small connection with the world, but out here it hasn't produced much contact. I get primarily Japanese-language shows, some Australian cricket matches, and lots of born-again Christian hoopla from America's deep South.

Being free of human contact is one of the most compelling reasons for me to make the effort to journey this far from civilization. It is extremely rare in this day and age to be able to get so remote. Other than the beach drift indicating that man does exist somewhere out there, we have seen no vapor trails, no cruise boats, no fishermen, nothing that would lead us to believe that anyone but us is alive.

Just four weeks before, we know this place only by rough, distant, out-of-date maps. Now we knew it more intimately than anyone on the planet. From up here, as I retrace our routes between the islands, the deep blue seas below look so calm, the rip tides like gentle white slashes. All of those days of ferocious winds and rain are, for the moment, completely forgotten.

Given the day—the Fourth of July, remember—I make a small personal toast with a thermos cup of hot Gatorade. To a single sentiment, something that motivates me everyday, no matter where I am, but was a particularly helpful belief out here, propelling this team safely into the middle of the Bering Sea and up this tall mountain. "To independence," I say quietly.

EPILOGUE

We are inside our tents, fog-bound, at nine o'clock the morning of July 7 when we hear a distinct, if atypical sound: The *putt-putt-putt* of a motor cutting through the low clouds. Don Graves and his *Miss Pepper* were back. Early, in fact. We are surprised he was on time because the weather the previous couple days, ever since we came down from atop Mount Cleveland, were bad—foggy, rainy, cold. We were fully prepared for Graves to be late by a day or more, especially since the pickup date had been chosen so randomly. We counted our food and figured we had enough to last—barely—another five days.

Pulling his rubber Zodiac ashore, dressed like Santa Claus in his red survival suit, Graves passes big smiles all around. I think he is happier—more surprised?—to find us alive and well than we are that he actually showed up, and on time.

"So, how was it?" he asks, knowing he won't get a simple, or quick, response. Our energies are focused on breaking down camp. We were so convinced he wouldn't arrive we didn't bother to take down our tents or pack up our dry bags for the last time.

As we pack, he talks. "It was a straight, smooth shot out here, and I hope it's the same on the way back. Much different than when I returned after dropping you off, that's for sure. That was a nightmare. The seas were even more rough going back than they were coming out.

"And man, do I have a treat for you onboard—steaks, beer, eggs, wine, donuts! I'll start cooking as soon as we are loaded up."

It takes less than two hours to shuttle our gear and kayaks out to the waiting *Miss Pepper*. Once on board, the motor warming and anchor being lifted, a quiet falls over the four of us even as Don continues to gab. Though we are all ready to return to another pace of life, to get out of these dry suits and fleece, to sleep on a real mattress, we aren't completely without regrets as we motor out from Applegate Cove, past Skiff Cove and toward Samalga Pass.

As we advance along the edge of Chuginadak, past the cave where the puffin smacked me in the head and the deep cliff-side ravine where we saw our lone sea otter, I ask Graves to slow the boat. I want to soak in these islands for just a little longer, before they became only memory. I doubt I will ever return to this place, and for an instant I wish we had 25 more days to explore them further.

It is always disconcerting when you spend a few weeks in the wilderness and are then dumped back into civilization. What bothers me most right away is the sound of the boat's engines. For the past month we never slept more than 100 feet from the ocean, and its sound, the crashing of waves, the rolling of the sea, became part of our consciousness. It was particularly resonant on our last camp, at Applegate Cove, where we slept for several nights within feet of the rolling surf and continual slap of the Bering Sea. It lulled us, woke us, calmed us, excited us, and it feels odd to be leaving that omnipresent reverberation behind.

I would like to report that the snowcapped peaks of the volcanoes of the Islands of Four Mountains saluted as we drove away, but they did not. Just as when we arrived, the entire scene was buried beneath a heavy fog.

"Fitting, don't you think," I say to Barry as we settle into the cushioned bench seats of the motor boat and stare out the window. "It is amazing. If you didn't know these islands were here, if you hadn't seen them as we have, it would be easy for them to stay hidden from man forever. Maybe that's the way they like it."

During the course of our travels I wondered to myself, and out loud with my teammates, how you judge an expedition like ours a "success" or "failure." For me, as we clear the final point of land and enter Samalga Pass, I can only think of our experience as a success. We saw all of the islands in their entirety, exploring them by foot and by sea. We climbed the tallest volcano. We made all the crossings and not once overturned a boat, my biggest fear before we arrived. We never had to put into practice all those lessons learned about how to survive hypothermia.

Scott already voiced his disappointment that we hadn't circumnavigated each of the islands. He felt by doing so we would have truly set a mark for future expeditions to match. During our last few nights on Applegate I tried to explain to him that I didn't think he should be worried about setting such precedents. This was not a place for competitions, for record-setting. This was a place to limit risk. I reminded him of something we'd talked about on the ferry between Homer and Dutch Harbor, that merely coming back safely from such a place is reward enough. While he said he agreed, I sensed it wasn't wholehearted.

For me, the confidence gained in coming to such a remote place and living in it, trying to understand it, and returning from it is plenty of success. Today, as I travel the country showing my slides from the trip, I'm thrilled when someone approaches me afterward and admits, "I always wondered where the Aleutians were, and now I know."

A month after our return to Dutch Harbor, Don Graves was hired again to make a run out to the Islands of Four Mountains, straight back to Chuginadak. This time his clients were Montana-based environmental consultants, on contract for the Department of Defense, hired to investigate any environmental harm done by the WWII-era weather station on the island. The government had gotten wind of our discovery of the World War II plane, thanks to a phone call report I made to NATIONAL GEOGRAPHIC's Website, and contacted us immediately, asking if we would provide them with the coordinates of the plane. Sean sent them the latitude and longitude. They claimed they wanted to find the plane, to see if there were any lingering "environmental concerns" as a result of its crashing in such a remote place. I was struck by the coincidence of our having just been there and their seeming rush to return, and I asked if they could send me a copy of the report they were to write up.

A year later they did send a copy of the report made to the Department of Defense.

A month after we left Applegate Cove a team of two had made the round-trip to Chuginadak, with Don Graves aboard the *Miss Pepper*, and had successfully found the site of the weather station. They did not, however, make it to the downed plane, due to typically bad weather. Their round trip lasted just 32 hours.

Their biggest concern about our find was the potential for still-live ammunition and/or bombs. After consulting with military historic experts they concluded that the biggest threat was not what we took to be the unexploded bomb, which they guess might have been an oxygen canister rather than the 100-pound bombs or 325-pound depth charge normally carried aboard the King Fisher. Their bigger concern—for anyone, government agency or private entrepreneur, who may be interested one day in attempting to recover the valuable plane—is the 20-50 mm caliber ammunition used by the rear-mounted machine guns that are most likely still lying around the plane. Needless to say, we didn't see, or step on, any of them.

A year after we returned from the Islands of Four Mountains, each of us went on to adventures on our own and together. I made small explorations into the mountains of southern Cuba and the coastline of Brazil. Barry and I traveled together by sea kayak to the reefs off Belize and San Blas islands off Panama. Sean returned to open arms at his law office (shaving his beard before returning) and dove immediately into the tests required to become a small airplane pilot. He and Barry took a motored canoe 500 miles down the Yukon River. Scott is still selling shoes up and down the West Coast and plotting future solo and two-man adventures.

Again thanks to the financing help of the National Geographic Expeditions Council, Barry and I—and three others—have organized another sizable sea kayak adventure for the spring of 2001. This one will take us 800 miles down the coast of north Vietnam, from the Chinese border to south of Danang.

The inspiration for that trip was a direct result of our experience in the Aleutian Islands. I wanted some place hot, with lots of paddling and a living culture. It should provide all of that.

Recently, I ran into sea kayaking guru Derek Hutchinson, on a beach near Port Townsend, Washington. He was demonstrating new kayaks and paddles bearing his signature.

As he broke down his four-part paddle, water and sand running out of its interior, I thanked him belatedly for the inspiration. If not for his mention of this beautiful, inspiring part of the world, we might never have ventured there ourselves. He remembered seeing the islands through his binoculars and was impressed that we had gotten out there, and back, safely.

"I was a little disappointed that you took doubles, though," he said. "Not really much of a sport that way, is it?" Hitting me up for a couple bucks so he could buy a hamburger from a beachside vendor, he was off, down the beach, followed by a couple youngsters smitten by his reputation.

APPENDICES

APPENDIX A

Islands of the Four Mountains – *Lat 52° 52' N Long 169° 47' W*

Itinerary

Sunday, June 13, 1999 – leave Dutch Harbor aboard the *Miss Pepper* (4 p.m.)

Monday, June 14 – arrive North Cove, Kagamil (6:30 a.m.) – *52° 59' N 169° 42' W*

Tuesday, June 15 – North Cove, Kagamil (cross to Uliaga – *53° 03' N 169° 46' W*)

Wednesday, June 16 – North Cove, Kagamil

Thursday, June 17 – North Cove Kagamil

Friday, June 18 – Eagle Camp, Kagamil

Saturday, June 19 – Eagle Camp, Kagamil

Sunday, June 20 – Eagle Camp, Kagamil

Monday, June 21 – Skiff Cove, Chuginadak – *52° 50' N 169° 49' W*

Tuesday, June 22 – Skiff Cove, Chuginadak

Wednesday, June 23 – Skiff Cove, Chuginadak

Thursday, June 24 – Skiff Cove, Chuginadak

Friday, June 25 – Applegate Cove, Chuginadak

Saturday, June 26 – Carlisle Island – *52° 53' N 170° 03' W*

Sunday, June 27 – Carlisle Island

Monday, June 28 – Herbert Island – *52° 45' N 170° 07' W*

Tuesday, June 29 – Herbert Island

Wednesday, June 30 – Herbert Island

Thursday, July 1 – Herbert Island

Friday, July 2 – Applegate Cove

Saturday, July 3 – Applegate Cove

Sunday, July 4 – Applegate Cove (summit Mt. Cleveland)

Monday, July 5 – Applegate Cove

Tuesday, July 6 – Applegate Cove

Wednesday, July 7 – pick up by the *Miss Pepper* (9 a.m.)

APPENDIX B

Sponsors & Equipment

Adventure Medical Kits

Backcountry Pantry – freeze-dried food

Bertram-Mann – chambray shirts

Black Diamond – ropes, ice-axes, backpacks

Bolle Diffusion France – polarized sunglasses

Cascade Designs – Therm-a-Rest, Sweetwater Filters, SealLine Dry Bags, Platypus Hydration Systems

5.10 – water shoes and hiking boots

Gath – helmets

Kelty Pack Co – duffles and backpacks

Kokatat – Gore-Tex dry suits and one-piece Polartec liners

Lake Viry Fishing Club – survival prune juice

Lotus Designs – PFDs (life jackets)

Lowe Alpine Systems – fleece jackets

Magellan — GPS

Mountain Hardware – tents, sleeping bags, parkas and pants, Windstopper fleece jackets and pants, thermal wear, gloves, fleece hats

Mountain Surf – spray skirts

MSR – stoves, cooksets, dromedary bags

National Geographic Expeditions Council – funding and support

Necky – tandem Nootka Outfitter kayaks

Oobe – casual clothes, hats, fleece

Outdoor Research – stuff sacks, thermos, hats

Patagonia – aquafurs, molten core pants, aquaclavas, black hole duffles, Skanoraks

Princeton Tec Sportlights – headlamps and safety beacons

Salamander – gloves, throwbags

Seals/Take It Outside – spray skirts, camera skins

Suunto – watches, compasses

Werner – paddles

APPENDIX C

FOOD INVENTORY

Breakfast

Oatmeal, Granola, Coffee, Tea, Prunes, Raisins, Dried fruit, Honey, Brown sugar, Almonds

Lunch

Dried salmon, Gu, Clif Bars, Balance Bars, Gatorade, Mixed nuts, Pita bread, Peanut butter & Jelly, Turkey & fish jerky, Soup mixes (variety)

Dinner

Pasta, Rice, Couscous, Baked bread, Macaroni & cheese, 48 packs of freeze-dried dinners

Miscellaneous

Olive oil, Soy sauce, Pick-a-Pepa, Yucatan hot sauce, 2 pints Southern Comfort, 1 pint Black Velvet, 1 flask of Prune d'Viry brandy, 8 cigars (Davidoff), French chocolate (various)

APPENDIX D
BIBLIOGRAPHY

Adney, Edwin Tappan & Chapelle, Howard I., *The Bark Canoes and Skin Boats of North America*, Smithsonian Institution Press, 1983

Alaska Geographic Society, *The Aleutian Islands*, 1995, *Alaska's Volcanoes*, 1991, *Unalaska/Dutch Harbor*, 1991

Alekseev, A.I., *The Destiny of Russian America, 1741-1867*, The Limestone Press, 1990

Armstrong, Robert H., *Guide to the Birds of Alaska*, Alaska Northwest Books, 1995

Bangs, Cameron C., M.D., Wilkerson, James, M.D., Hayward, John S., M.D., *Hypothermia, Frostbite and other Cold Injuries*, The Mountaineers, 1986

Black, Lydia, *Glory Remembered, Wooden Headgear of Alaska Sea Hunters*, Alaska State Museums, 1991

Brinck, Wolfgang, *The Aleutian Kayak*, Ragged Mountain Press, 1995

Brower, Kenneth, *The Starship and the Canoe*, Perennial Library, 1978

Burch, David, *Fundamentals of Kayak Navigation*, Globe Pequot Press, 1999

Castleman, Deke & Pitcher, Don, *Alaska-Yukon Handbook*, Moon Publications, 1997

Diaz, Ralph, *Complete Folding Kayaker*, Ragged Mountain Press, 1994

Dowd, John, *Sea Kayaking, A Manual for Long-Distance Touring*, Greystone Books, 1997

Dyson, George, *Baidarka, The Kayak*, Alaska Northwest Books, 1999

Fitzhugh, William W. & Crowell, Aron, *Crossroads of Continents, Cultures of Siberia and Alaska*, Smithsonian Institution Press, 1988

Ford, Corey, *Where the Sea Breaks Its Back*, Alaska Northwest Books, 1998

Forgey, Wm. W. M.D., *Hypothermia: Death by Exposure*, ICS Books, Inc., 1985

Garfield, Brian, *The Thousand-Mile War*, University of Alaska Press, 1995

Halliday, Jan, *Native Peoples of Alaska*, Sasquatch Books, 1998

Hanson, Jonathan, *Complete Sea Kayak Touring*, Ragged Mountain Press, 1998

Hendrickson, Robert, *The Ocean Almanac*, Doubleday, 1984

Hrdlicka, Alex, *The Aleutian and Commodore Islands and Their Inhabitants*, Wistar Institute of Anatomy and Biology, 1945

Hudson, Ray, *Moments Rightly Placed, An Aleutian Memoir*, Epicenter Press Inc., 1998

Hutchinson, Derek C., *Eskimo Rolling*, Globe Pequot Press, 1999

_____, *Expedition Kayaking on Sea & Open Water*, Globe Pequot Press, 1995

Kemp, Peter (editor), *The Oxford Companion to Ships and the Sea*, Oxford University Press, 1988

Khlebnikov, K.T., *Notes on Russian America, Parts II – V: Kad'iak, Unalashka, Atkha, The Pribylovs*, The Limestone Press, 1994

Kushnarev, Evgenii G., *Bering's Search for the Strait, The First Kamchatka Expedition 1725-1730*, Oregon Historical Society Press, 1990

Langdon, Steve J., *The Native People of Alaska*, Greatland Graphics, 1993

Laughlin, William S., *Aleuts, Survivors of the Bering Land Bridge*, Holt, Rinehart and Winston, 1980

MacLeish, Sumner, *Seven Words for Wind*, Epicenter Press Inc., 1997

McCracken, Harold, *God's Frozen Children*, Doubleday, Doran & Company, 1930

Mitchell, Robert J. Lt., *The Capture of Attu*, University of Nebraska Press, 2000

Muller, Gehard Friedrich, *Bering's Voyages: The Reports from Russia*, University of Alaska Press, 1995

Naske, Claus-M. & Slotnick, Herman E., *Alaska, A History of the 49th State*, University of Oklahoma Press, 1987

Nordby, Will (editor), *Seekers of the Horizon, Sea Kayaking Voyages From Around the World*, Globe Pequot Press, 1989

Pratt, Verna E., *Field Guide to Alaskan Wildflowers*, Alaskakrafts, 1996

Rearden, Jim, *Koga's Zero, The Fighter that Changed World War II*, Pictorial Histories Publishing Company, Inc., 1995

Robertson, Dougal, *Survive the Savage Sea*, Sheridan House, 1994

Rourke, Norman Edward, *War Comes to Alaska, The Dutch Harbor Attack, June 3-4, 1942*, Burd Street Press, 1997

Veniaminov, Ivan, *Journals of the Priest Ioann Veniaminov in Alaska, 1823-1836*, University of Alaska Press, 1993

_____, *Notes on the Islands of the Unalashka District*, The Limestone Press, 1984

Walker, Spike, "Working on the Edge," St. Martin's Press, 1991

_____, *Nights of Ice*, St. Martin's Press, 1997

Williams, Margaret, *The Boater's Weather Guide*, Cornell Maritime Press, 1990

Willis, Clint (editor), *Rough Water, Stories of Survival from the Sea*, Mainstream Publishing, 1999

APPENDIX E
FINDING A MUMMY
(from Corey Ford's *Where the Sea Breaks its Back*)

Ford's account of a 1950s team which discovered some of Kagamil's mummies, by accident:

The party had been gathering bird specimens on Kagamil, working their way along the south shore of the island, when they heard a blue fox barking at them from a cave some 50 yards above the water. They marked the location by a live fumarole which was sending a steady jet of steam through a fissure in the rocks beside the cave, and climbed the loose mass of tumbled boulders to the entrance, a narrow V-shaped orifice. Mingled with the sulfurous odor of the fumarole was a curious death smell, which issued from the mouth of the cave. The fox had fled, but the object on which it had been chewing lay at their feet. It was a section of human arm.

Laboriously they wriggled and squeezed feet first into the vault. The ceiling was so low they could not stand upright, and caked with a hard white mineral deposit. The floor was littered with rubble, loose rocks, pieces of bone, the scat of numerous foxes, all of it covered with a fine fluffy brown dust, as soft as lint, which rose around their boots as they crept forward. It was uncomfortably warm in the cave – the dirt in places was actually too hot to touch – and the strange fetid smell gagged them. They crawled in single file on their hands and knees, hugging the wall for guidance in the pitch blackness. Abruptly the leader halted with a grasp of fright. A hand reaching from the wall had raked its fingers across his cheek.

He struck a match. Before him, in the flickering light, he saw the withered arm of a mummy protruding from the dirt. It had been partly dug out of its earthly tomb by the ravenous foxes; the exposed portion of its leathery face had been eaten away, but the part still buried was intact.

The match went out; someone lit a second. Beyond them they made out another sunken grinning face, and still another. Both sides of the cave were lined with dry bodies, as far as they could see. Once they had been stacked in tiers, one upon another, supported by racks of drift-wood. Most of them had been dislodged and violated by foxes, and one or two mummies had been dragged onto the floor of the caves. They were of all ages; adult males and females, children even a premature birth in a basket of pleated grass. Each body had been clothed in otter fur or a bird-skin parka, and wrapped in sea lion hide, which was laced together with thongs of twisted kelp. They wore ivory ornaments around their necks and in their cheeks. One wrinkled monkey-face had a jaunty feather stuck through the lobe of his left ear.

All around them were crude artifacts, torn matting, shreds of woven mummy wrappings, bones, trinkets. Part of a skin kayak, interred with its owner, lay overturned on its side; paddles, war shields, stone lamps, delicate grass baskets were spilled in the dust. Still buried in the wall as a carved wooden dish, filled with the dried wings of birds, proba-bly a funeral offering; an ornithologist in the party recognized the feathers of the pine grosbeak. A solitary skull lay in a wicker basket lined with moss, shiny as an Easter egg, the top of the head neatly split by a stone ax.

APPENDIX F

UNWRAPPING A MUMMY

(from Harold McCracken's *God's Frozen Children*)

The following descriptions are quoted from one of three American Museum of Natural History anthropological publications prepared under the direction of Dr. Clark Wissler, Ph.D., Curator in Chief of the Department of Anthropology and Archeology of the museum. Two mummies, a child and a chief, both taken from a cave on Kagamil in the 1920s, are inspected:

Of the two complete bodies received by the museum, that of the chief, specified by McCracken and Wyer as No. 1, was brought with some of the wrappings still about it, and the bundle of the mummy specified as No. 4, a child, was practically intact...

The Unwrappings of No. 4. The bundle rested on a flat wooden frame, and was encircled by a wooden hoop. Perhaps the best method of describing the wrappings is in the order in which they were removed, naming the layers in accordance with the diagram.

On top were two pieces of twined grass fabric, the selvages lapping over each other along the center of the bundle. The design and technique of the two pieces is the same. Under this fabric, to the left of the feet of the body, were four wooden spoons, a small empty wooden box, and a shell.

When the grass fabric is removed, a blanket, or possibly the remains of a garment of gutskin, was revealed, which extended far down on the left side, but was disintegrated on the right. At the right side of the bundles, under the gutskin blanket, was a rolled-up fur garment of a child. Beside it lay a conical openwork bag split down one side, in which the garment had apparently originally been placed and from which it had fallen when the bag split.

Under the gutskin blanket was . . . a covering of sea-otter skin dou-
bled and wrapped around the body so that the fur surface appeared
on both the inside and outside. A few fragments of fringe adhering to
it indicated that it might have been part of a garment. A bundle of
crude fabric, moss, and grass lay in a deep fold of the fur at the left,
and was probably part of the bedding described below which had been
forced into the fold.

Under the fur a twined fabric was wrapped about the mummy and
folded under the head, and directly under this another coarser fabric
was wrapped about the body from left to right, with the overlapping
edge tied to the under one with a piece of sinew.

Next to this was the body itself, covered with two gutskin garments,
one on the trunk and one over the head.

The body rested on a bedding of grass and moss, under which was
a woven grass fabric. One of the curious "shaft sections" lay beneath
this and another layer of grass and moss, mixed with fragments of
coarse fabric.

All of this rested on a partly disintegrated sealskin drum, still
attached in places to the burial hoop, while hoop and all lay on the
wooden tray.

The Unwrapping of No. 1. Only the wrappings directly about the
body of the chief, mummy No. 1, remained, and these were consider-
ably different from those about the body of the child, No. 4.

Part of a birdskin garment with the feather side in covered the head
and face and extended somewhat down the back. Beneath this and
over the face was a rectangle of gutskin strips with sinew skins attached
to it, and under the strips a small piece of very fine woven fabric. Lastly
there was a birdskin mask which must originally have covered the entire
face, since fragments were found about the mouth, but of which only

enough remained to cover the eyes. The feathers of the mask were turned toward the face, and at the left side it was tied with a fine twisted sinew cord to the ear, as it probably was originally at the right side. Under the neck was a small piece of very fine woven fabric, and in the lower lip was a labret of discolored jade.

A conical woven bag rested on the chest of the chief. Each limb was wrapped in a rectangle of woven fabric secured with sewing. The leg coverings extended over the foot and were turned up over the sole, forming a rough boot. The arm coverings extended from under the armpits to the wrist. The right hand was flexed, and sewed up in a separate piece of fabric, but the left hand was extended and exposed.

The body lay on pieces of woven fabric, and fragments of sealskin and straw, evidently the remains of some wrappings which had previously been removed, adhered to its underneath and were pressed into the folds of the mummy skin in some parts.

...Special attention should be called to the remarkably fine needlework and decorative bands used to embellish the grave garments. The Aleuts are still famous for their fine baskets, mats, and needlework, but the work of to-day is not equal to the high standard of early days nor the objects found in the burial. The garments of fur were decorated with embroidery and fur fringes. The almost microscopically small scale upon which some of the work is projected is truly astonishing. At best one needs a reading glass to see the details. We know from early accounts that this work was done with stone tools and bone needles.

ACKNOWLEDGMENTS

First and foremost I must thank my teammates Barry Tessman, Sean Farrell, and Scott McGuire for their combined skills, patience, and toughness, all necessary in order for us to get to and return from such a remote, beautiful, *out there* place.

This expedition would have been stillborn but for the support of the National Geographic Expeditions Council, particularly its director Rebecca Martin, Susan Reeve, Laura-Ashley Allen, Julie Rushing, Karen Sligh, and Jennifer Vernon.

The team at *National Geographic Adventure,* which first published my story about the trip, got it from the very beginning, that this was *real* adventure as opposed to some other types out there masquerading as the same: John Rasmus, Mark Jannot, David Dunbar, Lynne Sanford, Sabine Meyer, Nell Hupman, Caryn Davidson, Kalee Thompson, and Katie McDowell. And at the National Geographic Society: Margaret Burnette, Maryanne Culpepper, Lori Dynan, David Hamlin, Mike Heasley, Rainier Jenns, Bruce McElfrish, Greg McGruder, Sean Markey, Peter Miller, Ray Miller, Susannah Moore, Holly Saunders, Horace Shansab, and Lynn Wallace.

Though it was our first expedition together, my friends at Mountain Hardwear also got it and I look forward to the next one, the one after that and all those to come undertaken with their strong support, especially Jack Gilbert, Jennifer Slaboda, Jamie Tipton, Chris Strasser, Martin Zemitis, Paul Kramer, Victor Ichioka, and Geoff Sacco.

We had support from the best manufacturers in the industry (see page 252) and I would specifically like to thank the folks who founded, manage and promote those companies: Sarah Alcorn, Reed Bartlett, Nancy Prichard Bouchard, Diane Bertramm, Robert Bolle, Alan Boulter, Brad Brock, Philippe Ceas, Craig Cottle, Dave Cozzone, Philip Curry, Jess Donoho, Ric Gath, Spike Gladwin, Jennifer Gombas, Shelley Furrer, Craig Lanford, Ron MacAbee, Jordy Margid, John Mason, Tom Merritt, Jim Meyers, Mike Mowery, Tom Myers, Ann Obenchain, Grant Sanders, Jane Sievert, Andy Stone, Anna Schreiber, Mike Smith, Jennifer Van Homer, Amy Quirk-Weiss, and Dr. Eric Weiss.

In Dutch Harbor, despite spending much of our time there suffering from stress related to too little time and too much to do, we made great friends in Bob Adams, Jeff Dickrell, Don and Chris Graves, Jeff Hancock and Carol Bunes, Dr. Rick Knecht, Burke Mees and Dan Parrett. Along the road to the Aleutians and this book I had specific and varied support from a great cast of editors, scientists and friends: Tom Bie, Jeff Blumenfeld, Eugene Buchanan, Andreina de Bei, George Dyson, Sven Haakens, Loren Hayden, Stephen Loring, Adele McNicholas, Tom Miller, and Anne-Marie Russell.

Like expeditions, books are a team effort and at National Geographic Books I am happy to have great teammates in Nina Hoffman, Kevin Mulroy, Johnna Rizzo, Nancy Feresten, and Suzanne Fonda. Thanks to John Paine for helping me put all the words in good order. And to my longtime friend and agent, Stuart Krichevsky, for making sure those words have an opportunity to get *out there* in the first place.

Few stories are written about the mates left behind to tend the fires while their opposite is away on adventure. What do you know about Mrs. Shackleton, for example? For her own variety of skills, patience, toughness—and love—I thank my own Mrs. Shackleton, Brigitte Bolle´.